SPSS Manual

to accompany

Susan A. Nolan/Thomas E. Heinzen
Statistics for the Behavioral Sciences

Robert Weathersby
Eastern University

WORTH PUBLISHERS

SPSS Manual
by Robert Weathersby
to accompany
Susan A. Nolan and Thomas E. Heinzen: ***Statistics for the Behavioral Sciences***

© 2008 by Worth Publishers

All rights reserved.

The contents, or parts thereof, may be reproduced for use with ***Statistics for the Behavioral Sciences***, by Susan A. Nolan and Thomas E. Heinzen, but may not be reproduced in any form for any other purposes without prior written permission of the publisher.

ISBN-10: 1-4292-2086-4
ISBN-13: 978-1-4292-2086-6

Printed in the United States of America

First Printing 2007

Worth Publishers
41 Madison Avenue
New York, NY 10010
www.worthpublishers.com

CONTENTS

Preface   iv

CHAPTER 1   An Introduction to Statistics and Research Design: The Basic Elements of Statistical Reasoning

CHAPTER 2   Descriptive Statistics: Organizing, Summarizing, and Graphing Individual Variables

CHAPTER 3   Visual Displays of Data: Graphs That Tell a Story

CHAPTER 4   Probabilities and Research: The Risks and Rewards of Scientific Sampling

CHAPTER 5   Correlation: Quantifying the Relation Between Two Variables

CHAPTER 6   Regression: Tools for Predicting Behavior

CHAPTER 7   Inferential Statistics: The Surprising Story of the Normal Curve

CHAPTER 8   Hypothesis Testing With z Tests: Making Meaningful Comparisons

CHAPTER 9   Hypothesis Testing with t Tests: Comparing Two Groups

CHAPTER 10   Hypothesis Testing With One-Way ANOVA: Comparing Three or More Groups

CHAPTER 11   Two-Way ANOVA: Understanding Interactions

CHAPTER 12   Beyond Hypothesis Testing: Confidence Intervals, Effect Size, and Power

CHAPTER 13   Chi Square: Expectations versus Observations

CHAPTER 14   Beyond Chi Square: Nonparametric Tests with Ordinal Data

PREFACE

This Manual is designed to show students how to perform the statistical procedures discussed in *Statistics for the Behvioral Sciences* using SPSS. It provides applications and exercises for nearly all chapters of the text. Step-by-step instruction describing how to carry out statistical analysis using SPSS are also provided. The data sets which accompany some of the exercises within this manual can be downloaded from the book's companion Web site: www.worthpublishers.com/nolanheinzen1e

I would like to thank the Worth Publishers team who were involved in this project, including Christine Ondreicka, Jenny Chiu, and Stacey Alexander for their dedication in coordinating various aspects of the editorial and production processes.

Robert Weathersby

CHAPTER 1

AN INTRODUCTION TO STATISTICS AND RESEARCH DESIGN

The Basic Elements of Statistical Reasoning

EXERCISE 1
NAMING VARIABLES AND DATA ENTRY

The goal in this first exercise is to become familiar with the program by getting some practice with naming variables and data entry.

- Launch SPSS. You may either select the SPSS icon from the start menu at the lower left corner of the screen or you may double-click the SPSS shortcut icon on your desktop. When the application has finished loading, the screen should be similar to the one below. The window in the center of the display is called a dialog window (or dialog box) in SPSS. You may opt to skip this one by checking the box in the lower left corner of the window.

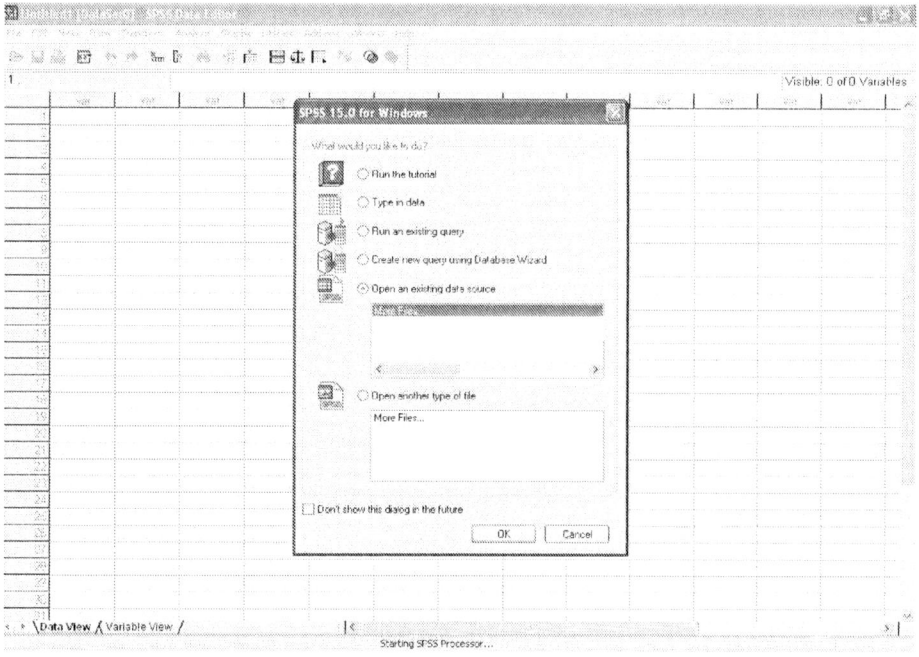

- From the list of options under "What would you like to do?" select the round radio button next to **Type in data**, and click **OK** to cause this dialog window to disappear.

You are now looking at the spreadsheet–like **Data View** window of the SPSS **Data Editor**. The cell in the upper left corner of the window should be highlighted (outlined with a bold border), indicating that it is the active cell. We could enter a data value in this cell and others, but we would be getting ahead of ourselves. First, we'll name and define the variables.

THE VARIABLE VIEW WINDOW

- There are two tabs at the lower left corner of the screen. Select the **Variable View** tab to access the **Variable View** window. The cell in the upper left corner should be the active (highlighted) cell:

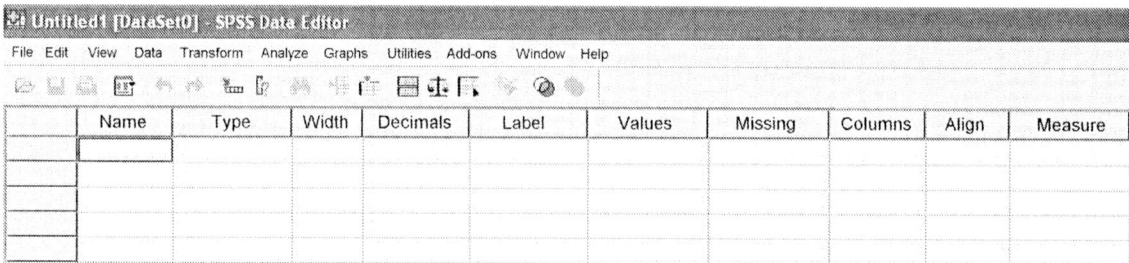

Naming and coding the independent variable

- With the cursor in the first cell, type **Condition** as the name of the independent variable. Press the **Enter** key. Notice that a small gray box appeared in the **Type** cell next to the word **Numeric**. Click on the gray box to produce the **Variable Type** dialog window. The window shows that the selected (default) variable type is **Numeric**; that's why this word appears in the cell under **Type**.

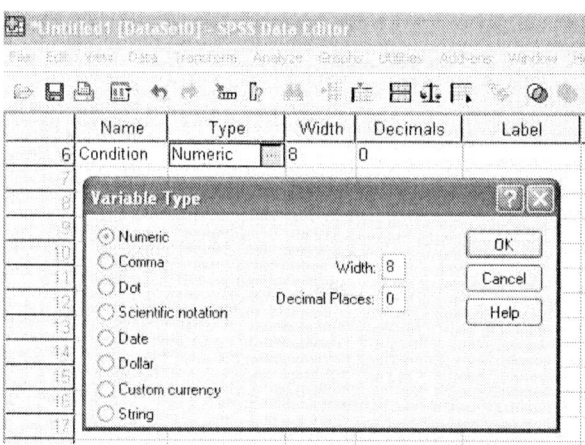

You will rarely, if ever, need to use any of the other choices, so leave the default selection as it is and click **OK** to return to the Variable View window. Leave the **Width** set at 8 but change the **2** in the **Decimals** column to **0**, because the values that you'll enter for the condition variable will be whole-number codes that represent the names of the two conditions (levels of the independent variable).

- Click in the cell under **Label** and type a descriptive label for the condition variable (without the quotation marks): "1 = intruder; 2 = no intruder." Click in the first cell in the **Values** column; a gray box should appear. Click on the gray box to produce the **Value Labels** dialog window. Enter "1" as the first **Value:** and press the Tab key on the keyboard to move the cursor to the **Label:** field. Type "intruder" (without the quotation marks) and click the **Add** button to enter the value and its label. The value and its label should appear as **1 = "intruder"** in the large field below. Now repeat the process, entering "2" as the second Value: and "no intruder" as its label. Again, click the **Add** button to enter the code value and label. When you have completed both labels, the Value Labels dialog window should appear as follows:

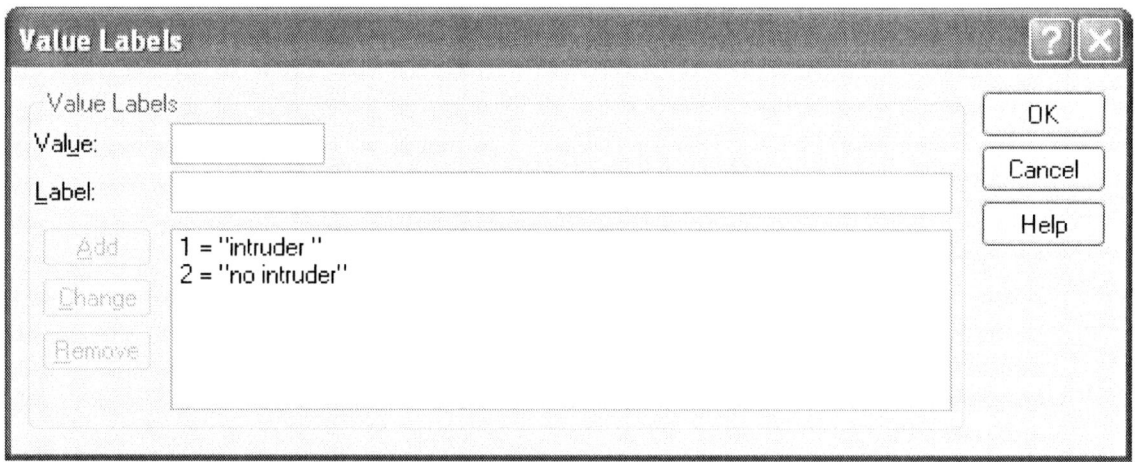

- Click **OK** to return to the **Variable View** window.

We may ignore the **Missing** and **Columns** menu options for now. By default the values that you enter in the Data Editor will be aligned in the right side of each cell. If you like, you may replace "Right" with "Center" (or "Left") by typing a **c** (or an **l**) in the first cell under **Align**. The last column heading, **Measure**, allows you to identify the scale (**Scale**, **Ordinal**, or **Nominal**) used to measure the variable entered in that row. Select **Nominal** to indicate that the codes you'll enter represent the names of the two levels of the independent variable. Note, however, that the analysis is not affected by the choices displayed in this column; they are useful only as reminders of the types of variables entered in each row.

Naming the dependent variable

- In the second row under **Name** type **Departure time** as the name of the dependent variable. Unless you encounter an error of some sort, your screen should look like this.

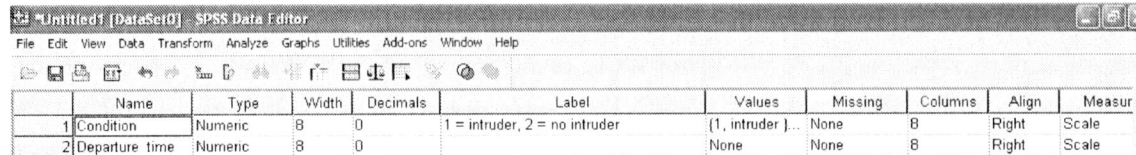

Well, I set you up to encounter an "error of some sort." As you discovered, the space that you typed between "Departure" and "time" is an "illegal character."

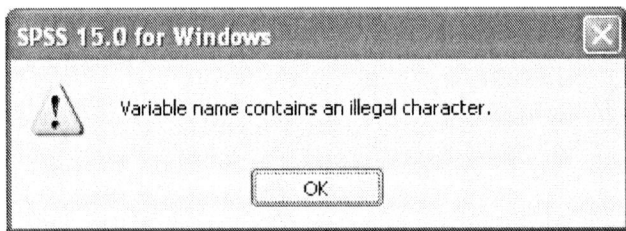

- Click **OK** to remove the error warning window and type **Departure_time** (with an underscore character replacing the space) as a legal name for the dependent variable. Set **Decimals** to **0**, and under **Label** type "Time in seconds to exit parking space." When you are finished, the Variable View window should be similar to the following:

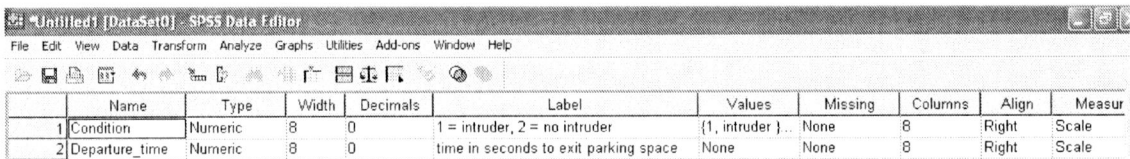

CHAPTER 1 ■ AN INTRODUCTION TO STATISTICS AND RESEARCH DESIGN

Click on the **Data View** tab to return to the Data View window of the Data Editor. Before entering data, you should save the data file by selecting **Save As...** from the **File** menu at the top left corner of the menu bar.

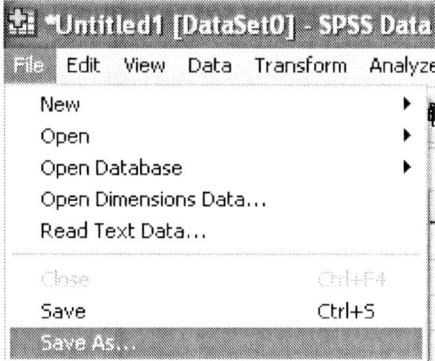

When the **Save Data As** dialog window appears, the cursor should be blinking in the **File name:** field at the bottom of the window. Follow the steps in the figure to save the file.

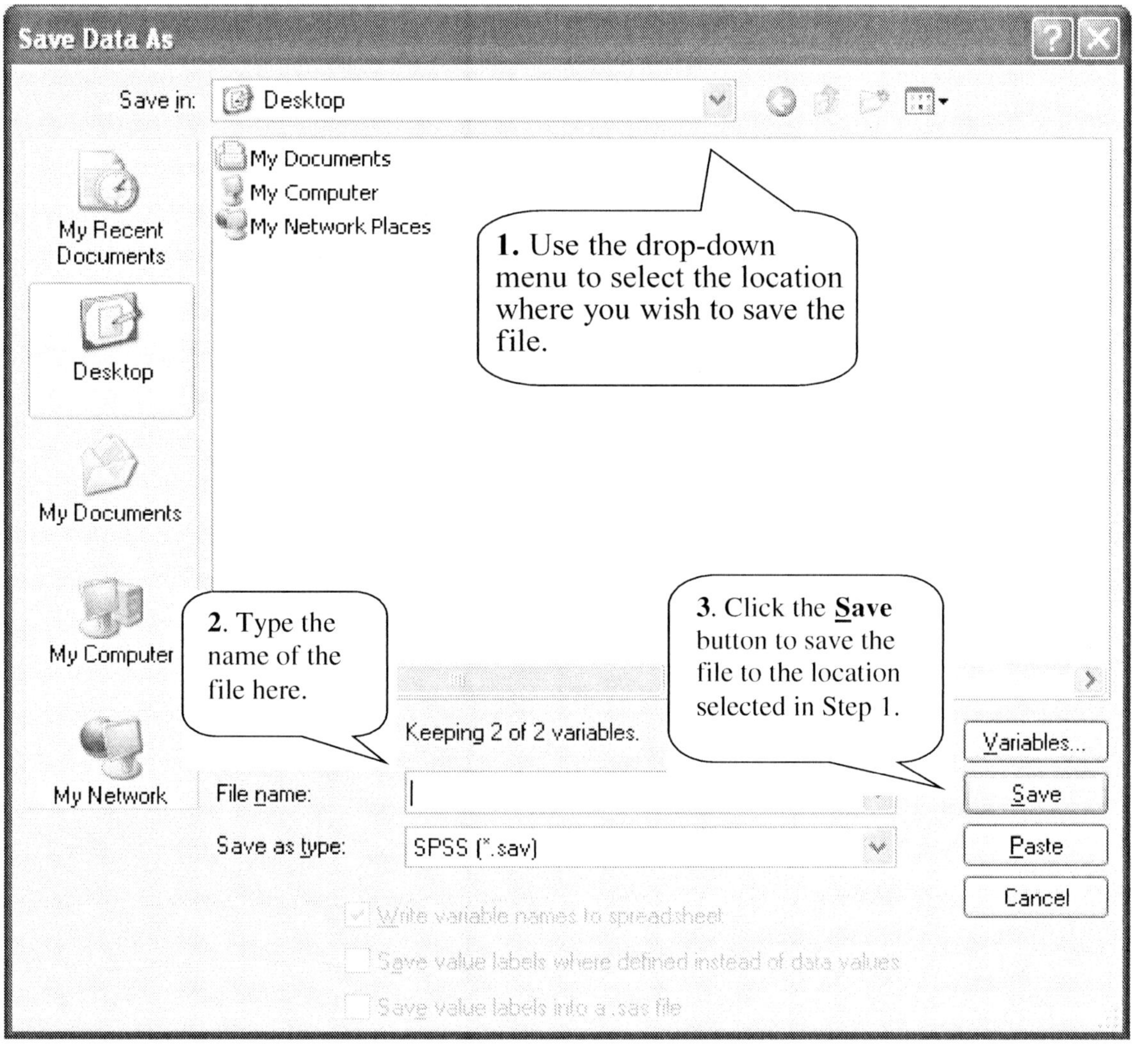

1. Use the drop-down menu to select the location where you wish to save the file.

2. Type the name of the file here.

3. Click the **Save** button to save the file to the location selected in Step 1.

THE DATA VIEW WINDOW OF THE DATA EDITOR

You should see **Condition** and **Departure_time** displayed as the first two variable ("var") names at the top of the window.

- Move the cursor until it is directly over **Condition**; the variable label should appear in a pale yellow box just below the variable name and remain on the screen for about 5 seconds.

- As a shortcut to entering the **Condition** codes, type a "1" (without the quotation marks) in the first cell under Condition, then press the Enter key to enter the value. Now click on the cell that you just entered the "1" in, right–click, and select Copy from the drop-down menu.

- Hold down the left mouse button as you drag the cursor through cells 2–25. Release the left mouse button, right–click, and select **Paste** from the drop-down menu to paste the "1" into those cells.

CHAPTER 1 ■ AN INTRODUCTION TO STATISTICS AND RESEARCH DESIGN

- Type a "2" in cell 26 and repeat the previous sequence (p. 1-6) to paste a "2" into cells 27–50.

The data that you will enter (below) are a subset of the data collected by student observers in a quasi–replication of the first two studies reported by Ruback and Juieng (1997).

Condition	Departure_time	Condition	Departure_time	Condition	Departure_time	Condition	Departure_time
1	31	1	28	2	27	2	65
1	24	1	25	2	45	2	35
1	63	1	41	2	17	2	25
1	32	1	18	2	19	2	29
1	22	1	7	2	17	2	43
1	36	1	15	2	12	2	13
1	34	1	27	2	38	2	17
1	74	1	14	2	26	2	18
1	12	1	56	2	34	2	19
1	40	1	45	2	25	2	7
1	20	1	75	2	58	2	76
1	20	1	22	2	16	2	20
1	17			2	12		

- Now enter the values for the dependent variable **Departure_time** in the order shown. When you've finished entering the data, the first 10 rows of your Data View window should be similar to the one below.

Ruback & Juieng Data for SPSS Exe

File Edit View Data Transform Analyze

1 : Condition   1

	Condition	Departure_time
1	1	31
2	1	24
3	1	63
4	1	32
5	1	22
6	1	36
7	1	34
8	1	74
9	1	12
10	1	40

Although typing numbers into the **Data Editor** may seem to be a dull task, you should not underestimate the importance of careful data entry. Common data entry errors include:

1. Double data entry—that is, entering the same data value on consecutive data entries.

2. Skipping a data entry.
3. Either pressing too lightly, or forgetting to press, the Enter key between data entries.
4. Confusing digits that are similar in appearance such as "3" and "8."
5. Repeating a digit—that is, typing "933" instead of "93."

USING THE EXPLORE PROCEDURE TO IDENTIFY OUTLIERS

The last error will show up as a data entry with too many digits. For example, suppose that the value "76" (case 49) was mistakenly entered as "766." We'll use the Explore procedure to look for possible outliers.

From the **Analyze** menu, select **Descriptive Statistics** ▶ **Explore...** .

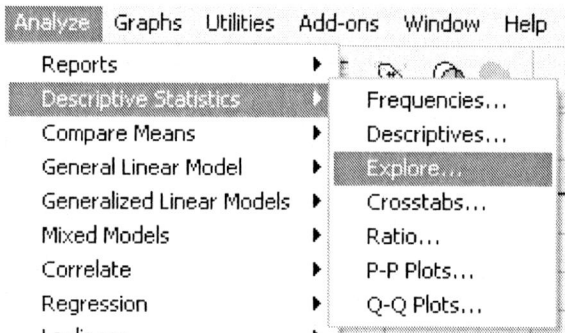

- When the **Explore** dialog window appears, select **Departure_time** and click the ▶ button to move this variable into the **Dependent List:** field. Locate the **Display** section in the lower left corner of the window and click on the round radio button next to **Statistics**.

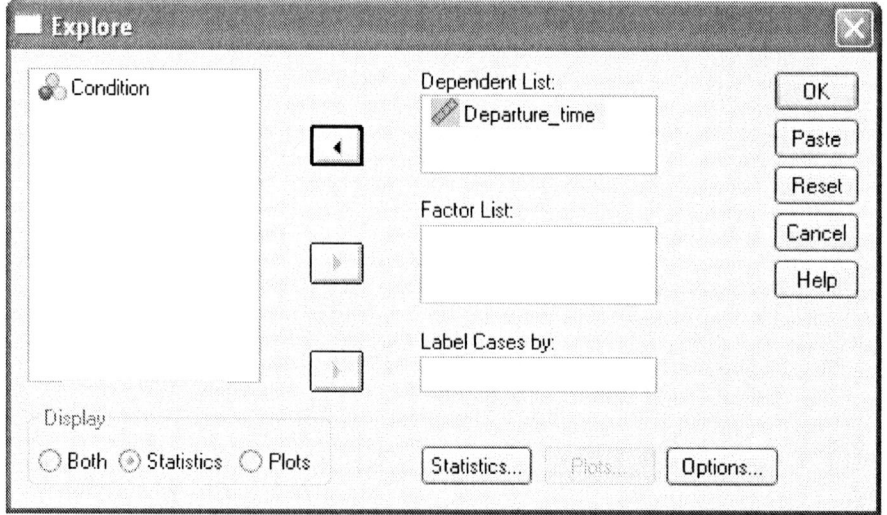

CHAPTER 1 ■ AN INTRODUCTION TO STATISTICS AND RESEARCH DESIGN   1-9

- When the dialog window looks like the one at the bottom of the previous page, click on the **Statistics...** button (in the center of the window on the bottom row) to produce the **Explore: Statistics** dialog window.
- In the **Explore: Statistics** dialog window, select **Outliers** as shown below. Then click **Continue** to return to the **Explore** dialog window.

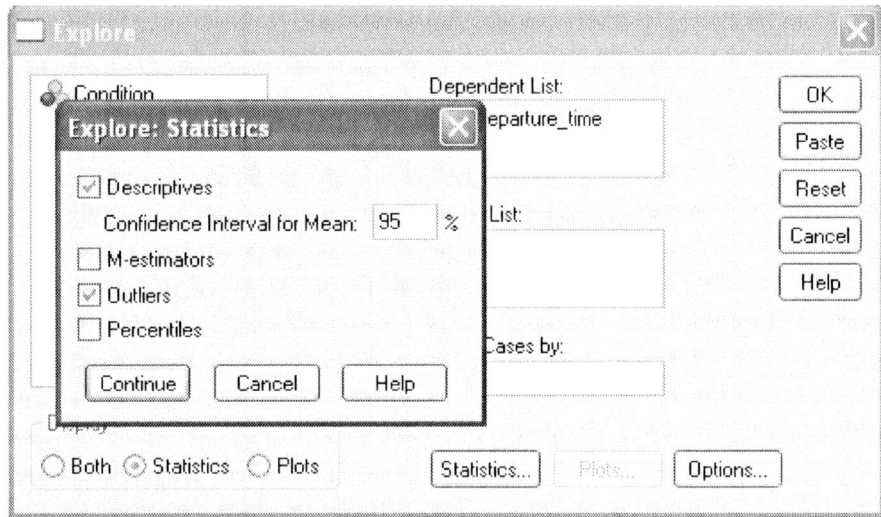

- Now click **OK** to produce the output.

You should see a **Descriptives** table followed by an **Extreme Values** table in the Output pane of the SPSS Viewer. You can use the Descriptives table to check the **Minimum** and **Maximum** data values to see if either is outside the range of the data values. Outliers may be more easily identified in the Extreme Values table, where they may be compared with the highest and lowest 5 values in the dataset.

Descriptives

			Statistic	Std. Error
Departure_time	Mean		44.02	14.920
	95% Confidence Interval for Mean	Lower Bound	14.04	
		Upper Bound	74.00	
	5% Trimmed Mean		28.96	
	Median		25.00	
	Variance		1130.306	
	Std. Deviation		105.500	
	Minimum		7	
	Maximum		766	
	Range		759	
	Interquartile Range		22	
	Skewness		6.804	.337
	Kurtosis		47.404	.662

If you know the range of the data, the presence of outliers may be detected by inspecting the minimum and maximum values in the Descriptives table.

Extreme Values

			Case Number	Value
Departure_time	Highest	1	49	766
		2	24	75
		3	8	74
		4	39	65
		5	3	63
	Lowest	1	48	7
		2	18	7
		3	38	12
		4	31	12
		5	9	12

Outliers are perhaps more easily detected in a list of the highest and lowest values in a dataset.

EXERCISE 2
MERGING FILES

As noted previously, the data that you entered in Exercise 1 are a subset of the data collected by student observers in a field exercise designed to disclose whether drivers exiting their parking spaces take longer to leave when an "intruder" is waiting for the space. In this exercise we will merge all the data collected by students over five semesters into a single data file. The files are named **Parking Data (Spring, 200X)**, where X = 2-6.

- Open the file named **Parking Data (Spring, 2002)**.
- From the **Data** menu, select **Merge Files ▶ Add Cases...**

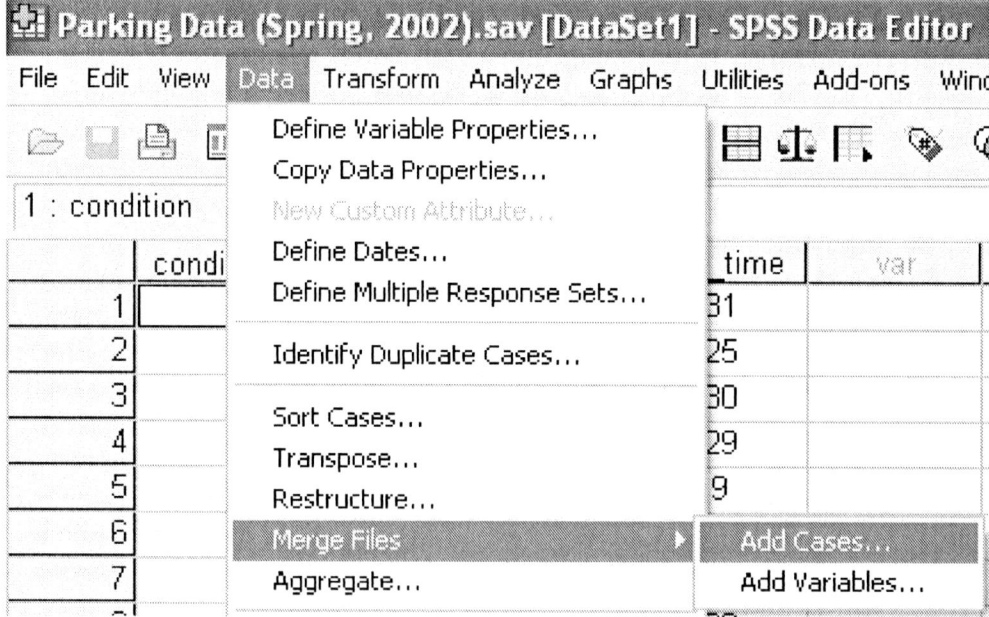

- When the **Add Cases to** dialog window appears, select the radio button next to **An external SPSS data file** then click on the **Browse...** button.

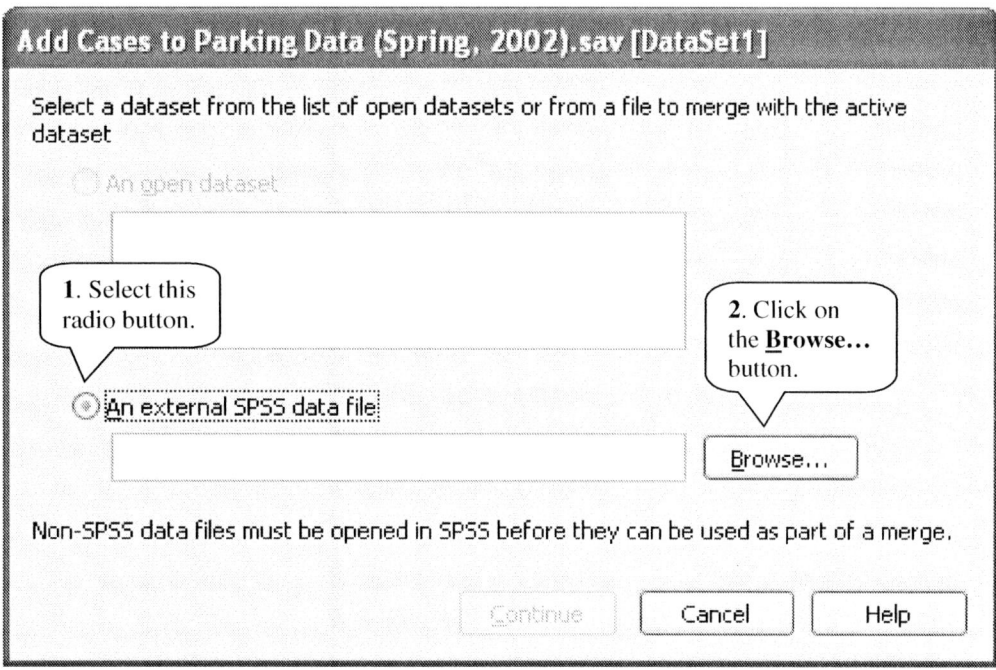

- From the **Add Cases: Read File** dialog window, select **Parking Data (Spring, 2003)** and click the **Open** button.

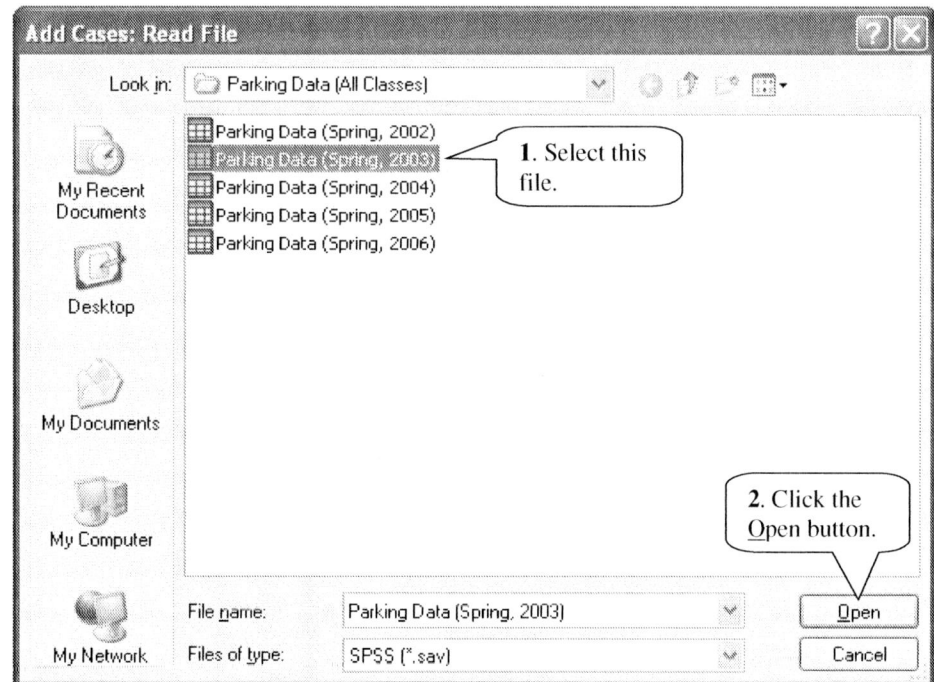

- Clicking the **Open** button returns you to the **Add Cases to** dialog window. The **Parking Data (Spring, 2003)** file should be listed in the external data file field.

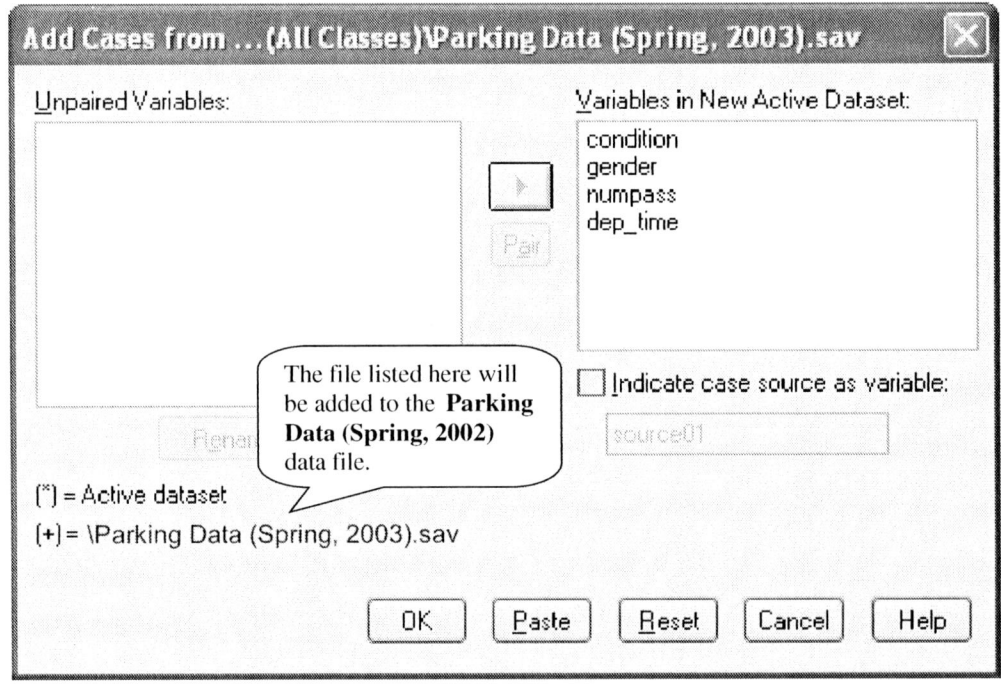

- Click **Continue** to produce the **Add Cases from ...** dialog window.

The file listed here will be added to the **Parking Data (Spring, 2002)** data file.

CHAPTER 1 ■ AN INTRODUCTION TO STATISTICS AND RESEARCH DESIGN

- Click **OK** to add **Parking Data (Spring, 2003).sav** to the Parking Data (Spring, 2002) data file.
- Now repeat the 6 steps below to add each of the remaining three data files to the open dataset.
  1. From the **Data** menu, select **Merge Files ▶ Add Cases...**
  2. When the **Add Cases to** dialog window appears, select the radio button next to **An external SPSS data file**, and then click on the **Browse...** button.
  3. From the **Add Cases: Read File** dialog window, select **Parking Data (Spring, 200X)** and click the **Open** button.
  4. Clicking the Open button returns you to the **Add Cases to** dialog window. The Parking Data (Spring, 200X) file should be listed in the external data file field.
  5. Click **Continue** to produce the **Add Cases from ...** dialog window.
  6. Click **OK** to add **Parking Data (Spring, 200X).sav** to the Parking Data (Spring, 2002) data file.
- When you have merged all five files, save the merged files under a new name such as **Parking Data (Merged Files)**.

EXERCISE 3
USING SELECT CASES TO DELETE "DIRTY DATA"

In this exercise we will remove unwanted data from the merged parking data files.

- From the **Data** menu, select the **Select Cases...** option.

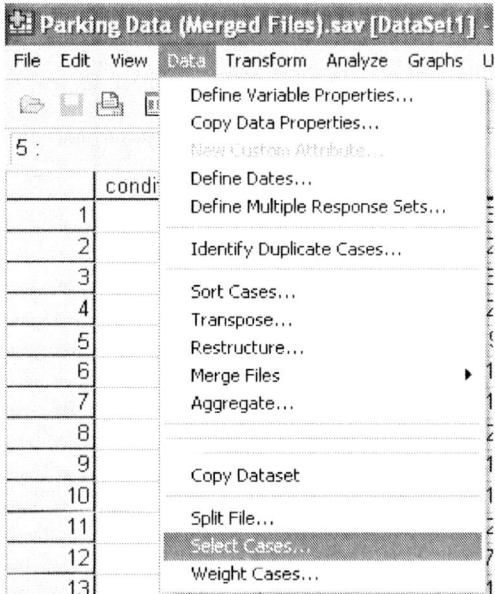

- When the **Select Cases** dialog window appears, click on the radio button next to **If condition is satisfied**. Then click on the **large If...** button to produce the **Select Cases: If** dialog window. (*Note:* The window was cropped to fit on the page.)

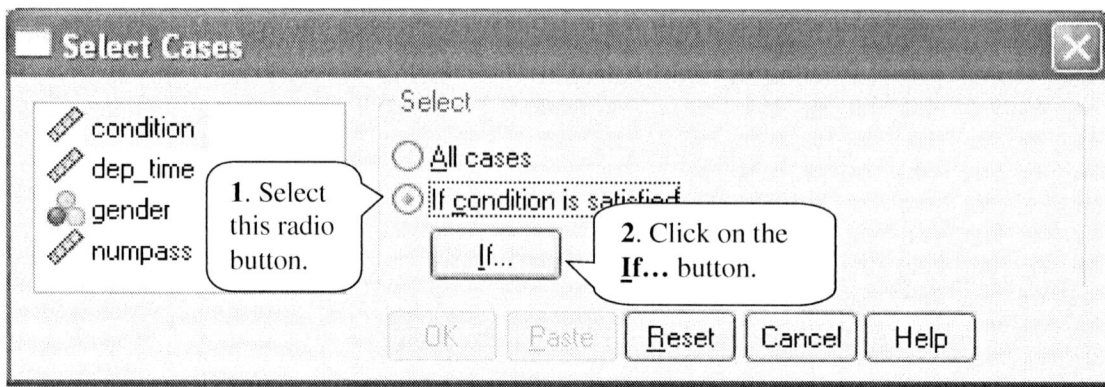

- When the **Select Cases: If** dialog window appears, select **dep_time**, then click the [▸] button to move the dep_time variable into the field at the top of the window. Now position the cursor to the right of dep_time and type "**<= 120**" (without the quotation marks). The command instructs SPSS to select the cases whose departure times were not more than 2 minutes. This selection criterion is based on the original study by Ruback and Juieng (1997):

The three drivers who waited in their car for more than 2 min were not included in the data because the researchers assumed those drivers had certain time-consuming tasks to complete before leaving (e.g., waiting for another shopper or looking at a map). (p. 823)

- The window should now appear as follows:

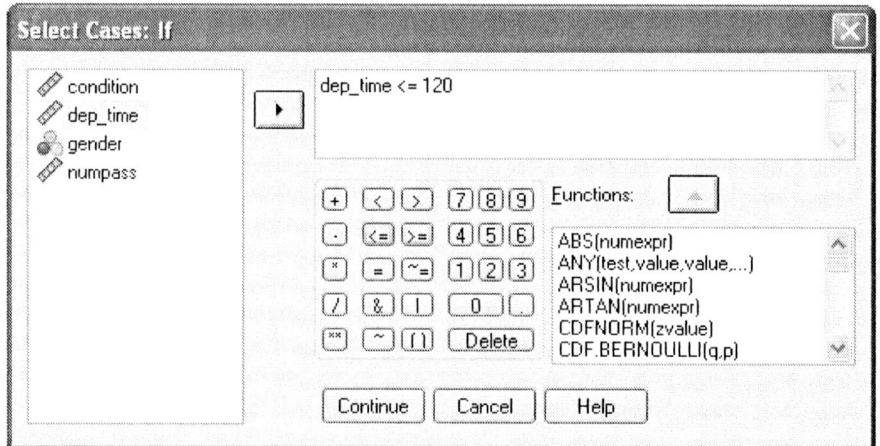

CHAPTER 1 ■ AN INTRODUCTION TO STATISTICS AND RESEARCH DESIGN   1-15

- Click **Continue** to return to the **Select Cases** dialog window. Locate the Output section near the bottom of the window and select the radio button next to **Delete unselected cases**. This will remove all cases with departure times longer than 2 minutes from the data set.

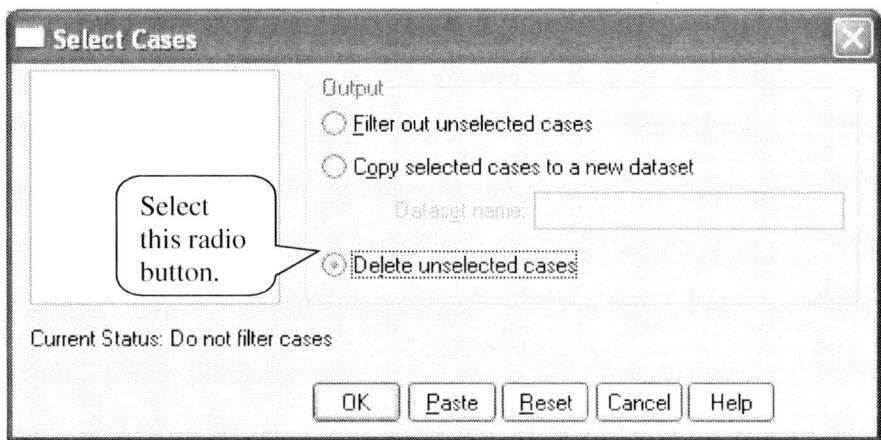

- Click **OK** to execute the case selection command. **Save** the file. We will use this file to complete exercises in other chapters.

CHAPTER 2

DESCRIPTIVE STATISTICS

Organizing, Summarizing, and Graphing Individual Variables

1. Go to http://www.norusis.com/ and download the "corrected data CD for release 15." Launch SPSS and open the file **gssnet.sav** from the downloaded folder. This file contains a random subset of cases from the General Social Survey, a national survey of randomly selected households that has been conducted every two years since 1972.

   From the **Analyze** menu, **select Descriptive Statistics ▶ Frequencies...** . When the **Frequencies** dialog window appears, select **Age of respondent** and move this variable into the **Variable(s):** field as shown:

   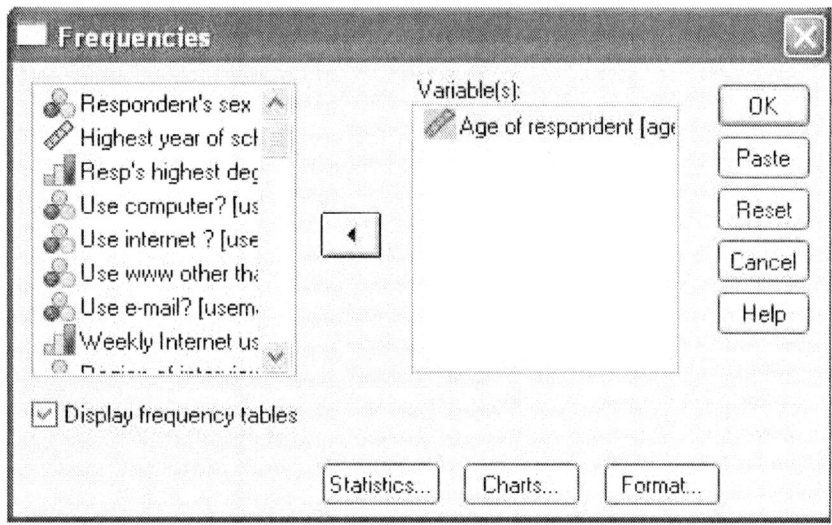

   Click on the **Statistics...** tab to open the **Frequencies: Statistics** dialog window. Find the **Central Tendency** section and select **Mean, Median,** and **Mode,** then locate the **Dispersion** section and select **Std. deviation, Variance,** and **Range.** Finally, under **Distribution** select **Skewness** and **Kurtosis** before clicking **Continue** to return to the **Frequencies** window.

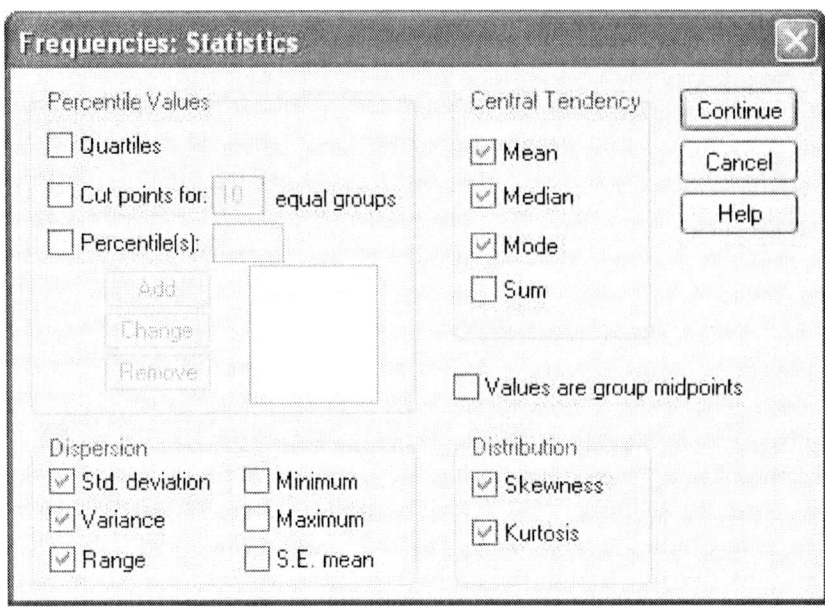

Deselect the **Display Frequencies** option, that is, make sure this option is NOT checked. Otherwise, the output will include a frequency table listing all of the ages from 18 to 89. Click **OK** to produce the output.

   a. Explain how the sign of the **Skewness** statistic may be predicted by comparing the values of the **Mean**, the **Median**, and the **Mode**.

   b. What is the relationship between the **Std. Deviation** and the **Variance**?

2. Students were asked during the first class of an introductory course in statistics to "Use a scale of 0 (*no anxiety*) to 10 (*extreme anxiety*) to rate your level of math anxiety." The self-ratings of 87 students are displayed below. From the **File** menu select **New ▶ Data**. Click on the **Variable View** tab at the bottom of the screen to display the **Variable View** window and define the variable as follows: **Name** = "Math_Anxiety," **Decimals** = 0, and **Label** = "Self-ratings of math anxiety (0 = no anxiety, 10 = extreme anxiety)." Now click on the **Data View** tab to display the **Data View** window and enter the data.

4	1	8	7	8	6	8	8	6
6	5	3	3	7	9	4	6	8
7	5	7	6	8	5	6	7	3
5	5	10	2	7	5	7	6	7
9	4	3	8	3	4	4	5	10
4	4	7	2	7	2	7	8	10
8	2	0	8	8	1	4	5	7
2	0	6	10	2	8	1	8	
7	3	10	6	5	7	6	8	
7	6	6	5	10	4	4	5	

The **Bar Charts** option in SPSS should be used when the variable is measured on a nominal or ordinal scale, whereas the **Histograms:** option is selected when the variable is measured on an interval or ratio scale. Rating scales such as this one are generally regarded as an interval scale of measurement.

3. Select **Analyze ... Descriptive Statistics ▶ Frequencies...** to display the **Frequencies** dialog window. Make sure that the **Display frequency tables** option (lower left corner) is selected. Select the variable displayed in the left field and either click the triangle (▶) or double-click the variable name to move it into the **Variable(s):** field on the right side of the window. Select the **Statistics...** tab at the bottom of the window to display the **Frequencies: Statistics** dialog window. Find the **Percentile Values** section and select **Quartiles**, then **Continue** to return to the Frequencies dialog window. Now select the **Charts ...** tab to display the **Frequencies: Charts** dialog window. Under **Chart Type** select **Histograms:** then click **Continue** to return to the Frequencies dialog window. Click **OK** to produce the output.

4. a. Identify the score at the **75th percentile**.

   b. The 75th percentile is also known as _____.

   c. Identify the score at the **25th percentile**.

   d. The 25th percentile is also known as _____.

5. a. Compute the **interquartile range**.

   b. Describe the interquartile range in a way that does not refer to any of the terms from question 4 above.

6. a. Identify the score at the **50th percentile**.

   b. Provide two other names for the **50th percentile**.

ANSWERS

1.

a. In all positively skewed distributions, the value of the mean exceeds that of the median, whereas in all negatively skewed distributions, the value of the median exceeds that of the mean.

b. The standard deviation is the square root of the variance.

2.

Statistics

Math_anxiety

N	Valid	87
	Missing	0
Percentiles	25	4.00
	50	6.00
	75	8.00

Math_anxiety

		Frequency	Percent	Valid Percent	Cumulative Percent
Valid	0	2	2.3	2.3	2.3
	1	3	3.4	3.4	5.7
	2	6	6.9	6.9	12.6
	3	6	6.9	6.9	19.5
	4	10	11.5	11.5	31.0
	5	11	12.6	12.6	43.7
	6	12	13.8	13.8	57.5
	7	15	17.2	17.2	74.7
	8	14	16.1	16.1	90.8
	9	2	2.3	2.3	93.1
	10	6	6.9	6.9	100.0
	Total	87	100.0	100.0	

Histogram

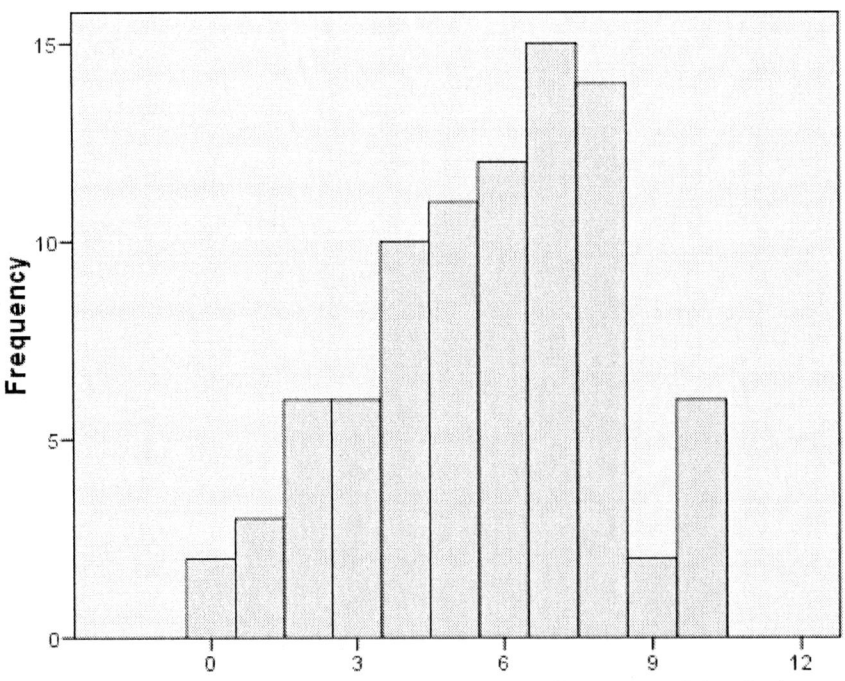

Self ratings of math anxiety on the first day of statistics class (0 = no anxiety, 10 = extreme anxiety)

Mean =5.69
Std. Dev. =2.47
N =87

4. a. The score at the 75th percentile is **8**.
   b. The 75th percentile is also known as the **third quartile** (or **Q3**).
   c. The score at the 25th percentile is **4**.
   d. The 25th percentile is also known as the **first quartile** (or **Q1**).
5. a. The interquartile range is computed by subtracting Q1 from Q3: 8 – 4 = **4**.
   b. The interquartile range is the **middle 50%** of the scores in a distribution.
6. a. The score at the 50th percentile is **6**.
   b. Two other names for the 50th percentile are the **second quartile** (**Q2**) and the **median**.

# CHAPTER 3

VISUAL DISPLAYS OF DATA

Graphs That Tell a Story

In this exercise we will use SPSS to create a graph. We will create this visual display of data, we will observe the 10 points listed in the section *How to Build a Graph: Dos and Don'ts* on p. 118 in the text as well as the guidelines for the preparation of figures from the *Publication Manual of the American Psychological Association* (2001).

CONSTRUCTING A HISTOGRAM TO DISPLAY FREQUENCY DATA

Launch SPSS. If you have not yet disabled the opening **What Do You Want To Do?** dialog window, then click **OK** to open an existing data source. If you have disabled the opening window, then select **File, Open ▶ Data...** from the SPSS Data Editor menu. Either method will produce the **Open Data** dialog window (on the next page). Click on the button to access the **Look in:** drop-down menu of drives and folders. Navigate to the folder where you saved the merged data file from the Chapter 1 exercises, and click the **Open** button to access the contents of the folder.

3-2 SPSS Manual

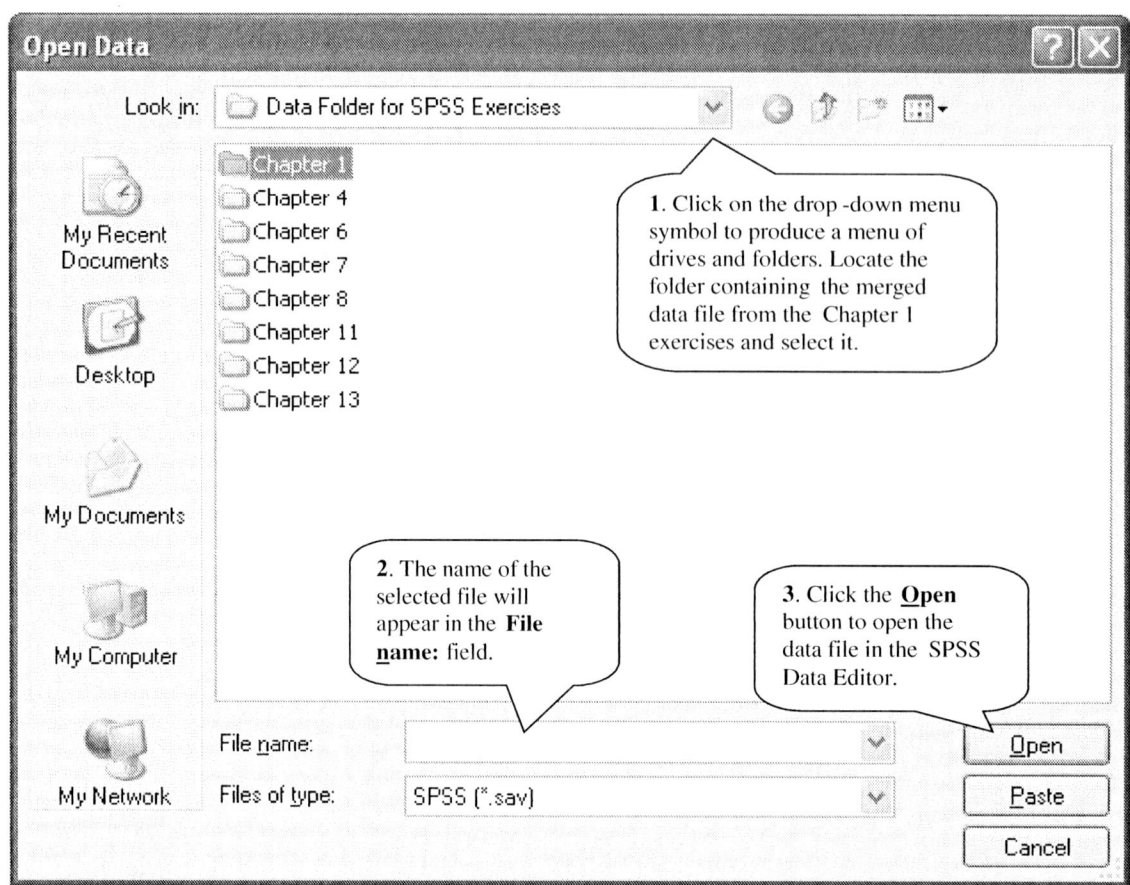

- Select **Graphs, Chart Builder...**

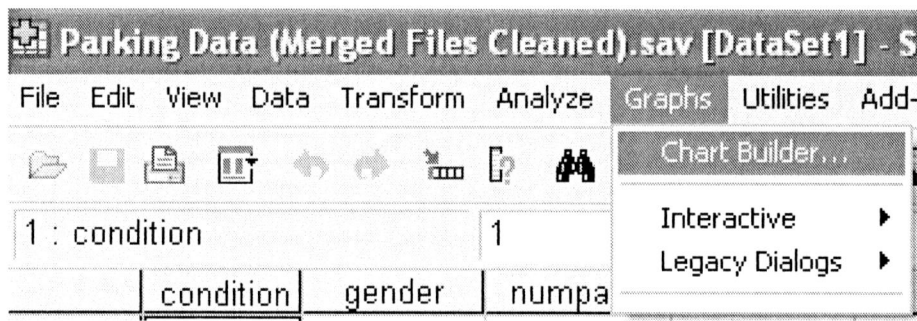

- ... to produce the first **Chart Builder** dialog window. If the variable properties were defined when they were first entered in the **Variable View** window, it will not be necessary to define them at this step.

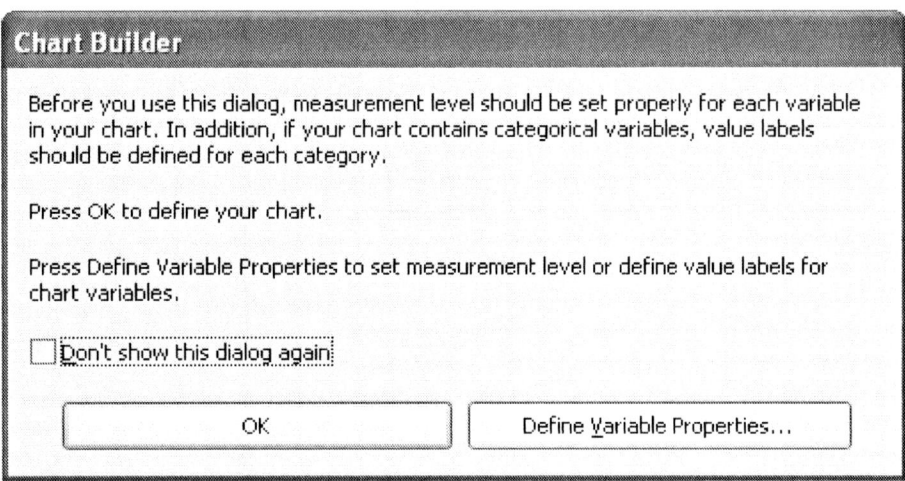

- Click the box next to **Don't show this dialog again**. If you should ever need to access the **Define Variable Properties...** dialog window, you may do so by selecting it from the Data menu in the Data Editor.

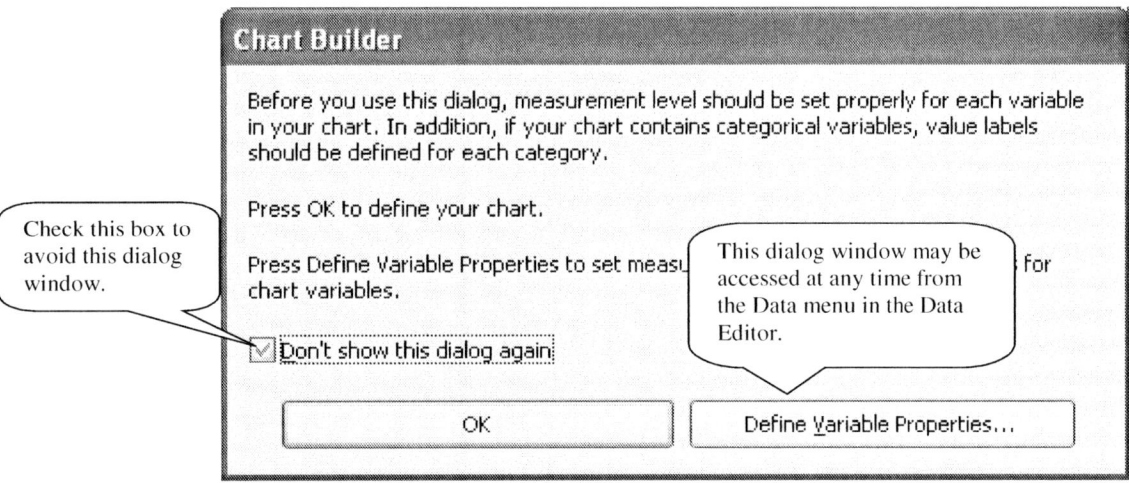

- Click **OK** to access the second **Chart Builder** dialog window. Selecting **Histogram** from the **Choose from:** list produces an array of histograms in the chart gallery window on the right. Move the cursor over the simple histogram and watch the cursor change from an arrow to a pointing hand. Select the simple histogram from the chart gallery as shown, then hold down the left mouse button and drag it into the large chart preview field at the top of window.

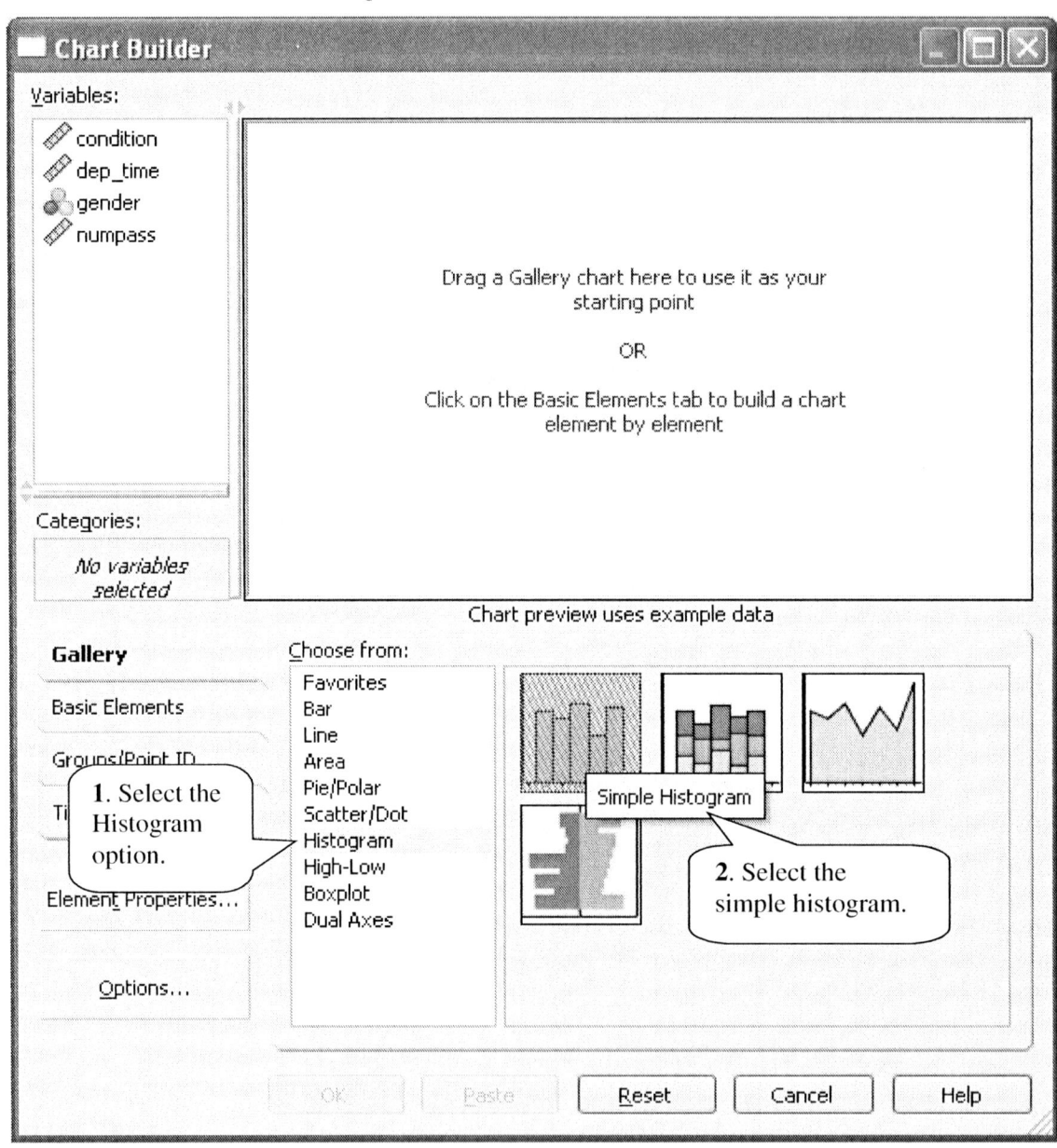

- Select **dep_time** from the list of **Variables:** and drag this variable into the **x-axis?** field in the chart preview area.

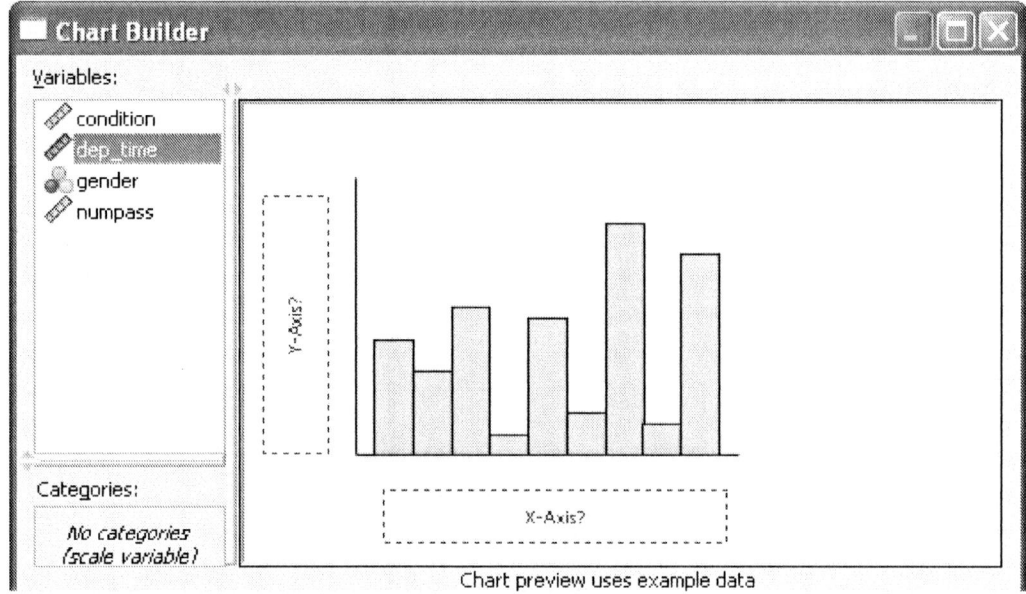

- Click the **OK** button to produce the histogram. The default chart options in SPSS result in a histogram like the one below. The annotations identify the elements of the chart that should be edited or deleted.

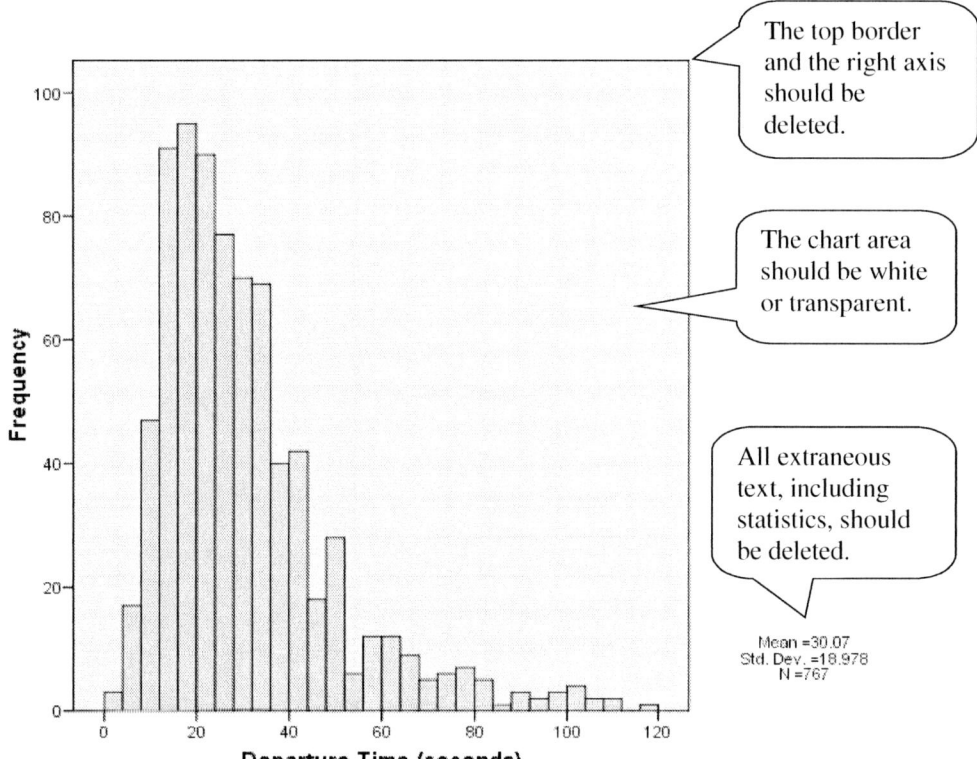

The top border and the right axis should be deleted.

The chart area should be white or transparent.

All extraneous text, including statistics, should be deleted.

- To access the SPSS **Chart Editor**, you may double-click on any part of the chart or right-click and select **SPSS Chart Object ▶ Open**.

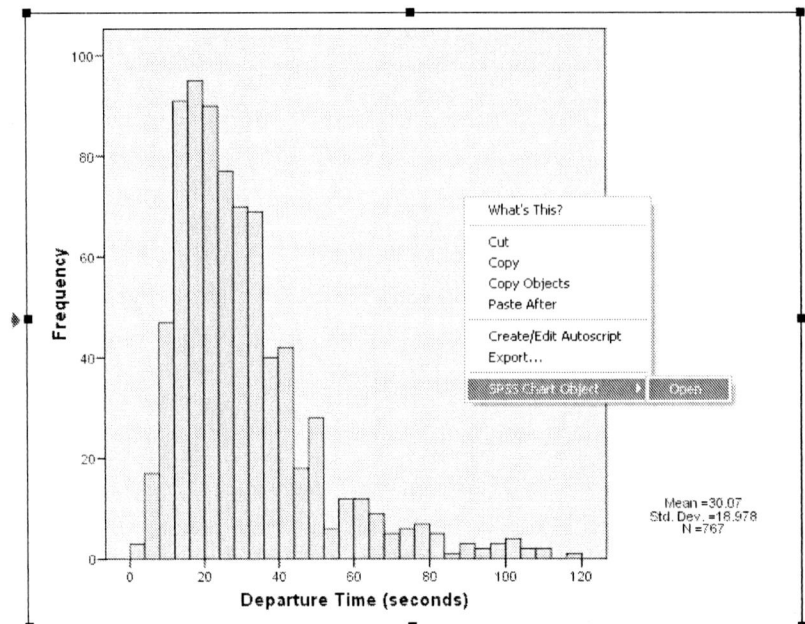

- In the **Chart Editor** double click on the chart to produce the **Properties** dialog window.

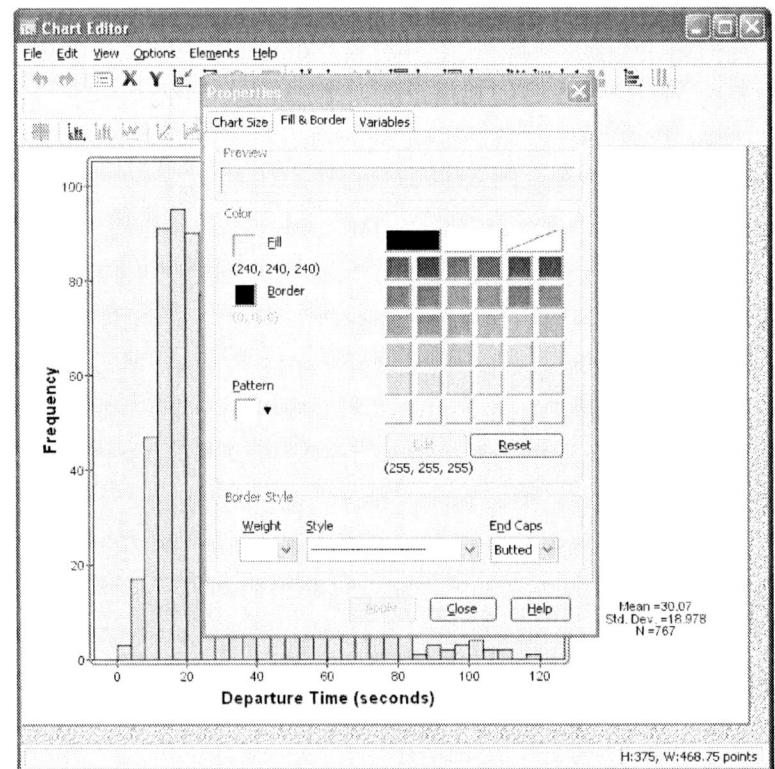

CHAPTER 3 ■ VISUAL DISPLAYS OF DATA 3-7

- In the **Properties** window, click on the box to the left of **F̲ill**, then select **Transparent** to replace the light gray background with a transparent background. Now click on the box to the left of **B̲order**, then select Transparent to remove the top border and right axis of the chart. Click on the **A̲pply** button, then the **C̲lose** button to close the window and return to the **Chart Editor**.

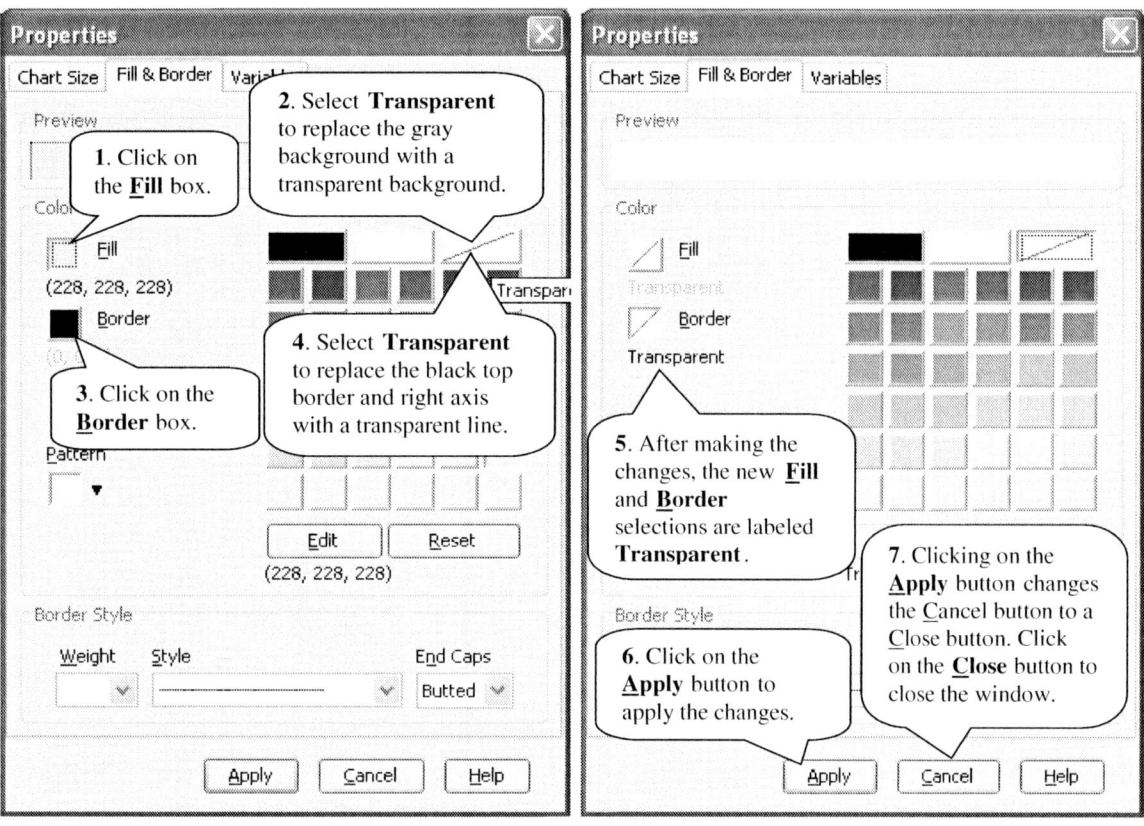

- Right-click on the statistics text and select **Delete** from the menu.

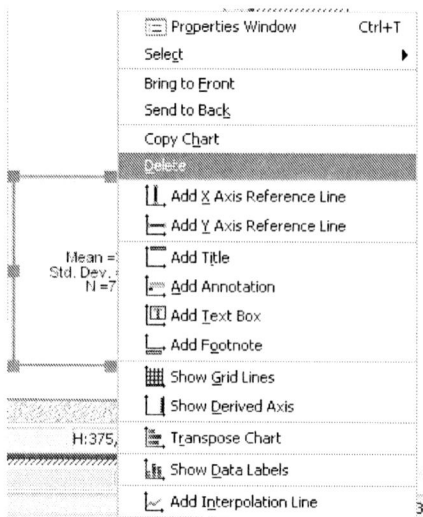

- After completing the edits just described, the histogram should appear as follows.

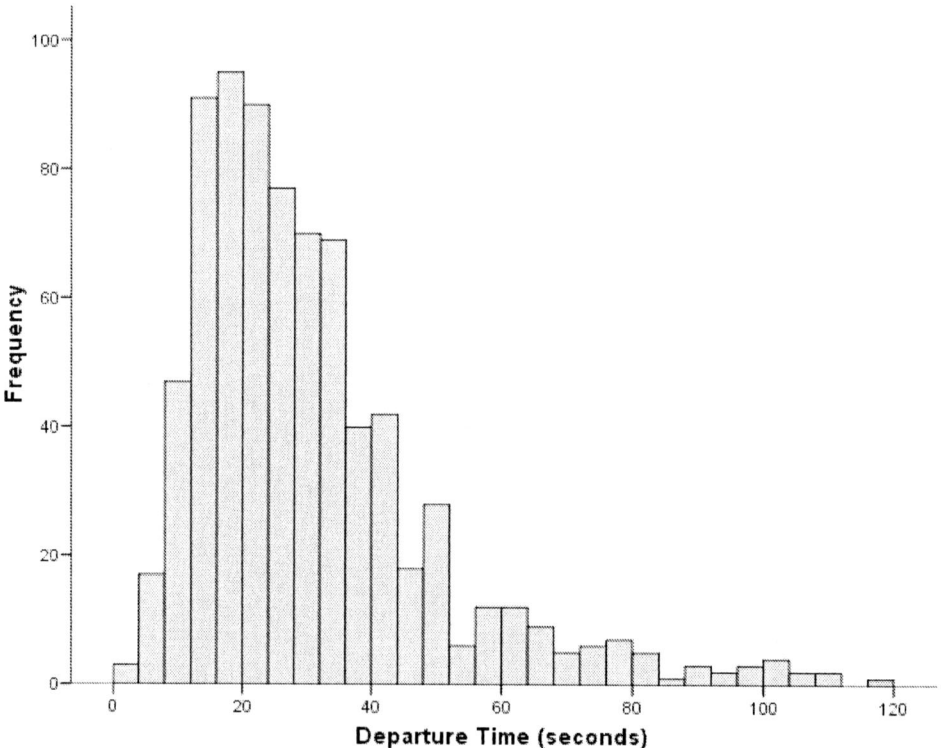

- You may continue to edit the chart to change the color and or border of the bars. Double-click the chart (or right-click and select **SPSS Chart Object ▶ Open**) to access the **Chart Editor**. Then either double-click on one of the bars (or right-click and **Select ▶ All Histogram Bar**) to bring up the Properties dialog window.

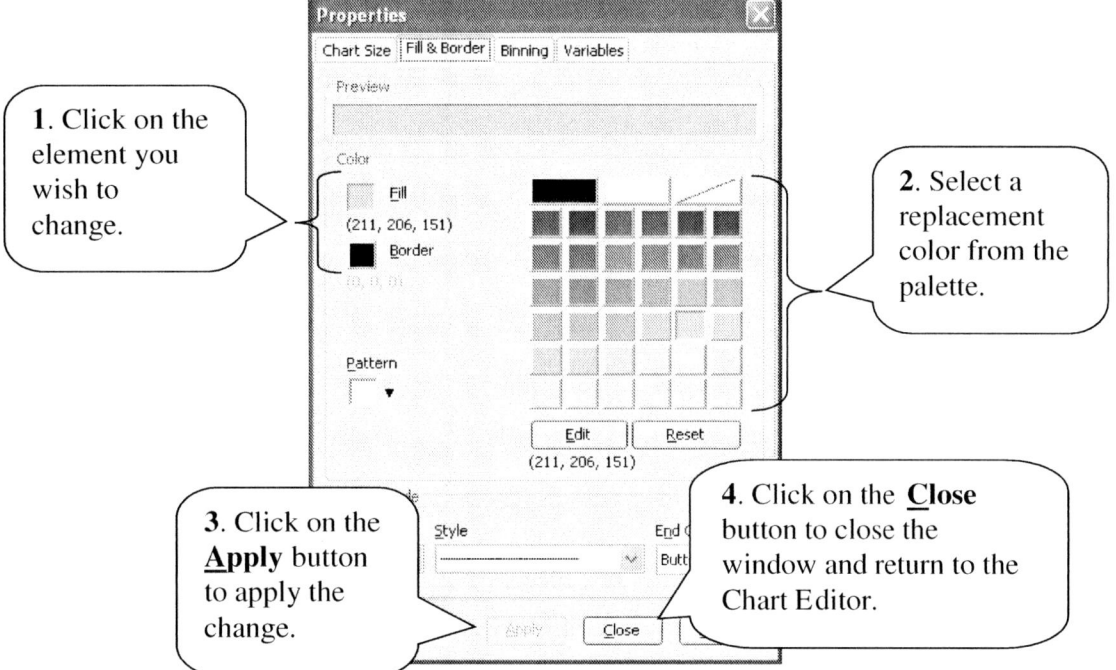

- To change any element of any chart within the **Chart Editor**, double-click on that element to access the **Properties** dialog window, then select the tab for that element. For example, to change either the horizontal or vertical axis scale, double-click on the axis or one of the axis labels to bring up the Properties dialog window, then select the **Scale** tab.

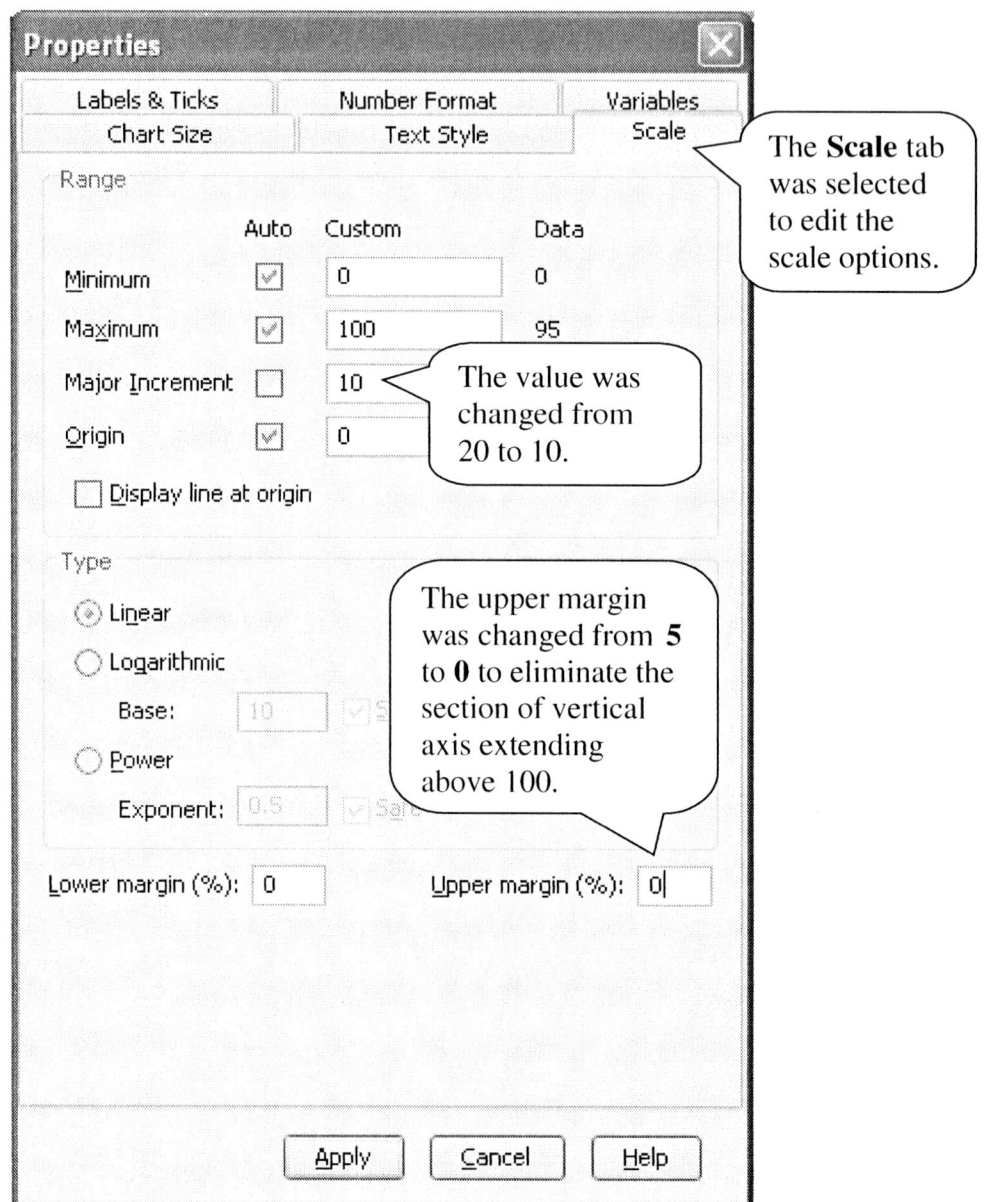

- After changing the vertical and horizontal axes, your completed histogram should be similar to the one below:

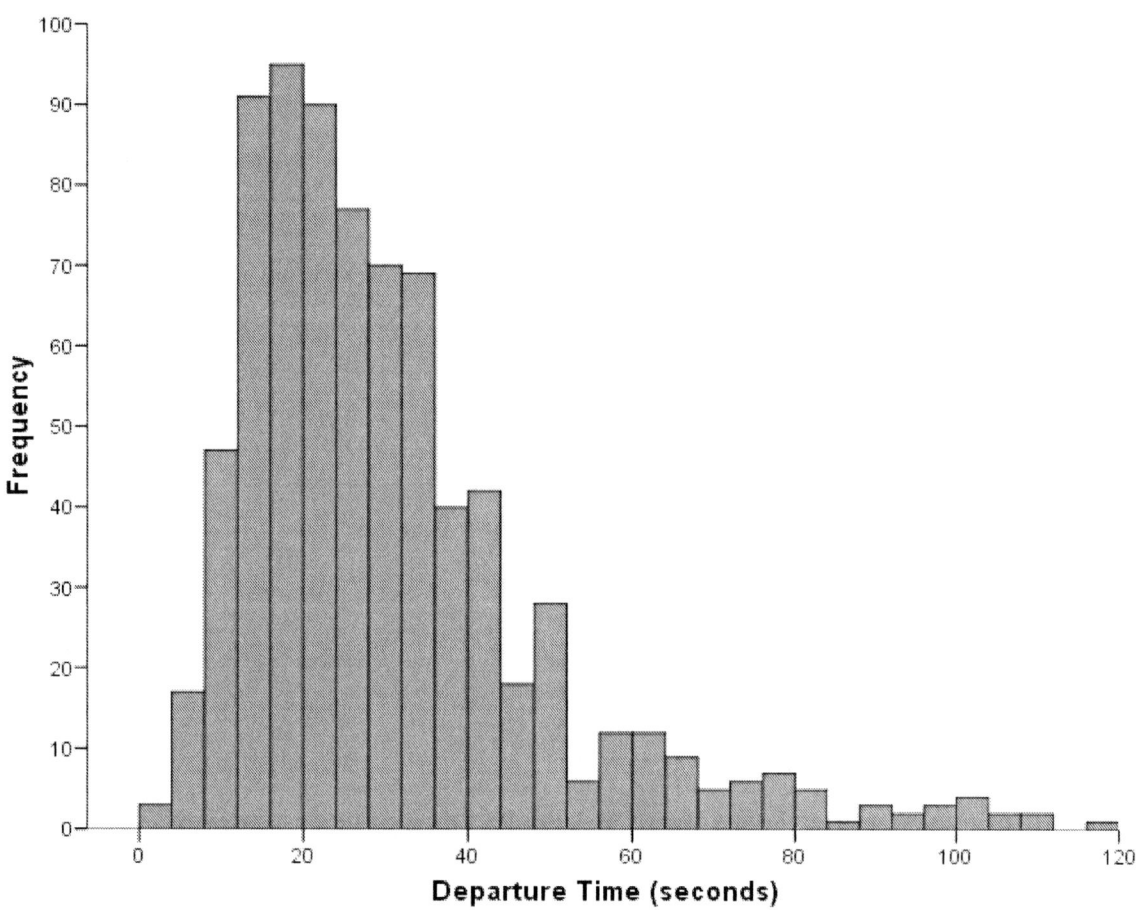

CHAPTER 4

PROBABILITIES AND RESEARCH

The Risks and Rewards of Scientific Sampling

EXPECTED RELATIVE-FREQUENCY PROBABILITY

EXERCISE 1

Launch SPSS and select **Type in data** from the list of "What would you like to do?" options. First, we'll do some things "by hand" and then use the syntax language of SPSS to do them for us.

Go to the **Variable View** window and enter the names of four variables: **Trial, Outcome, Sum,** and **Proportion**. The **Type** of each variable is **Numeric** and **Decimals** should be set to **2** for *Proportion*, zero for the others as shown below.

	Name	Type	Width	Decimals	Label
1	Trial	Numeric	8	0	
2	Outcome	Numeric	8	0	
3	Sum	Numeric	8	0	
4	Proportion	Numeric	8	2	

- Go to the **Data View** window. You should see *Trial, Outcome, Sum,* and *Proportion* listed as the names of the first four variables. Type **1** in the first row under Trial. Press the Enter key until the cursor is on Row 100 (this is the "by hand" part); type **100** in the first column in that row.

- From the **Transform** menu, select **Compute Variable...** to produce the **Compute Variable** dialog window. Type **Trial** in the **Target Variable:** field, then type **lag(trial) + 1** in the **Numeric Expression:** field.

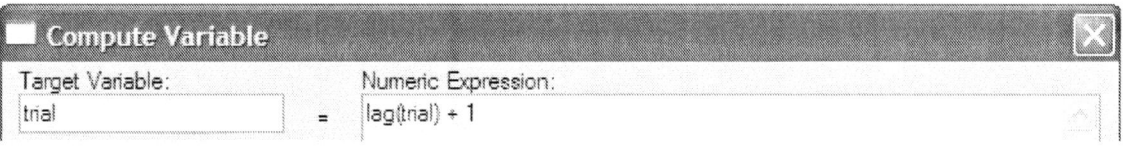

- Now click the **If... (optional case selection condition)** button (it's in the bottom left corner of the window and looks like this: [If...]) to produce the **Compute Variable: If Cases** window. Click the radio button next to **Include if case satisfies condition:** and type **missing(trial)** in the condition field.

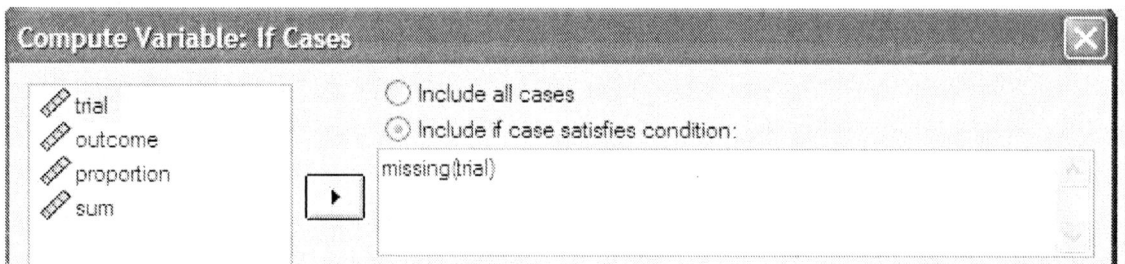

The only two values of Trial so far are 1 and 100, so 98 of them are "missing." The expression **lag(trial) + 1** adds 1 to the value of trial in the previous row, the row that "lags" behind by 1. So, the combination of lag(trial) + 1 and missing(trial) will fill the blank ("missing") cells under Trial with the values 2 through 99.

- Click **OK** to produce the **Change existing variable?** query, then click **OK** to fill the blank cells under Trial.

- Open the **Compute Variable...** window again and type **Outcome** in the **Target Variable:** field. Scroll down the **Function group:** window and select **Random Numbers** to access the **Functions and Special Variables:** list. Select **Rv.Binom** and click the [▲] button to move this function into the **Numeric Expression:** window. Replace the first **?** with **1** and the second **?** with **.5 or 0.5** (typing the zero makes it easier to see the decimal). The expression should read **RV.BINOM(1,0.5)**.

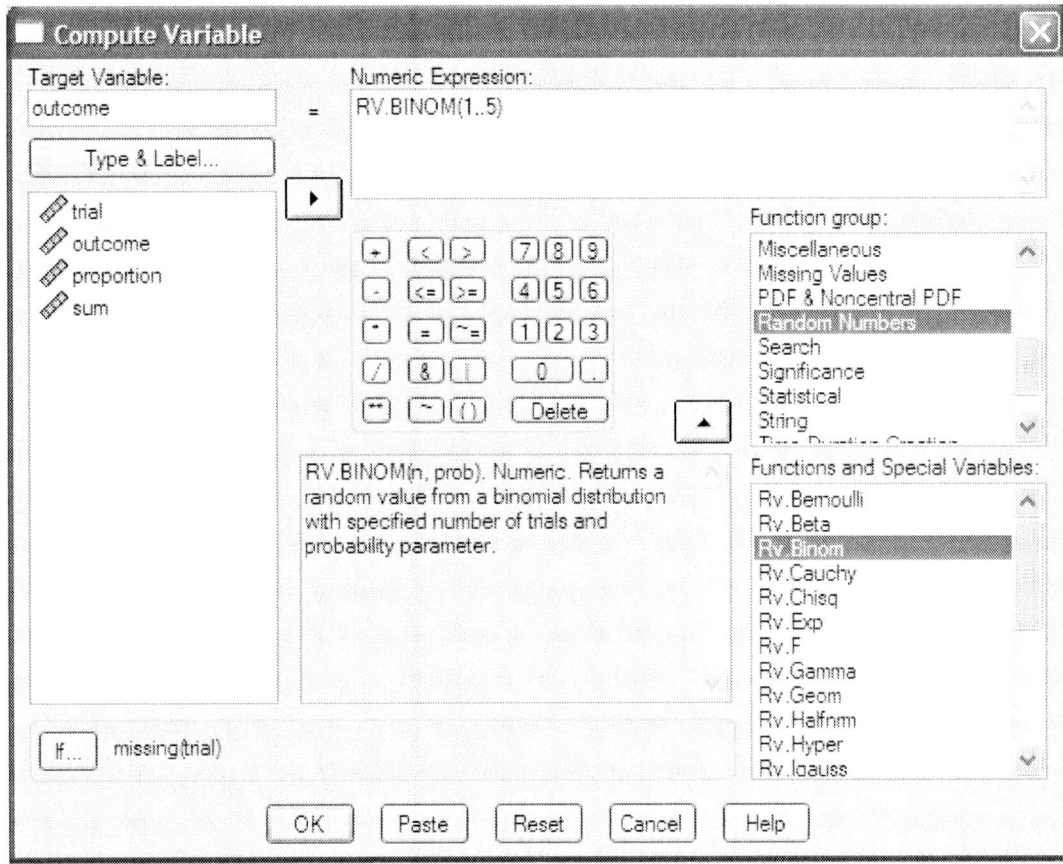

You may skip the selection of the Rv.Binom function and just type the function and arguments into the numeric expression window. The first argument specifies the number of trials (1) and the second argument specifies the probability of observing a success on that trial (0.5). So, you are using RV.BINOM to simulate a single coin toss. Because there are 100 values of the Trial variable, you are simulating 100 coin tosses in all. Notice that the **If... (optional case selection condition)** radio button has the phrase **missing(trial)** instead of **(optional case selection condition)** printed to the right of the button. This means that the **Compute Variable: If Cases** dialog window is set to **Include if case satisfies condition:** from a previous step in this exercise.

- Click (what is now) the **If... missing(trial)** button to produce the **Compute Variable: If Cases** window and click the radio button next to **Include all cases**. Click **Continue** to return to the **Compute Variable** window. You should see the default phrase **(optional case selection condition)** next to the **If...** button.

- Click **OK** to produce the **Change existing variable?** query, then click **OK** to generate 100 outcomes of a coin tossing experiment. Each **1** that appears under **Outcome** is a success (e.g., a head or a tail, depending on which one is defined as a success).

- In the first row under **Sum** type the first value of **Outcome** (a 1 or a 0). Access the **Compute Variable...** window again and type **Sum** in the **Target Variable:** field. In the **Numeric Expression:** field type **lag(sum) + outcome**.

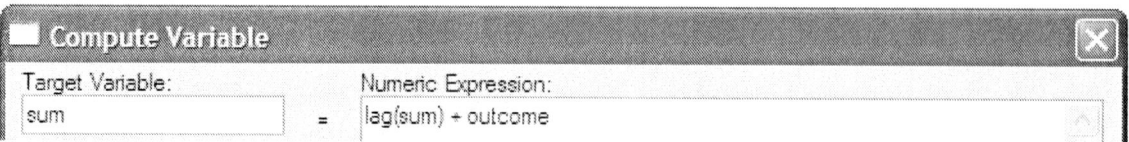

- Click [If...] to access the **Compute Variable: If Cases** window, select **Include if case satisfies condition:**, and type **missing(sum)** in the condition field.

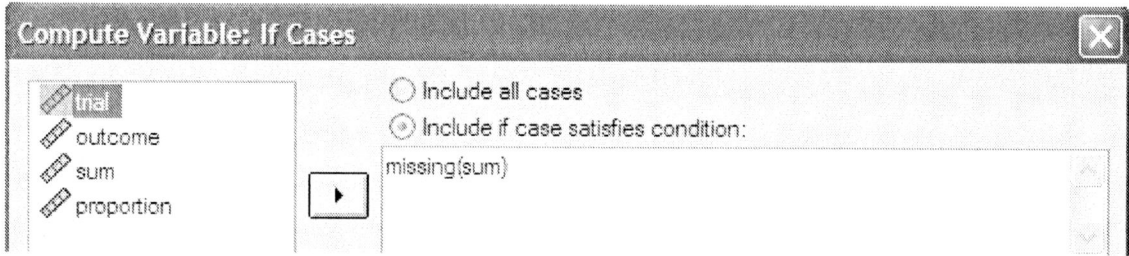

- Click **Continue** to return to the **Compute Variable** dialog window. When the Compute Variable dialog window appears, click **OK** to produce the **Change existing variable?** query, then click **OK** to fill the blank cells under **Sum**. The Sum variable maintains a running total of the number of successes (outcomes that equal 1). Check the values in this column to make sure you understand the values of the Sum variable.

- Access the **Compute Variable...** window again and type **Proportion** in the **Target Variable:** field. In the **Numeric Expression:** field type **sum/trial**. Click [If...] to access the **Compute Variable: If Cases** window, and click the radio button next to **Include all cases**.

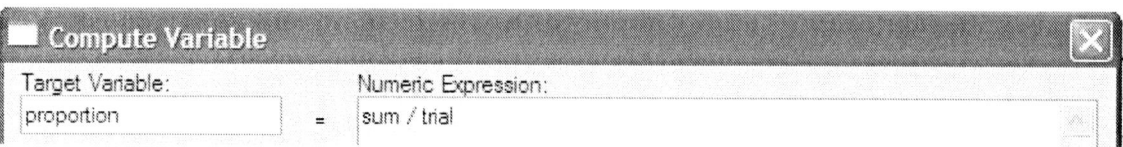

- Click **Continue** to return to the **Compute Variable** window, then click **OK** to produce the **Change existing variable?** query, then click OK again to fill the cells under **Proportion**. If the values of Proportion are single digits, go to the **Variable View** window and make sure that **Decimals** is set to **2**. Each value of proportion is the proportion of successful trials to that point.

Assignment 1

Make a line graph of the change in proportion of successes over trials. From the **Graphs** menu select **Chart Builder...** to produce the Chart Builder dialog window. The first Chart Builder dialog window offers an opportunity to define the variable properties if you have not already done so. That won't be necessary in this exercise, so click **OK** to produce the second Chart Builder dialog window. From the **Gallery** of chart types (bottom half of the window), select **Line** and drag the **Simple Line** template (it's the leftmost template in the gallery; you'll see the label "Simple Line" appear when you move the cursor over the template) into the large chart preview field at the top of the window.

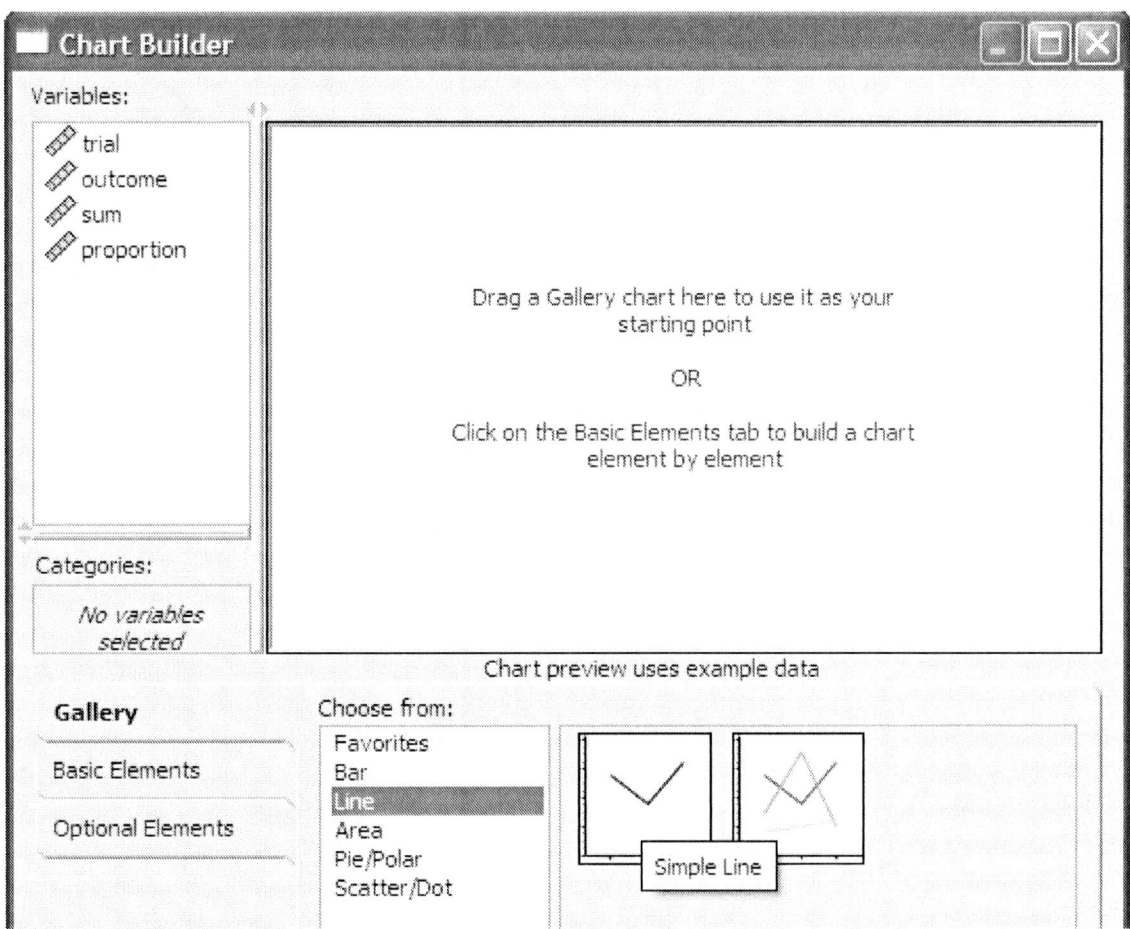

Select **Trial** and drag this variable to the **X-Axis?** field, then select **Proportion** and drag it to the **Y-Axis?** field. Click **OK** to generate the chart.

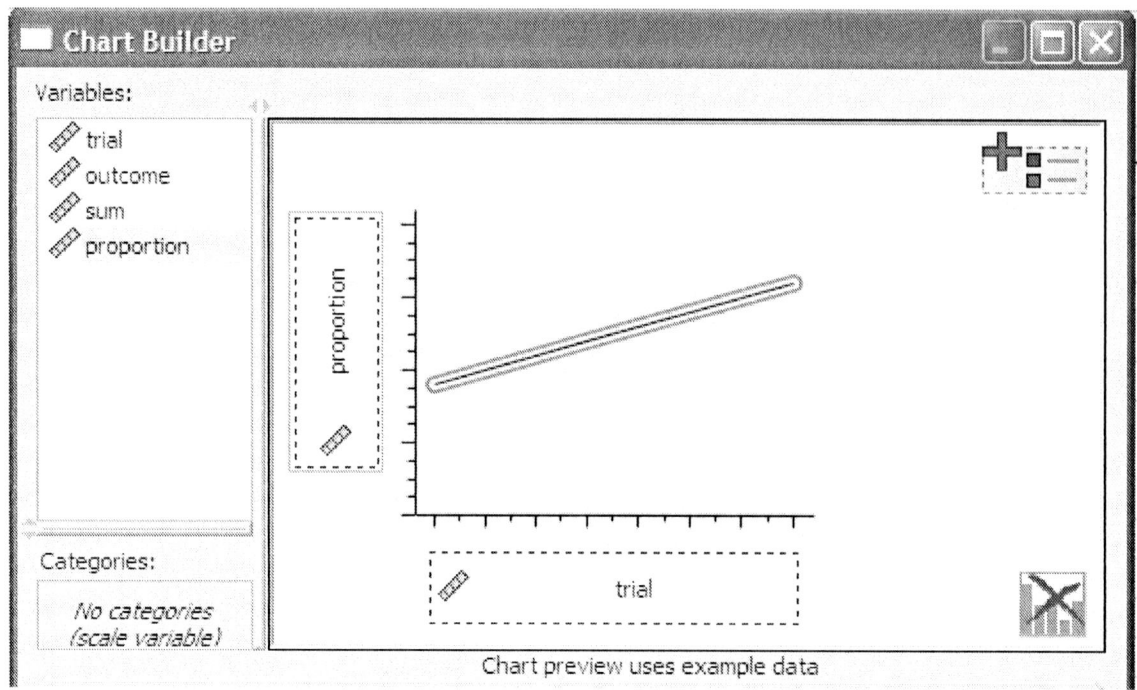

Questions

1. Describe the trend in the chart. What happens to the proportion of successes as the number of trials increases?
2. Explain the relation between the terms *relative frequency*, *proportion*, *percentage*, and *probability*.

EXERCISE 2

From the SPSS Data Editor **File** menu, select **Open ▶Syntax** to produce the **Open Syntax** dialog window.

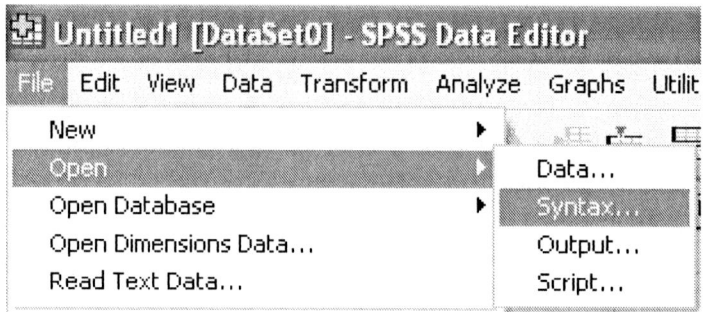

The current folder is identified in the **Look in:** drop-down menu at the top of the **Open Syntax** window:

Click the ⌄ button on the right to access the menu of accessible drives and folders. Navigate to the data folder and open the syntax file named **1000 trials of a coin-toss experiment**. You will see the following lines of syntax appear in the SPSS Syntax Editor window. Locate the **set seed = ######** line and replace each **#** character with a random digit.

```
new file.
* This program creates a new SPSS data file with four variables:
* trial, outcome, sum, and proportion. Each of the trials uses
* RV.BINOM(1,0.5) to simulate the outcome of a coin toss. Sum
* stores a running total of successful outcomes (e.g. "heads"),
* and proportion expresses sum as a proportion of trials.
* IMPORTANT: Replace the # characters below with a 6-digit random
* number to produce a unique sequence of outcomes each time you
* run the file.
set seed = ######.
input program.
* Need initial values of variables for lag function.
compute trial = 1.
compute outcome = rv.binom(1,.5).
compute sum = outcome.
compute proportion = sum.
end case.
      loop #trial = 2 to 1000.
            compute trial = #trial.
            compute outcome = rv.binom(1,0.5).
            compute sum = lag(sum) + outcome.
            compute proportion = sum/trial.
      end case.
      end loop.
      end file.
end input program.
formats proportion (f8.2).
execute.
```

To execute the syntax code, select **Run, All** from the **SPSS Syntax Editor** menu as shown below.

The syntax program will create a new file with the same four variables that you created in Exercise 1. The first 5 rows of your file should be similar to the one below.

	trial	outcome	sum	proportion
1	1	1	1	1.00
2	2	1	2	1.00
3	3	0	2	.67
4	4	1	3	.75
5	5	1	4	.80

Assignment 2

Follow the instructions for Assignment 1 to make a line graph for the new sequence of 1000 trials.

Question

3. Imagine that you are a gambler and you've made a wager with another individual about the outcomes of coin-toss experiments. You decide before the first coin toss who bets *heads* and who bets *tails* and each person defines that outcome as a success on every trial. Here's the wager: The person who bets *heads* has to pay the other person a dollar for every hundredth of a percentage point (0.01%) that the percentage of heads is below 50, whereas the person who bets tails has the same obligation if the percentage of tails is below 50. So, if the percentage of heads turns out to be 52.87, the person who bet tails would owe $287.

Would you rather define the length of the game as 100 trials or 1000 trials? Write a brief explanation of your answer. Be sure to refer to the graphs that you constructed for Assignments 1 and 2.

Exercise 3

Open and run the syntax file named **100,000 trials of a coin-toss experiment** and save the data file. Use the values in the data file to complete Assignment 3. Instead of scrolling down in this very large data file, use the **Go to Case...** command to quickly locate the cases (rows) that correspond to the trial numbers in the table. From the **Edit** menu, select the **Go to case...** command to produce the **Go To Case** dialog window. Type a trial number in the **Case Number:** field. Click **OK** to cause the requested row to appear at the top of the **Data Editor** window.

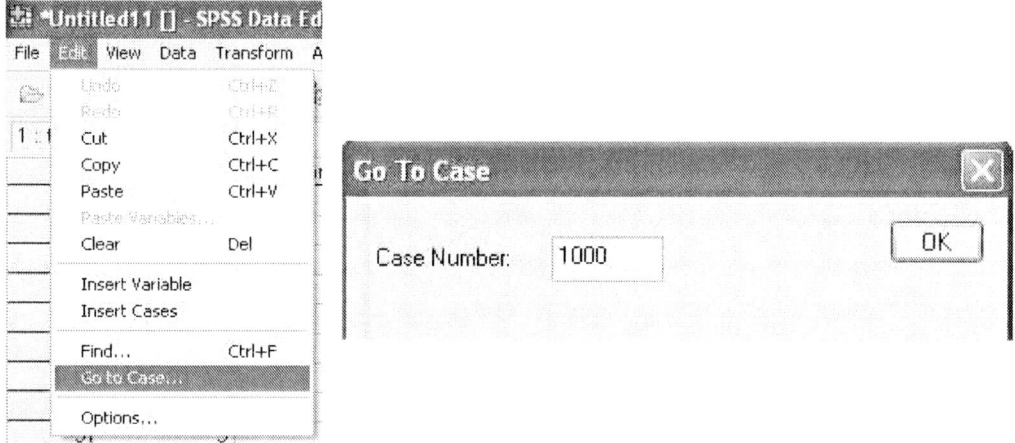

Assignment 3

Use the values in the data to complete the following table.

Trials	Sum	abs_error	rel_error
1			
10			
100			
1,000			
10,000			
100,000			

Individuals who exhibit the **gambler's fallacy** often support their belief by appealing to something called "the law of averages." After losing several games in a row, they may say something like, "I'm due for a win; it's just the law of averages." In mathematical statistics, the law of averages is more often called the *law of large numbers* or, more precisely, *the weak law of large numbers*. A paraphrase of the formal statement of the law of large numbers might read as follows: As the number of independent trials of a random process grows large, the deviation from expectation approaches zero. If the random process is tossing a coin, then the proportion of successes (e.g., heads) that you observe approaches the expected relative frequency probability as the number of coin tosses grows large. This is true, whether the expected relative frequency probability of success is exactly .5, or some other value such as .495 or .505.

The deviation from expectation is sometimes called *chance error*. You might express the law of averages in terms of chance error by stating that chance error decreases as the number of trials increases. Note, however, that this statement is true only if chance error is measured as a relative frequency or proportion. This statement is not true if chance error is measured in absolute terms such as the difference between the frequency of heads and the expected frequency of heads. If it is assumed that a coin is perfectly balanced, then one expects the relative frequency of heads to be .5

Question

4. Explain how the information in your completed table illustrates the *law of averages*. Be sure to address the relation between the number of trials and the values in the middle column as well as the relation between the number of trials and the values in the last column.

ANSWERS

1.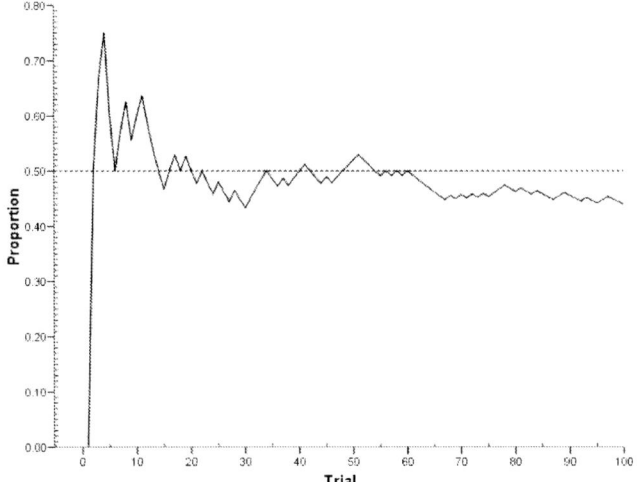

   The above graph shows the proportion of successes becoming less variable as the number of trials increases. However, the proportion of successes also appears to be deviating away from .5 (50%). Although the deviation away from .5 reflects a random process that may or may not be apparent in your chart, you should observe a similar reduction in variability. The reduction in variability is a function of sample size; as the size of the sample (number of trials) increases, variability decreases.

2. The terms *relative frequency* and *proportion* are interchangeable. In this context, both terms express the frequency of some outcome as a fraction of the total number of trials. A proportion may be expressed as a percentage by multiplying by 100. A *percentage* is simply the relative frequency with which an outcome occurs per 100 trials. These three terms may be used to express the *probability* of observing a particular outcome. When a percentage of outcomes is used to express the probability of an outcome, the phrase "percent chance" is typically used: "If you flip a coin enough times, the percent chance of observing a head is close to 50."

3. If you are a gambler, then you are probably a risk-taker so you'd rather base your wager on a game of 100 trials. That's because the deviation from the expected relative frequency of a successful outcome (.5) will usually be larger for a smaller number of trials. So, you stand to either win or lose more if you wager on 100 rather than 1000 trials. The line graph below shows that one of the gamblers would be losing about $600 if the game were limited to 100 trials, but only about $100 if the game were extended to 1,000 trials.

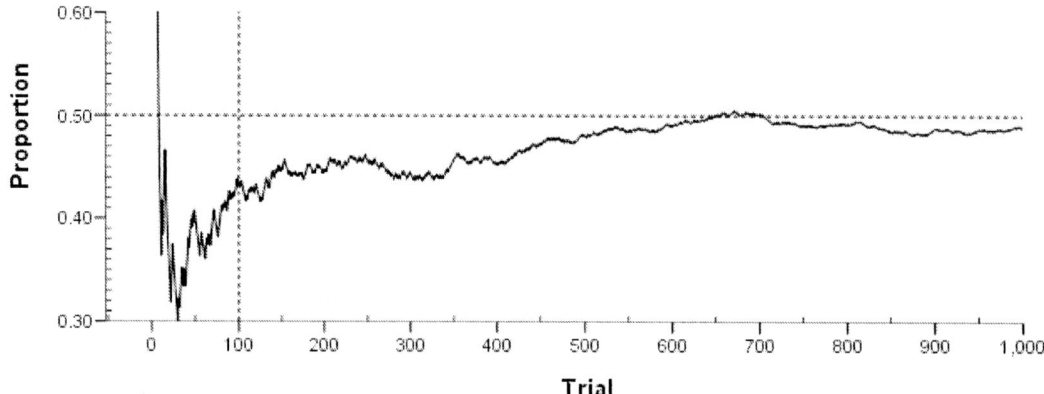

4. The numbers in the table will vary, of course, but the values in the last column should decrease with the number of trials as required by the "law of averages."

Trials	Sum	abs_error	rel_error
1	0	0.5	0.5
10	2	3	0.3
100	44	6	0.06
1,000	482	18	0.018
10,000	4961	39	0.0039
100,000	50020	20	0.0002

The law of averages states that the deviation from an expected frequency decreases as the number of trials grows large. However, this deviation must be expressed relative to the total number of trials—that is, as a relative frequency (last column) rather than a frequency (middle column).

CHAPTER 5

CORRELATION

Quantifying the Relation Between Two Variables

A graduate student assigned to teach her first class in introductory statistics for psychology majors wondered whether student performance on an exam would be related to class attendance. Accordingly, she kept a careful record of class absences before the first of three examinations in her class.

SPSS DATA ENTRY

Launch SPSS and select **Type in data** near the top of the list of menu options:

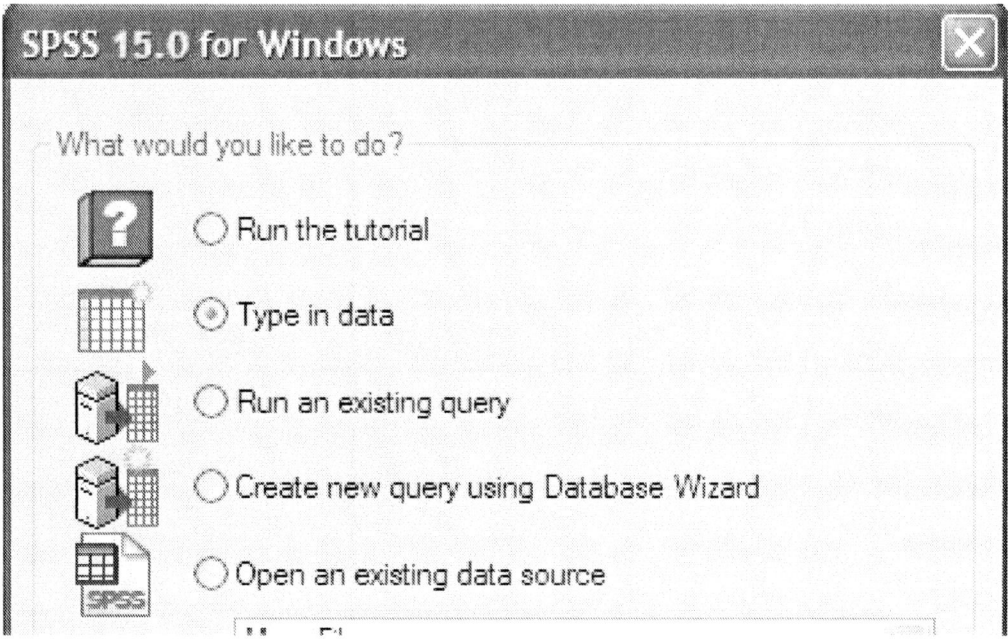

SPSS is fully launched when the spreadsheet–like **Data Editor** window appears. Click on the **Variable View** tab at the bottom of the screen to display the **Variable View** window:

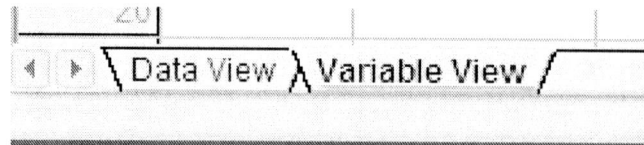

Type **Absences** in the first row of the first column of the Variable View window (under **Name**) and press the Enter key. Your screen should look like the one below, showing the default variable **Type** as **Numeric** and the default value of **Decimals** as "2." Do not change the variable type, but change the value of Decimals by clicking on the bottom arrow or just highlight the **2** and replace it by typing a **zero**. This value should be set to zero, because the number of class absences for each student is a **discrete** variable (one whose values can only be positive integers).

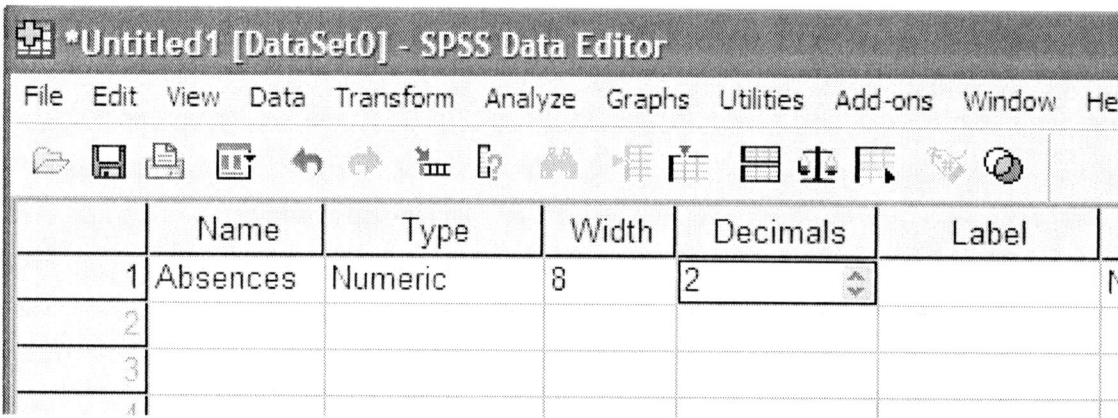

Now type **Exmscore** just beneath Absences and set Decimals to zero for this variable as well, because each student's score on the first exam has already been rounded to the nearest integer value. Before leaving the Variable View window, you should enter a description of each variable in the column under **Label**. Examples are shown below:

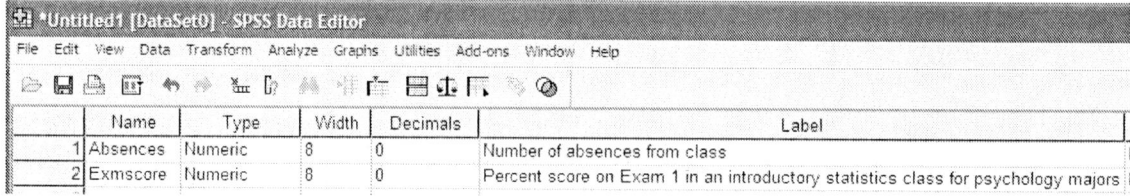

Now select the **Data View** window tab to return to the **Data Editor** window. You should see the names of the variables as headings for the first two columns (see below). If you do not see these names, review the previous steps and make sure that you've entered the names of the variables as instructed.

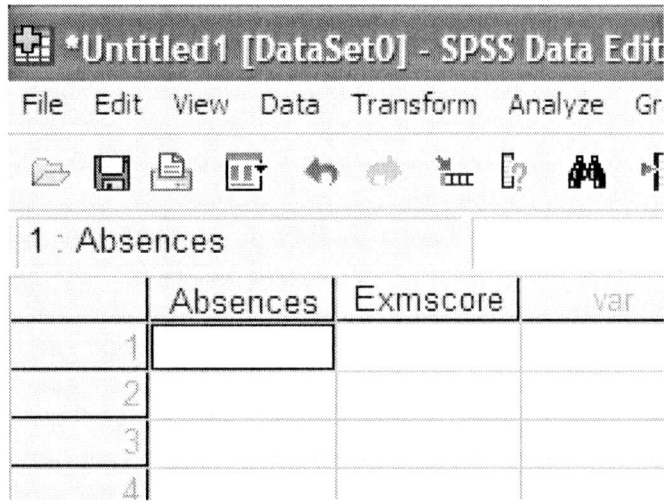

The data that you will type into the Data Editor window are displayed in the two columns on the next page. Absences is conceptualized as the "X" or **predictor** variable, because the instructor's interest is in determining whether a student's attendance record can be used to predict his or her exam score. The "Y" variable, Exmscore, is called the **criterion**, or dependent, variable.

The values in the X column should be typed in the Data Editor window in the column under Absences, and the values in the Y column should entered in the column under Exmscore. After entering all of the values, check to make sure that you entered them correctly in the order shown. When the data entry is complete, your screen should look like the one below on the right.

X	Y
0	86
1	85
0	81
0	79
0	78
0	75
1	67
1	65
2	63
0	63
2	61
1	60
1	52
2	51
2	48
2	47
1	43
2	43
2	40

Exercise 1

1. Select **Graphs, Scatter/Dot...** to access the **Scatter/Dot** dialog window.

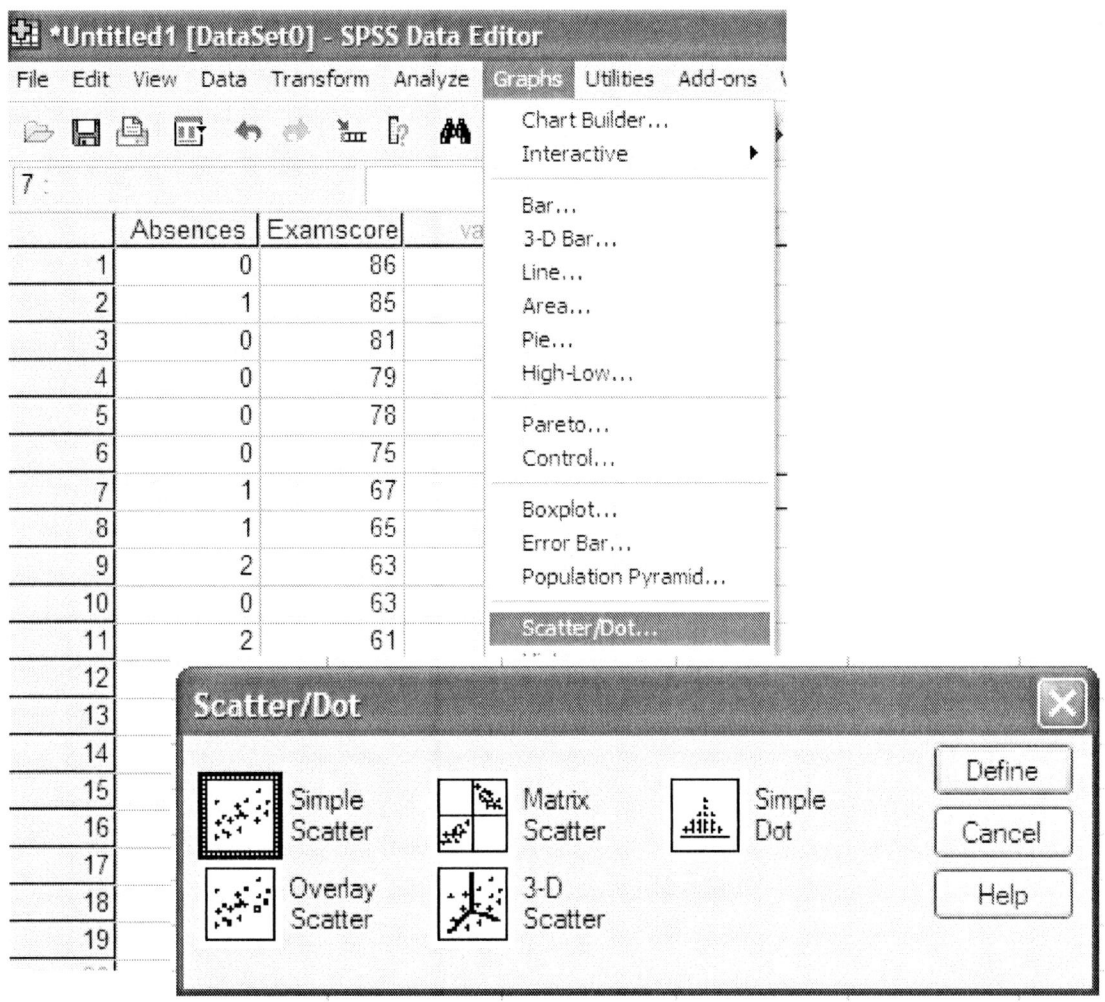

Select **Simple Scatter**, then click **Define** to bring up the **Simple Scatterplot** dialog window (below left). Now select **Absences** and click on the ▶ symbol to move this variable into the **X Axis:** field, then move **Exmscore** into the **Y Axis:** field (below right). Click **OK** to generate the output.

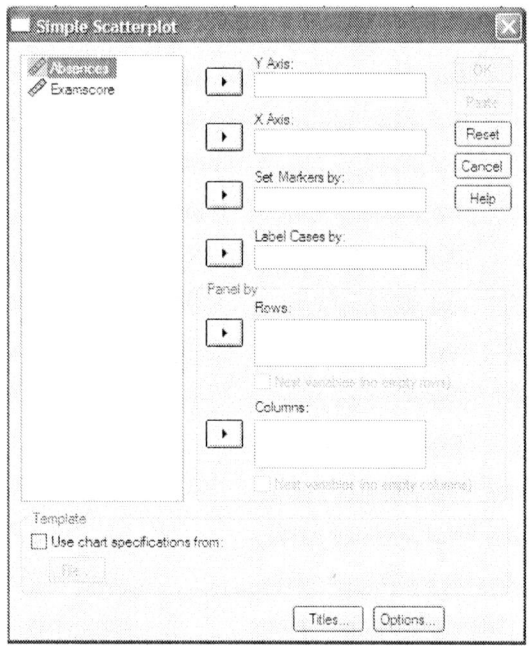 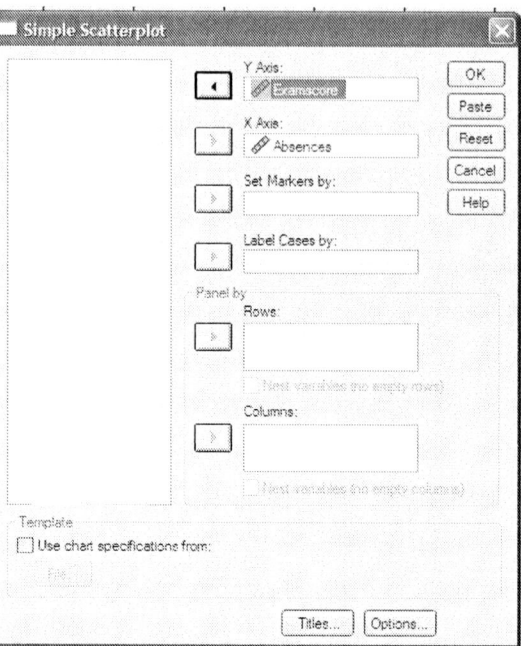

2. Describe the pattern in the scatterplot. Is it linear? Is the slope negative or positive?

3. Estimate the value of the correlation coefficient from the scatterplot and briefly explain your estimate.

4. Select **Analyze, Correlate ▶ Bivariate** (below left) to produce the **Bivariate Correlations** dialog window (below right).

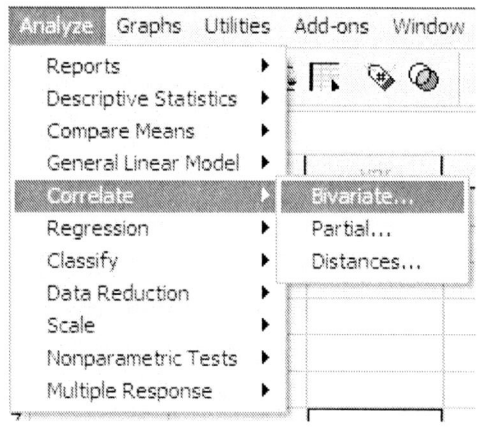 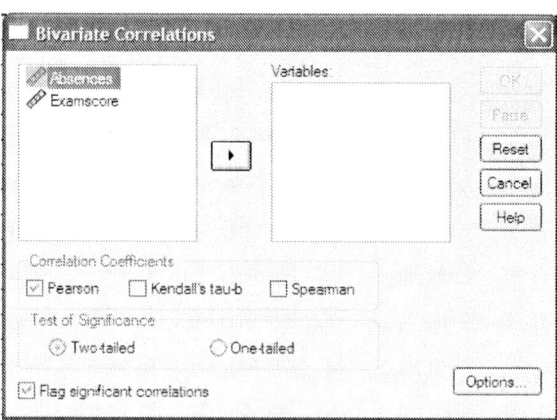

In the **Bivariate Correlations** dialog window, select both variables and move them into the **Variables:** field on the right side of the window. Make sure that the **Pearson** option under **Correlation Coefficients** is selected (see below). Click **OK** to generate the output.

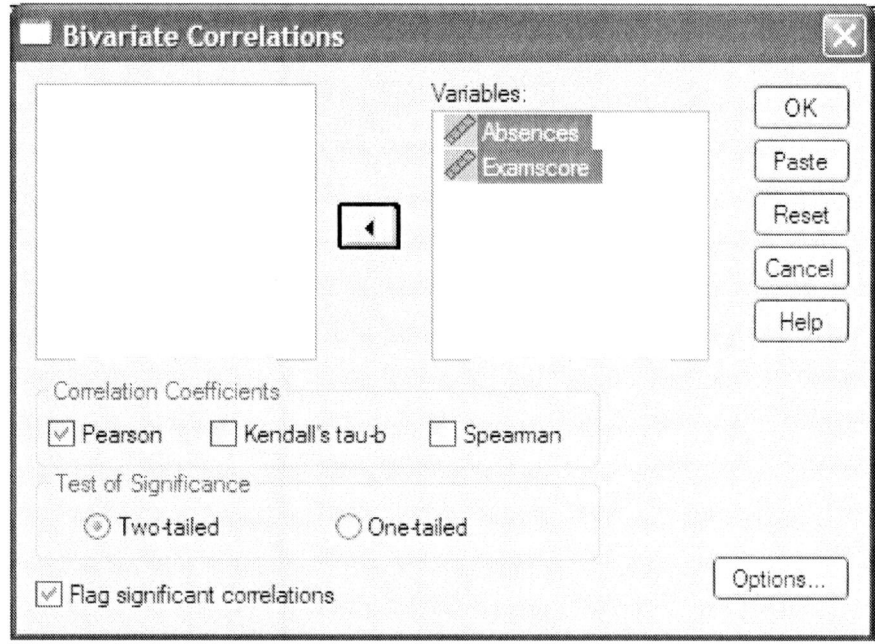

5. What is the value of the correlation coefficient? Was your estimate close? If your estimate wasn't close, revisit your explanation in **3** and explain how you went wrong.

6. What does the *magnitude* of the correlation coefficient reveal about the relationship between the two variables? What does the *sign* of the correlation coefficient reveal about the relationship?

Exercise 2

7. Add the following data values for the 20th student: **9** absences (she came to the first class and did not show up again until the day of the exam) and an exam score of **98**. Follow the instructions from Exercise 1-1 to produce a scatterplot of the data with this student added.

8. What term is used to describe the point that represents the added student?

9. Select **Analyze, Correlate ▶ Bivariate...** to compute the correlation coefficient for the data with this student added.

10. What is the effect of the addition of the new student's data on the sign and strength of the correlation coefficient?

Exercise 3

In this exercise, we'll exclude the cases with 2 or more absences before generating a scatterplot of the data with these cases removed.

- From the **Data** menu of the **Data Editor**, choose **Select Cases...**

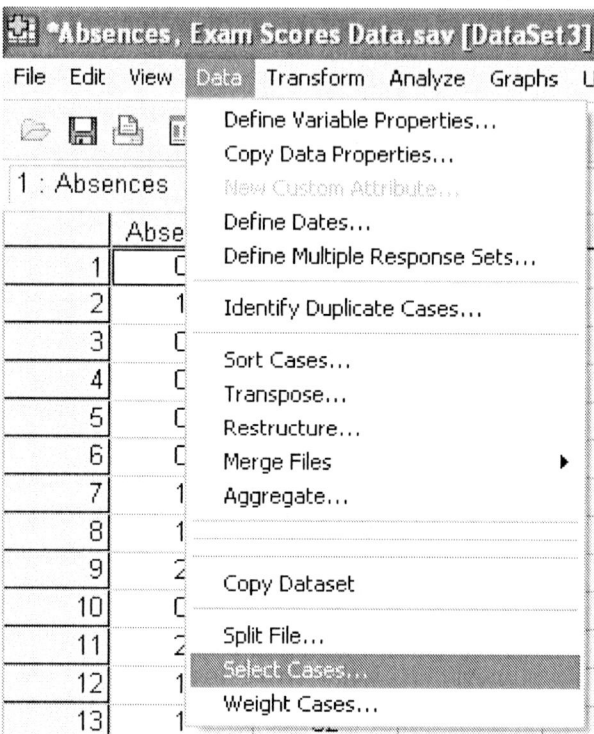

- This will produce the **Select Cases** dialog window. Click on the radio button next to **If condition is satisfied** as shown. Then click on the **If...** button (If...) just below.

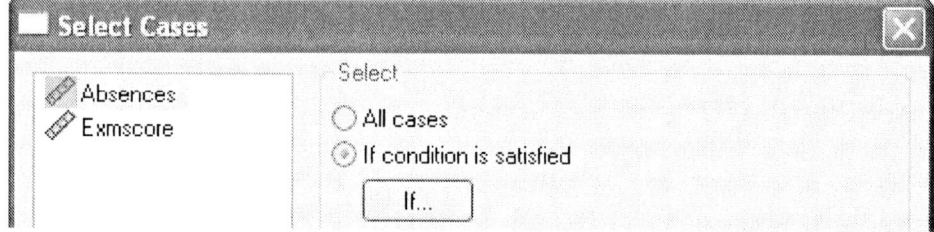

Clicking on the If... button produces the **Select Cases: If** dialog window. Type **Absences <= 1** as shown, then click **Continue** to return to the **Select Cases** dialog window.

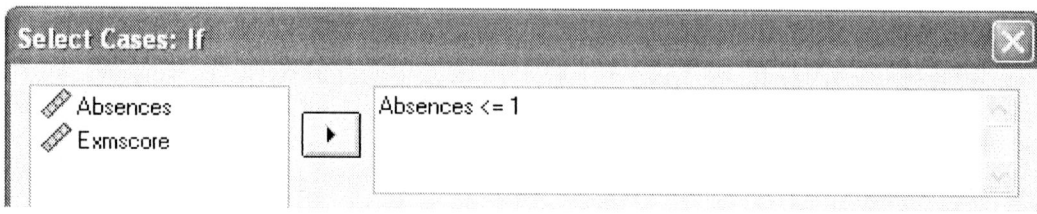

The **Select Cases** dialog should display **Absences <= 1** as the **If...** condition. If your dialog window looks like the one below, then click **OK** to return to the Data Editor.

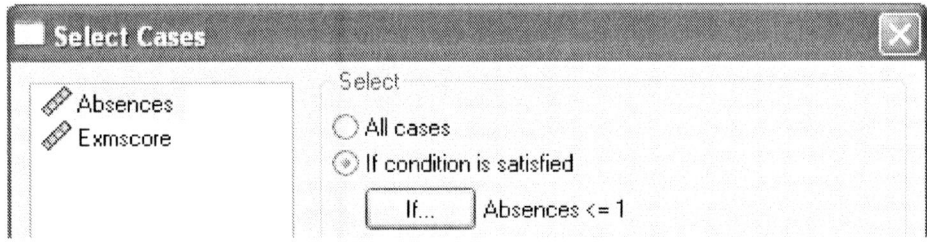

The Data Editor should be similar to the following. The forward slash (9) marks the cases with 2 or more absences that have been filtered (temporarily excluded) from the data set.

	Absences	Exmscore	filter_$
1	0	86	1
2	1	85	1
3	0	81	1
4	0	79	1
5	0	78	1
6	0	75	1
7	1	67	1
8	1	65	1
9	2	63	0
10	0	63	1
11	2	61	0
12	1	60	1
13	1	52	1
14	2	51	0
15	2	48	0
16	2	47	0
17	1	43	1
18	2	43	0
19	2	40	0
20	9	98	0

11. Follow the instructions from Exercise 1 to produce a scatterplot of the data with students with 2 or more absences removed.

12. Select **Analyze, Correlate ▶ Bivariate...** to compute the correlation coefficient for the data after removing the students with 2 or more absences.

13. Compare the correlation coefficient to the one that you computed in Exercise 2. What is the effect of excluding the students with 2 or more absences on the sign and strength of the correlation coefficient?

14. As discussed on p. 228 of the text, the change in the correlation coefficient occurred because the _____ of values of the absences variable was _____.

15. Does the correlation coefficient that you computed in Exercise 1 show that missing class causes students to make lower exam grades? Explain your answer.

ANSWERS

EXERCISE 1

1.

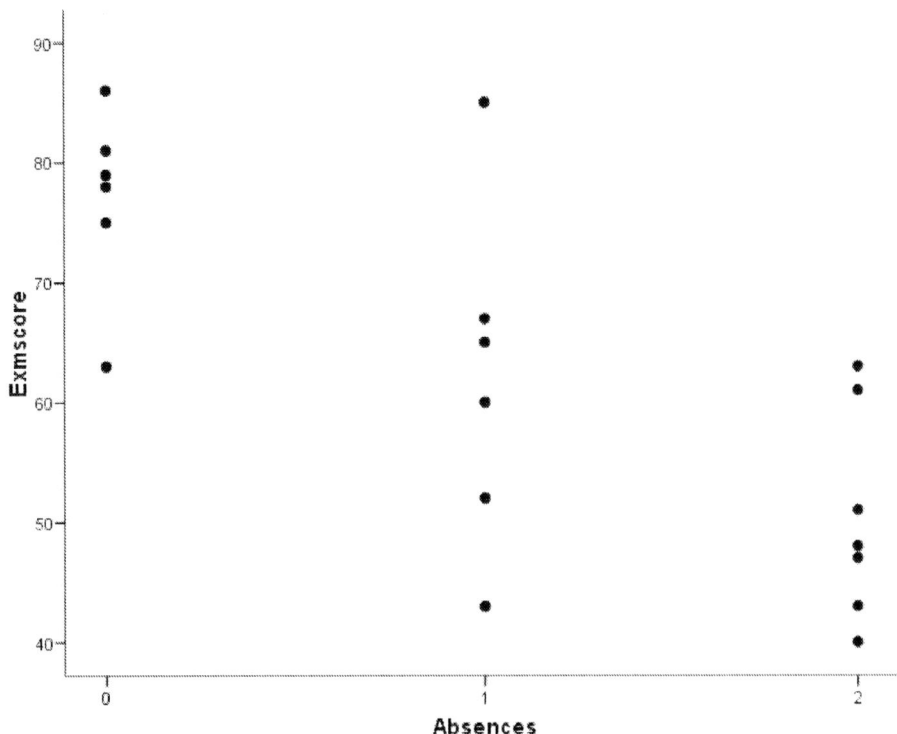

2. There is an apparent trend for students with fewer absences to earn higher exam scores, as may be expected. The relation between the variables is negative because a line drawn to fit the three columns of points would slope downward from left to right. You can visualize this pattern by connecting the middle of each cluster of points with an imaginary line.

3. The easiest part of the estimate is the sign, because estimating the magnitude (strength) of a linear relation from a scatterplot requires practice associating scatterplots with correlation coefficients, but a good estimate will be between $-.5$ and $-.75$.

4.
Correlations

		Absences	Exmscore
Absences	Pearson Correlation	1	-.747**
	Sig. (2-tailed)		.000
	N	19	19
Exmscore	Pearson Correlation	-.747**	1
	Sig. (2-tailed)	.000	
	N	19	19

** Correlation is significant at the 0.01 level (2-tailed).

5. From the SPSS output table, the correlation coefficient is –.747.

6. The *magnitude* of the correlation coefficient indicates the *strength* of the linear relationship between the variables. The strength of the relation may be roughly estimated by noting the typical distance between the points and a line drawn to fit the overall pattern of points. The closer the points to the line, the stronger the linear relation between the variables. The *sign* of the correlation coefficient indicates the *direction* (positive or negative) of the relation between the variables. This direction may be discerned from the slope of the pattern of points in the scatterplot. The sign of the slope will always be the same as the sign of the correlation coefficient.

EXERCISE 2

7.

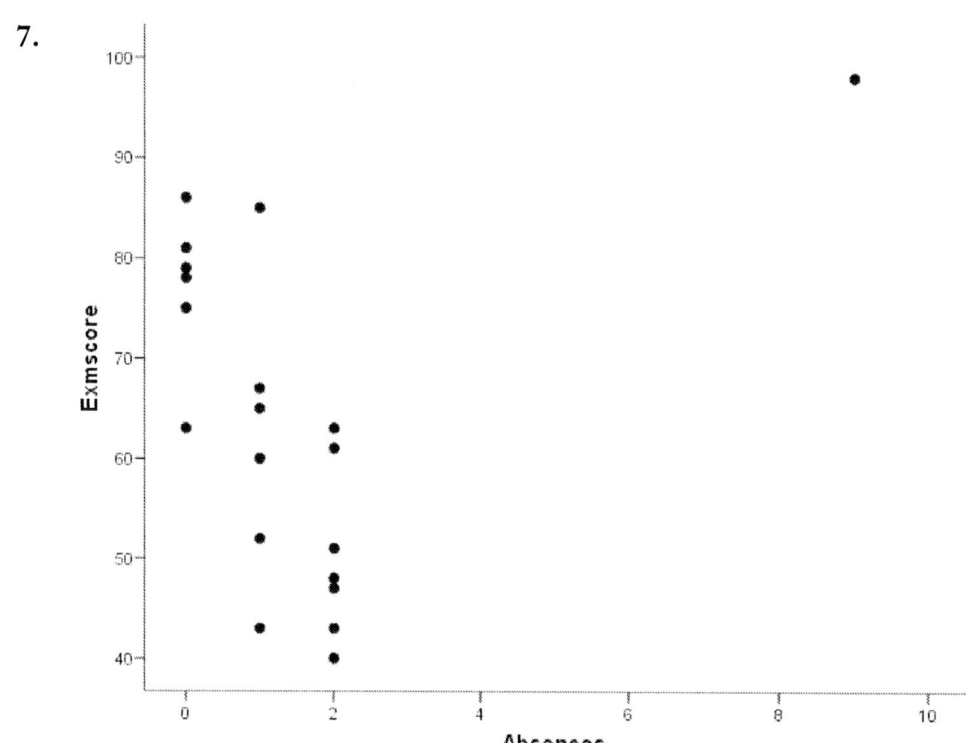

8. The added point is called an **outlier**.

9.

Correlations

		Absences	Exmscore
Absences	Pearson Correlation	1	.156
	Sig. (2-tailed)		.511
	N	20	20
Exmscore	Pearson Correlation	.156	1
	Sig. (2-tailed)	.511	
	N	20	20

10. The addition of the point representing the new student markedly reduced the strength and reversed the direction of the linear relation between the variables. The relation between the variables is grossly distorted by the outlier.

EXERCISE 3

11.
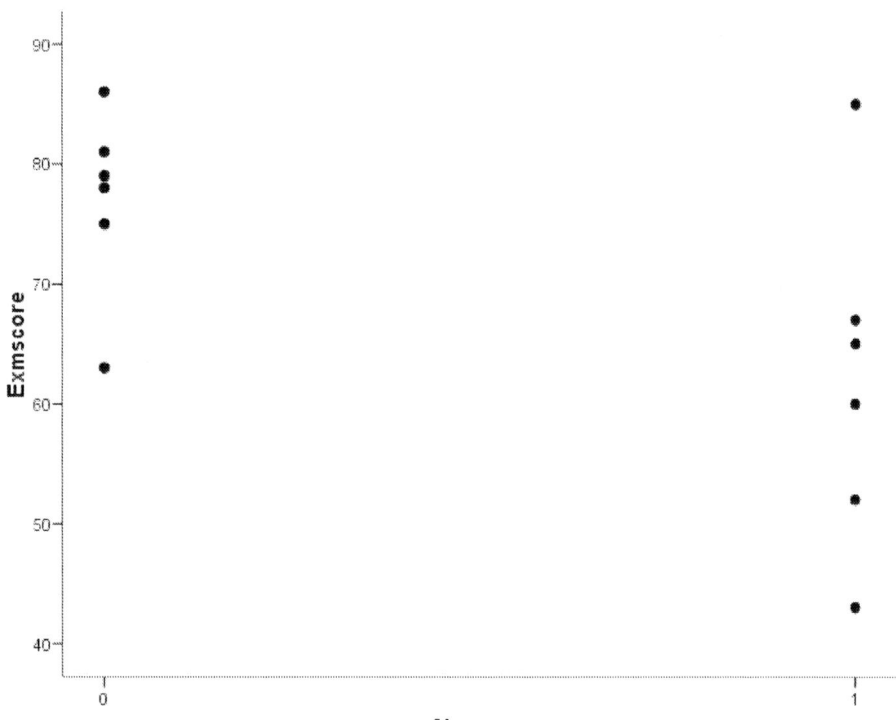

12.

Correlations

		Absences	Exmscore
Absences	Pearson Correlation	1	-.580*
	Sig. (2-tailed)		.048
	N	12	12
Exmscore	Pearson Correlation	-.580*	1
	Sig. (2-tailed)	.048	
	N	12	12

*Correlation is significant at the 0.05 level (2-tailed).

13. The removal of the students with two or more absences reduced the correlation coefficient from −.74 to −.58, indicating a reduction in the strength, but with no change in the direction, of the relation between the variables.

14. The change in the correlation coefficient occurred because the **range** of values of the absences variable was **restricted**.

15. The strong negative correlation between class absences and exam scores indicates that students with fewer absences earned higher exam scores, but says nothing about a causal relationship. Correlation is not causation. Even a perfect correlation can not be interpreted to mean that one of the variables is causally related to the other. In this example, a third variable, perhaps a character trait that we might call "conscientiousness," is responsible for good class attendance and competent performance on the exams.

CHAPTER 6

REGRESSION

Tools for Predicting Behavior

EXERCISE 1
PRODUCING A CORRELATION MATRIX

Launch SPSS. The default **"What would you like to do?"** menu option is **Open an existing data source**. Leave this option selected and access the **Statistics Grades (N = 72)** file on the data CD. The file includes scores on six variables for each of 72 students enrolled in an introductory statistics course. Four of the variables will be used in this exercise: scores on the verbal section of the SAT, scores on the math section of the SAT, self-reported ratings of math anxiety, and the final grade in the course. The values of these four variables for the first 15 cases from this file are displayed below.

SAT_Verbal	SAT_Math	Math_Anxiety	Final_Grade
560	540	4	92.42
680	690	5	94.29
590	420	9	91.31
580	470	4	88.57
580	480	8	82.63
700	720	2	95.69
480	450	7	85.72
600	630	5	91.69
460	410	5	71.69
630	600	4	96.39
600	600	2	94.83
750	710	0	83.80
510	430	3	71.52
660	580	6	84.21
570	570	8	85.01

Select **Analyze, Correlate, Bivariate...** to access the **Bivariate Correlations** dialog window.

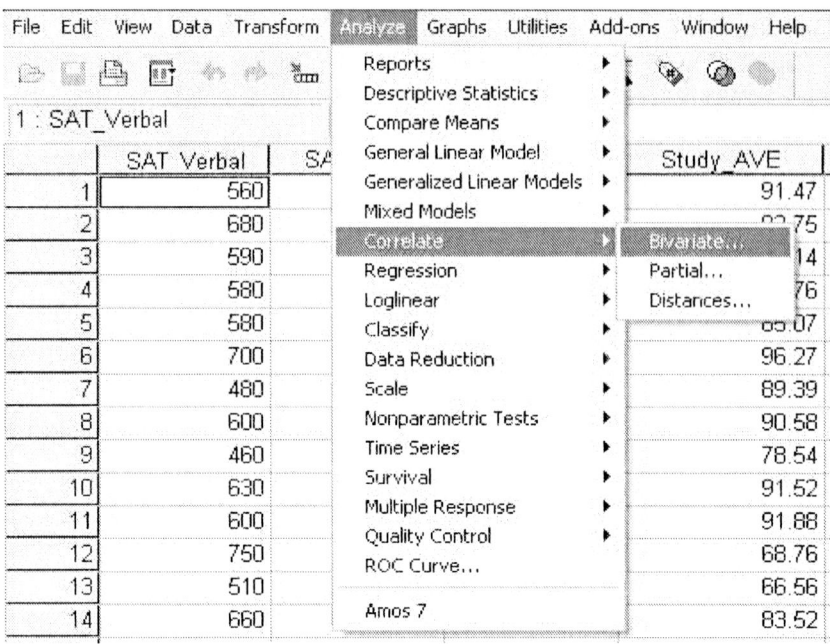

Select all four variables and click the ▶ button to move them into the **Variables:** field.

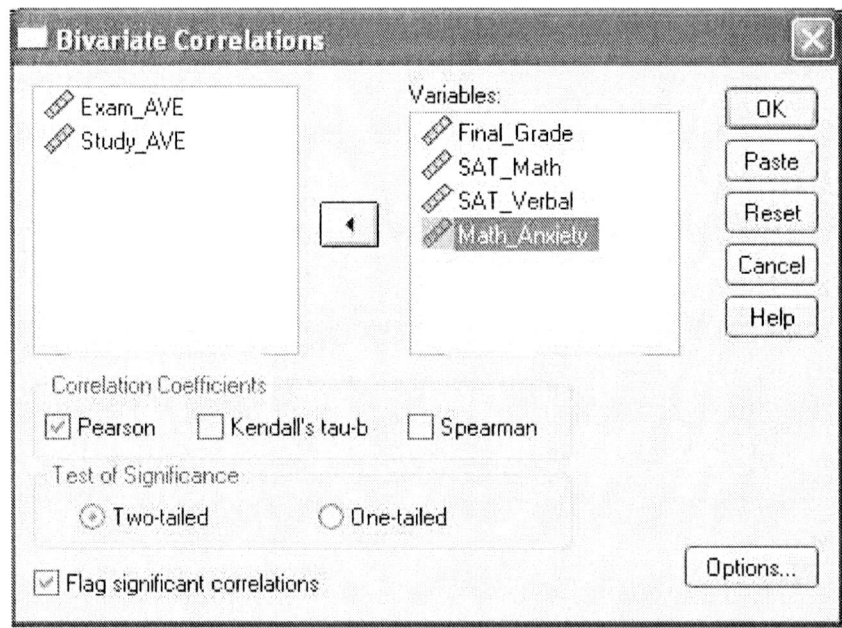

Click **OK** to generate the output. A table of correlation coefficients like the one produced by SPSS for this set of variables is called a *correlation matrix*. The correlations in the matrix are termed *zero-order correlations* to distinguish them from the higher-order correlations computed using the partial correlation procedure. In the social and behavioral sciences, the strength of a correlation was described by Cohen (1988) as follows: *strong* ($r = .5$ and above), *moderate* ($r = .3$ to $.49$), and *weak* ($r = .10$ to $.29$). The sign of r is ignored when assessing the strength of a correlation.

Questions

1. How many *unique* zero-order correlations are displayed in the correlation matrix?
2. Identify all of the unique pairs of variables by listing their names separated by a comma (e.g., SAT_Math, Final_Grade). In the column next to each pair of variables, identify the strength of the correlation between them by writing either "strong," "moderate," or "weak."

EXERCISE 2
SIMPLE LINEAR REGRESSION

In this exercise, you will run a simple linear regression to predict a student's final statistics grade from her or his score on the math section of the SAT. Score on the math section of the SAT (SAT_Math) was selected as the predictor, or independent, variable because this variable was most strongly correlated with the criterion, or dependent, variable, final statistics grade (Final_Grade). *Remember:* Correlations reveal potential, not actual, causal relations among variables. A high correlation, alone, can not tell us that having a higher score on the math section of the SAT causes a person to receive a higher final grade in statistics.

Select **Analyze, Regression ▶ Linear** to produce the **Linear Regression** dialog window.

In the **Linear Regression** dialog window, the term **Dependent:** appears at the top near the center of the window, and the term **Independent(s):** appears a little farther down. In simple linear regression, the values of the independent (or predictor) variable (X) are used to predict the values of the dependent (or criterion) variable, Y. Select **Final_Grade** and click the button to move this variable into the **Dependent:** field. Now move **SAT_Math** into the **Independent(s):** field. Click **OK** to generate the regression output.

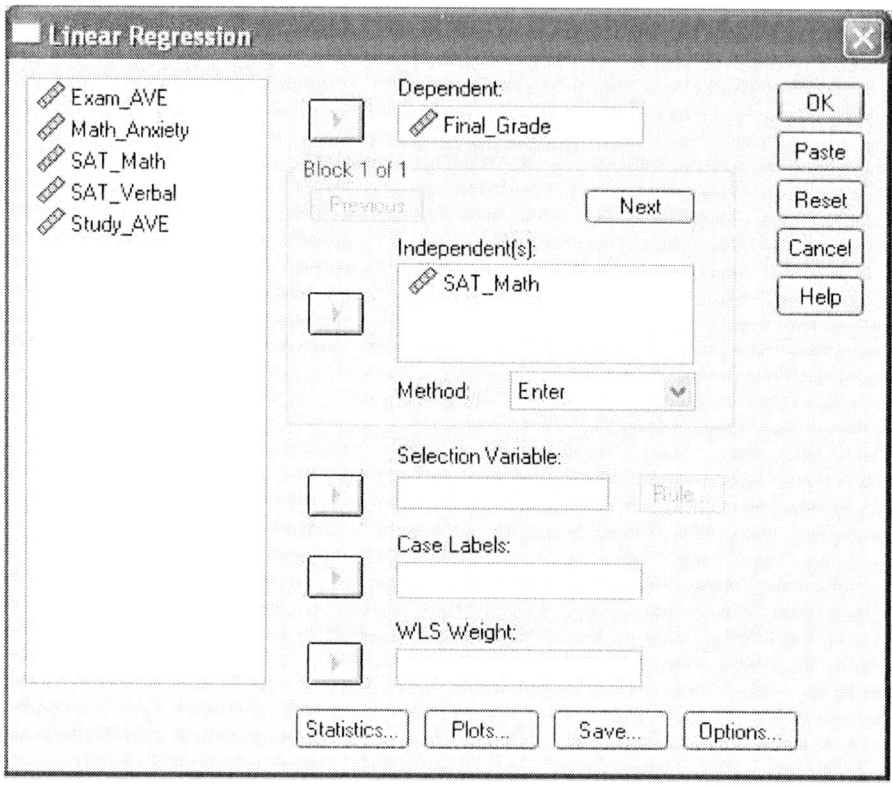

Questions

3. What is the name of the statistic whose symbol is R?
4. What is the value of R?
5. Interpret R; that is, describe what this statistic measures.
6. What is the name of the statistic whose symbol is R^2 (R Square in the Model Summary table)?
7. What is the value of R^2?
8. Interpret R^2; that is, describe what this statistic measures.
9. For each 1-point increase in a student's score on the math section of the SAT (SAT_Math) what is the change in the student's final grade in statistics (Final_Grade)?
10. Identify the name of the statistic whose value is the same as R.

EXERCISE 3
MULTIPLE REGRESSION

In this exercise, you will run a multiple linear regression to predict a student's final statistics grade from scores on the math and verbal sections of the SAT as well as self-reported ratings of math anxiety.

Select **Analyze, Regression ▶ Linear** to produce the **Linear Regression** dialog window. In the **Linear Regression** dialog window, **Final_Grade** should be in the **Dependent:** field and **SAT_Math** should be in the **Independent(s):** field. Select **SAT_Verbal** and **Math_Anxiety** and click the [▶] button to add these variables to the **Independent(s):** field. Click **OK** to generate the regression output.

Questions

11. Compare the values of R and R^2 from the simple and multiple regression analyses. What is the general effect of adding independent variables to the regression model?

12. Rank the three independent variables according to their relative strength in predicting final grade in statistics. (*Hint*: Look at the standardized regression coefficients.)

ANSWERS

EXERCISE 1

1. The correlation coefficients above the diagonal of autocorrelations (the 1's) are a mirror image of the correlations below the diagonal, so there are just 6 unique zero order correlations in the matrix.

		Final_Grade	SAT_Math	SAT_Verbal	Math_Anxiety
Final_Grade	Pearson Correlation	1	.557**	.547**	-.175
	Sig. (2-tailed)		.000	.000	.141
	N	72	72	72	72
SAT_Math	Pearson Correlation	.557**	1	.709**	-.497**
	Sig. (2-tailed)	.000		.000	.000
	N	72	72	72	72
SAT_Verbal	Pearson Correlation	.547**	.709**	1	-.330**
	Sig. (2-tailed)	.000	.000		.005
	N	72	72	72	72
Math_Anxiety	Pearson Correlation	-.175	-.497**	-.330**	1
	Sig. (2-tailed)	.141	.000	.005	
	N	72	72	72	72

**. Correlation is significant at the 0.01 level (2-tailed).

2.

Variables	Description of Relation
SAT_Math, Final_Grade	Strong
SAT_Verbal, Final_Grade	Strong
Math_Anxiety, Final_Grade	Weak
SAT_Math, SAT_Verbal	Strong
SAT_Math, Math_Anxiety	Moderate
SAT_Verbal, Math_Anxiety	Moderate

EXERCISE 2

Model Summary

Model	R	R Square	Adjusted R Square	Std. Error of the Estimate
1	.557[a]	.310	.300	5.68251

a. Predictors: (Constant), Score on the Math section of the SAT

ANOVA[b]

Model		Sum of Squares	df	Mean Square	F	Sig.
1	Regression	1015.876	1	1015.876	31.460	.000[a]
	Residual	2260.362	70	32.291		
	Total	3276.238	71			

a. Predictors: (Constant), Score on the Math section of the SAT
b. Dependent Variable: Final average in an introductory statistics course

Coefficients[a]

Model		Unstandardized Coefficients		Standardized Coefficients	t	Sig.
		B	Std. Error	Beta		
1	(Constant)	61.980	4.535		13.666	.000
	Score on the Math section of the SAT	.047	.008	.557	5.609	.000

a. Dependent Variable: Final average in an introductory statistics course

3. R is the symbol for the **multiple correlation coefficient**.
4. From the Model Summary Table, the value of R is **.557**.
5. The multiple correlation coefficient is a measure of the degree of linear relation among all of the independent variables and the dependent variable. R is computed as the correlation between the actual and predicted values of the dependent variable and thus can never be a negative value. In simple linear regression, R is the absolute value of the Pearson correlation coefficient computed for the independent and dependent variables.
6. The statistic R^2 is called the **coefficient of determination**.
7. From the Model Summary Table, the value of $R^2 = $ **.31**.
8. The coefficient of determination is a measure of the proportion of the total variability in the dependent variable that is "explained" or "determined" by the independent variable.
9. For each 1-point increase in a student's score on the math section of the SAT (SAT_Math), a student's final grade in statistics (Final_Grade) increases by **.047** points, the value of the slope (regression coefficient).

10. The value of the standardized regression coefficient (beta) is the same as that of the multiple correlation coefficient. This will always be the case when there is only one independent (predictor) variable.

EXERCISE 3

Model Summary

Model	R	R Square	Adjusted R Square	Std. Error of the Estimate
1	.607[a]	.369	.341	5.51586

a. Predictors: (Constant), SAT_Verbal, Math_Anxiety, SAT_Math

ANOVA[b]

Model		Sum of Squares	df	Mean Square	F	Sig.
1	Regression	1207.360	3	402.453	13.228	.000[a]
	Residual	2068.878	68	30.425		
	Total	3276.238	71			

a. Predictors: (Constant), SAT_Verbal, Math_Anxiety, SAT_Math
b. Dependent Variable: Final_Grade

Coefficients[a]

Model		Unstandardized Coefficients		Standardized Coefficients	t	Sig.
		B	Std. Error	Beta		
1	(Constant)	51.618	6.563		7.865	.000
	Math_Anxiety	.354	.312	.126	1.135	.260
	SAT_Math	.034	.012	.407	2.736	.008
	SAT_Verbal	.027	.012	.300	2.194	.032

a. Dependent Variable: Final_Grade

11. The value of the multiple correlation coefficient R increased from **.557** to **.607**, whereas the coefficient of determination R^2 increased from **.31** to **.369**. Adding independent variables to the multiple regression model always increases the values of R and R^2.

12. The strongest predictor of a student's final statistics grade is her or his score on the math section of the SAT (β = .407), followed by the score on the verbal section of the SAT (β = .3), and the student's self-reported rating of math anxiety (β = .126). It is important to remember that these are *relative* measures of predictive strength. The value of each standardized coefficient change with the addition of each new predictor variable.

CHAPTER 7

INFERENTIAL STATISTICS

The Surprising Story of the Normal Curve

STANDARDIZING A VARIABLE

In this set of exercises you will request that SPSS create a standardized variable by transforming raw scores (self-ratings of math anxiety) to **standard**, or **z, scores**. The formula for converting a raw score to a z score is:

$$z = \frac{X - \mu}{\sigma}$$

where,

X is a raw score
μ is the mean of the raw scores
σ is the standard deviation of the raw scores

A z score expresses a raw score in terms of the number of standard deviations between the raw score and the mean of the raw scores. Just as a yardstick measures distance in inches and feet, a z score measures distance in standard deviation units. The mean of the raw scores depicted in the figure below is 38, and the standard deviation is 4.

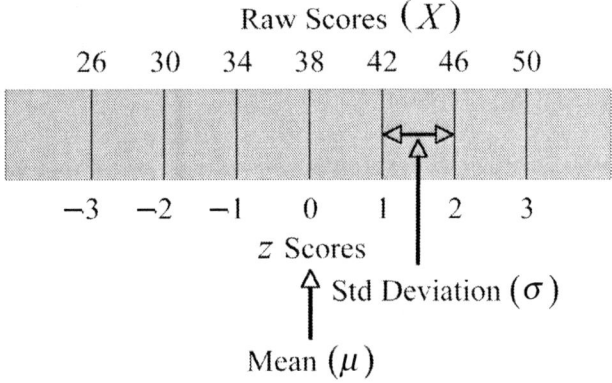

When raw scores represent measures of different variables it is necessary to standardize them before you can make meaningful comparisons between them. For example, it would be inappropriate to compare exam scores from an English class and a math class, because the content differs substantially and the classes may not be equally difficult. Thus, a seemingly low exam score in a difficult class may be relatively better than a higher score in a less difficult class. Standardizing the two exam scores enables a direct comparison between them. Here is an example. Suppose an English major is beaming after receiving a score of 93 on a midterm exam in her English literature course. Her best friend, a math major, is a little down after receiving a score of 77 on her midterm exam in a linear algebra course. Here are the relevant descriptive statistics for the two classes:

Class	μ	σ
English Literature	85	8
Linear Algebra	67	10

Is the English major's exam score better than her friend's score on the linear algebra exam?

Solution. Convert both scores to standard scores and compare them.

$$z_{English} = \frac{93-85}{8} = \frac{8}{8} = 1$$

$$z_{Math} = \frac{77-67}{10} = \frac{10}{10} = 1$$

As you can see, both scores are one standard deviation above the class mean, so they are equivalent.

EXERCISE 1

Launch SPSS. When the "**What do you want to do?**" window appears, select **Type in data**. Click on the **Variable View** tab at the bottom of the screen to display the Variable View window and define the variable as follows: **Name** = "Math_anxiety," **Decimals** = 0, and **Label** = "Self-ratings of math anxiety on the first day of statistics class."

	Name	Type	Width	Decimals	Label
1	Math_anxiety	Numeric	8	0	Self-ratings of math anxiety on the first day of statistics class

Click on the **Data View** tab to display the Data Editor and enter the following data.

4	1	8	7	8	6	8	8	6
6	5	3	3	7	9	4	6	8
7	5	7	6	8	5	6	7	3
5	5	10	2	7	5	7	6	7
9	4	3	8	3	4	4	5	10
4	4	7	2	7	2	7	8	10
8	2	0	8	8	1	4	5	7
2	0	6	10	2	8	1	8	
7	3	10	6	5	7	6	8	
7	6	6	5	10	4	4	5	

- From the **Analyze** menu, select **Descriptive Statistics ▶ Descriptives...** to produce the **Descriptives** dialog window.
- Select **Math_anxiety** and click the triangle (▶) to move the variable into the **Variable(s):** field.
- Click **Options** to produce the **Descriptives: Options** dialog window.
- Make sure that **Mean** and **Std. deviation** are the only statistics selected and click **Continue** to return to the Descriptives dialog window.
- Select the **Save standardized values as variables** option in the lower left corner of the window.
- Click **OK** to produce the output.
- Return to the **Data Editor** and notice the addition of the standardized variable.
- Use **Analyze, Descriptive Statistics ▶ Descriptives...** to determine the mean and standard deviation of the standardized variable. (Remember to *deselect* the **Save standardized values as variables** option in the lower left corner of the window; otherwise SPSS will generate a new variable named **ZZMath_anxiety**.)

Questions

1. What is the mean of the standardized variable?
2. What is the standard deviation of the standardized variable?
3. Do all samples of standard scores have the same mean and standard deviation? Put another way, are the mean and standard deviation the same for all distributions of *z* scores? Explain your answer.

SCALE SCORES

Any raw score may be standardized, then converted to a scale score using the formula:

$$\text{Scale Score} = z(\sigma) + \mu$$

where,

z is the standardized equivalent of a raw score
μ is the arbitrary mean of the scale scores
σ is the arbitrary standard deviation of the scale scores

The **T score scale** was developed to convert standard scores to a scale in which negative scores would almost never be observed. The arbitrary mean of the *T* score scale is 50 and the arbitrary standard deviation is 10. The following formula may be used to convert a *z* score to a *T* score:

$$T = z(10) + 50$$

EXERCISE 2

- From the **Transform** menu, select **Compute Variable...** to produce the **Compute Variable** dialog window.
- Locate the **Target Variable:** field in the upper left corner of the window and type **T_score**. Select **ZMath_anxiety** and click the triangle (▶) to move this variable into the **Numeric Expression:** field.
- Position the cursor to the right of ZMath_anxiety and type *** 10 + 50**. The Numeric Expression: field should look like this when you are finished:

   ZMath_anxiety * 10 + 50

- Click **OK** to produce the new variable **T_score**.
- Use **Analyze, Descriptive Statistics ▶ Descriptives...** to determine the mean and standard deviation of the *T* scores. (Remember to *deselect* the **Save standardized values as variables** option in the lower left corner of the window; otherwise SPSS will generate a new variable named ZT_score.)

Questions

4. What is the mean of the *T*_score variable?
5. What is the standard deviation of the *T*_score variable?
6. Are there any negative *T* scores? Why or why not? (*Hint*: Think of a negative *T* score in terms how far it would be from the mean.)

EXERCISE 3

In this exercise you will use the steps from Exercise 2 to express the self–ratings of anxiety on a new scale that has a mean of 200 and a standard deviation of 25. Choose a name for your new scale and type this name in the **Target Variable:** field. In the **Numeric Expression:** field, replace the mean and standard deviation of the *T* score scale with the mean and standard deviation of the new scale.

Question

7. What values on this new scale were assigned to individuals with self–reported anxiety scores of:

   a. 0?   **b.** 5?   **c.** 10?

THE CENTRAL LIMIT THEOREM

The purpose of this exercise is to use SPSS to conduct a series of exercises suggested by the *Experience It For Yourself* exercise described on pages 315 to 317 in the text. To demonstrate the central limit theorem (CLT), you will sample with replacement from a population of 140 student heights.

EXERCISE 4

From the **SPSS Data Editor**, select **File, Open ▶ Data...** . When the **Open Data** dialog window appears, navigate to the data CD and open the file **Height Data**. From the **Graphs** menu, select **Legacy Dialogs ▶ Histograms...** as shown:

When the **Histogram** dialog window appears, select **height** and click on the triangle (▶) to move this variable into the **Variable:** field. Click on the box next to **Display normal curve** to request a normal curve superimposed on the histogram of height data. Before clicking **OK** make sure that your window looks like the one displayed below:

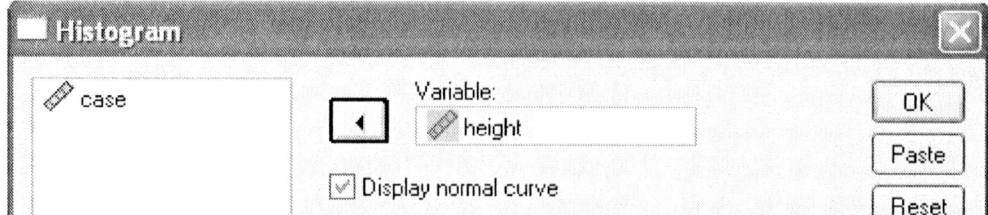

The histogram will appear in the **SPSS Viewer**. Notice that the shape of the histogram is not very closely approximated by the superimposed normal curve. However, regardless of the shape of the population distribution, the CLT guarantees that the distribution of all possible means from the population will be normal as long as the sample size is sufficiently large. We'll begin with 1,000 samples of size $N = 3$ to get an idea of what the sampling distribution of the mean looks like for a limited number of very small samples. Then we'll increase the sample size as well as the number of samples. The most efficient way to generate a large number of samples very quickly is to use SPSS syntax commands.

EXERCISE 5

From the SPSS Data Editor **File** menu, select **Open ▶ Syntax...**

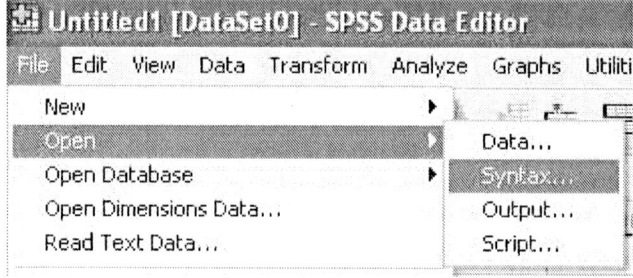

When the **Open Syntax** dialog window appears, navigate to the data CD and open the syntax file named **Sampling with replacement**. When the file is loaded into the syntax editor, you should see the following lines:

```
* This program creates 1000 samples of size n = 3, by sampling with
* replacement from an SPSS data file. Replace the # characters
* in the next line with random digits to generate unique samples.
```

```
set seed = ######.
input program.
loop sample = 1 to 1000.
    loop #case = 1 to 3.
        compute case = trunc(uniform(140))+1.
        end case.
    end loop.
    leave sample.
end loop.
end file.
end input program.
execute.
sort cases by case.

* IMPORTANT: The drive letter following the table subcommand line may
* have to be changed, depending on the location of the data file. The
* syntax is based on an assumption that the height data file is
* accessed from the data CD in drive D:\.

match files file = * /table = 'D:\Chapter 7\height data.sav' /by case.
sort cases by sample.
execute.

* The aggregate outfile = * command will replace the active dataset
* created by the program. If you wish to save the file produced by
the
* program, replace the asterisk with a file name.

aggregate outfile = *
    /break = sample
    /height_mean = mean(height).
```

To run the syntax program select **Run, All** from the Syntax Editor menu:

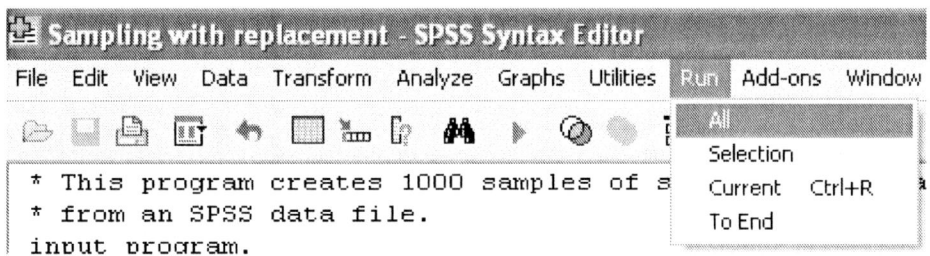

Executing these syntax commands will produce an aggregated data file with two variables, **sample** and **height_mean**. *Sample* has 1,000 values (from the second executable line of the syntax program) and *height_mean*

is the mean of each sample of 3 cases (specified in the third executable line in the program). The first five lines of the Data Editor should be similar to the following:

	sample	height_mean
1	1	62.33
2	2	62.33
3	3	67.00
4	4	63.33
5	5	63.67

Repeat the steps from Exercise 3 to construct a histogram of means of samples of 3 students. For this exercise the variable to be graphed is named **height_mean**. Move this variable into the **Variable:** field and be sure to request the normal curve before clicking **OK** to produce the histogram of sample means.

Questions

8. Compare the shapes of the population distribution and the distribution of 1,000 sample means. Which appears to be more similar to the normal curve?

9. Compare the mean of the distribution of sample means to the mean of the population. Are they similar or different? Now compare the population standard deviation to the standard deviation of the distribution of sample means (called the *standard error of the mean*, or just *standard error*). Explain your findings.

EXERCISE 6

Repeat Exercise 5, but before executing the syntax commands change the number of cases from 3 to 30 as follows:

```
loop #case = 1 to 30.
```

Questions

10. Compare the shape of distribution of means of samples of 3 students to the one that you just generated, based on samples of 30 students. Which appears to be more similar to the normal curve?

11. You should find that the mean of this distribution of sample means is very similar to the one based on samples of 3 students. However, the estimate of the standard error is different. Describe, then explain, this difference.

EXERCISE 7

Repeat Exercise 6, but this time change the number of samples from 1,000 to 10,000.

```
loop sample = 1 to 10000.
```

Ten thousand samples is appreciably closer to the infinitely large "all possible samples" required to build the sampling distribution of the mean. With a much larger number of samples, you should see a better fit of the normal curve to the sampling distribution of means. If you want to see a still better fit, increase the sample size to 60.

```
loop sample = 1 to 10000.
loop #case = 1 to 60.
```

As you increase the sample size, you should find that the shape of the sampling distribution of the mean becomes progressively more similar to the shape of the normal curve.

ANSWERS

1. The mean of the standardized variable is **0**.

2. The standard deviation of the standardized variable is **1**.

3. Just as all yardsticks are scaled in feet and inches, all z distributions are scaled in standard deviation units. Thus all distributions of standardized variables, regardless of the original scale of measurement, will have a mean of 0 and a standard deviation of **1**.

4. The mean of the T_score variable is **50**.

5. The standard deviation of the T_score variable is **10**.

6. Although not impossible, negative T scores are very rarely observed because such scores would be more than 5 standard deviations ($5 \times 10 = 50$) below the mean. Because most variables are approximately normally distributed, roughly **99%** of such distributions are within 3 standard deviations of the mean.

7. The values on the new scale assigned to individuals with self-reported anxiety scores of 0, 5, and 10 are shown in parentheses.

   a. 0? (**142**)   b. 5? (**193**)   c. 10? (**245**)

8. The normal curve is more perhaps a little more similar to the shape of the distribution of means of samples of 3 students than to the population distribution.

9. The mean of the distribution of sample means (64.89) is very similar to the mean of the population (64.84). This is in accord with the CLT. The population standard deviation (4.086) is almost double the standard deviation of the distribution of sample means (2.339). The latter value is an estimate of the standard error of the mean ($\sigma_M = \sigma / \sqrt{N} = 4.086 \sqrt{3} = 2.359$). The influence of extreme values is reduced when means replace individual scores, so the variability among means will always be less than the variability among individual scores.

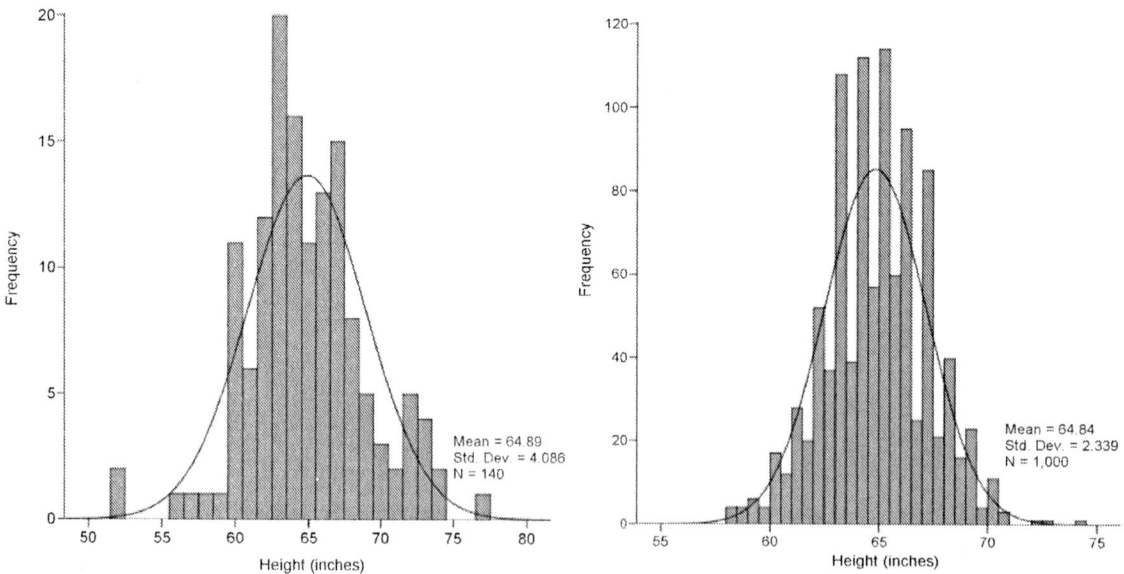

10. The normal curve is more similar to the shape of the distribution of means of samples of 30 students (below right) than to the shape of the distribution of means of samples of 3 students (below left). This is in accord with the CLT.

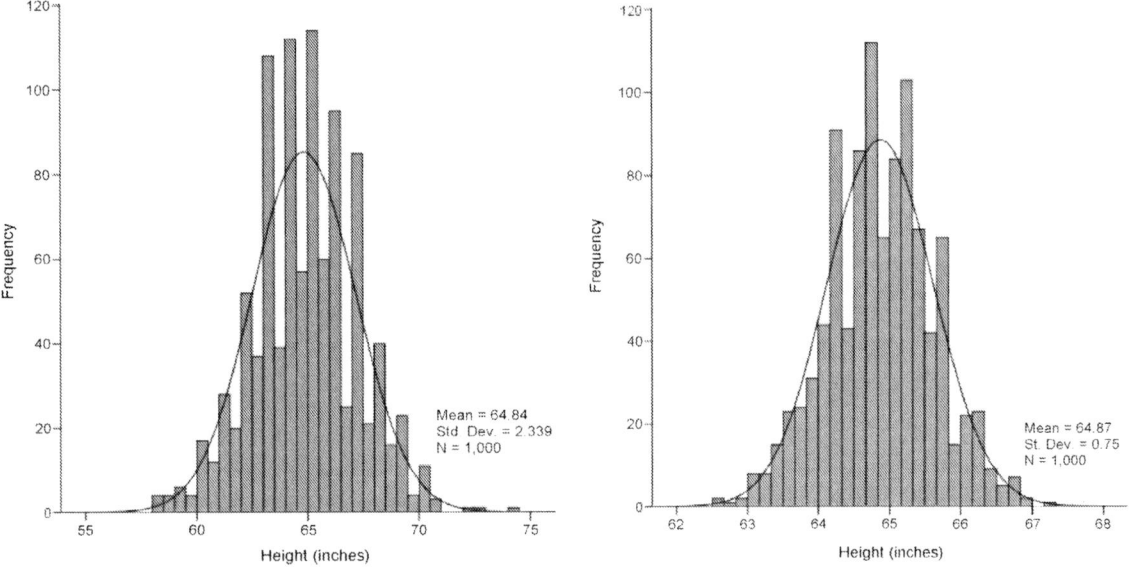

11. The estimate of the standard error is much smaller because the sample size is larger by a factor of 10. As sample size increases, variability decreases.

The histogram below was generated for 10,000 samples of $N = 100$ measures of height.

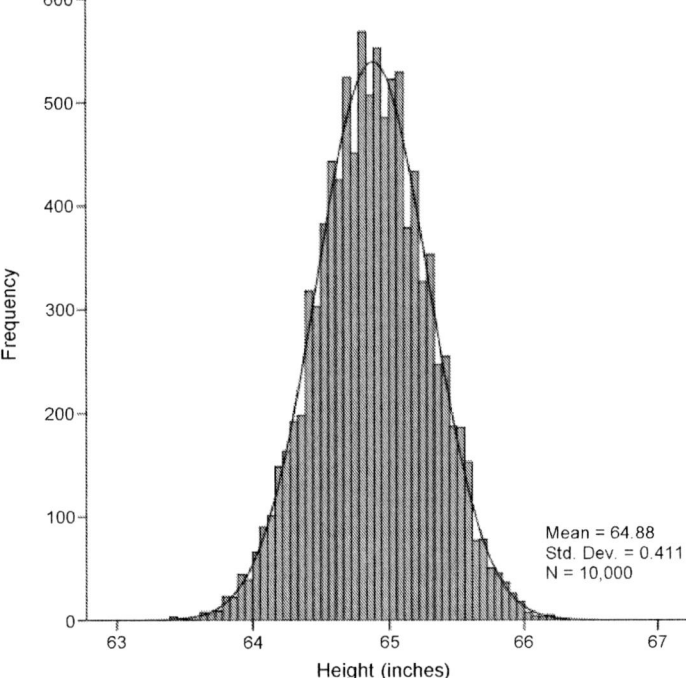

CHAPTER 8

HYPOTHESIS TESTING WITH z TESTS

Making Meaningful Comparisons

The general purpose of this set of exercises is to provide some hands-on experience testing the null hypothesis with z tests as described on pages 354–356 of the text. More specifically, we will examine the effect of increasing the sample size on the probability of rejecting the null hypothesis (see pages 356–358 in the text). We will use an SPSS syntax file to generate 1000 samples of hypothetical data from a normally distributed population with mean (μ) = 3.51 and standard deviation (σ) = 0.61. The syntax file simulates randomly selecting samples of different numbers of participants from this population, administering the Consideration of Future Consequences (CFC) scale to each participant in each sample, and recording the mean for each sample. The CFC scale was introduced on pages 14 and 15 of the text. Briefly, responses to each of the 12 items comprising the CFC scale range from 1 (*extremely uncharacteristic*) to 5 (*extremely characteristic*). Each respondent's CFC score is determined by summing the responses (1 to 5) to the items and dividing this sum by 12 to produce a mean score. Seven of the items are reverse scored, so higher scores indicate greater consideration of future consequences.

Exercise 1

- Launch SPSS. Select **Type in data** and click **OK**. From the **File** menu, select **Open ▶ Syntax...**

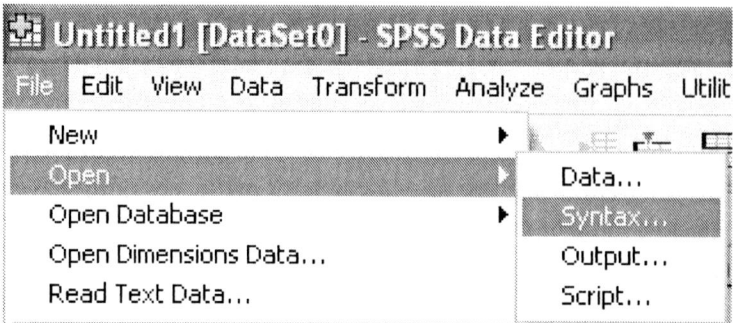

to produce the **Open Syntax** dialog window. Click the ⌄ button to access the **Look in:** drop-down menu and navigate to the folder named **Chapter 8**. Select the syntax file as shown in the truncated image of the window below, then click on the **Open** button to open the file in the SPSS Syntax Editor.

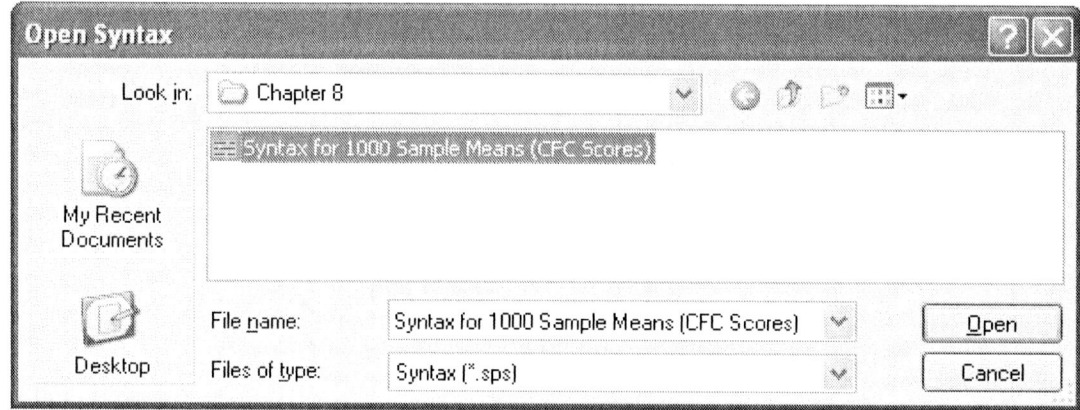

- You should see the following syntax file. Replace the # characters with a sequence of random digits. This will ensure that your samples of hypothetical CFC scores will be unique each time you execute the syntax code. The **input program** produces 1000 randomly selected samples of 5 CFC scores from a normal population with $\mu = 3.7$ and $\sigma = 0.61$. The **aggregate** command at the bottom of file computes the mean of each sample and stores this mean in a new file along with the number of the sample.

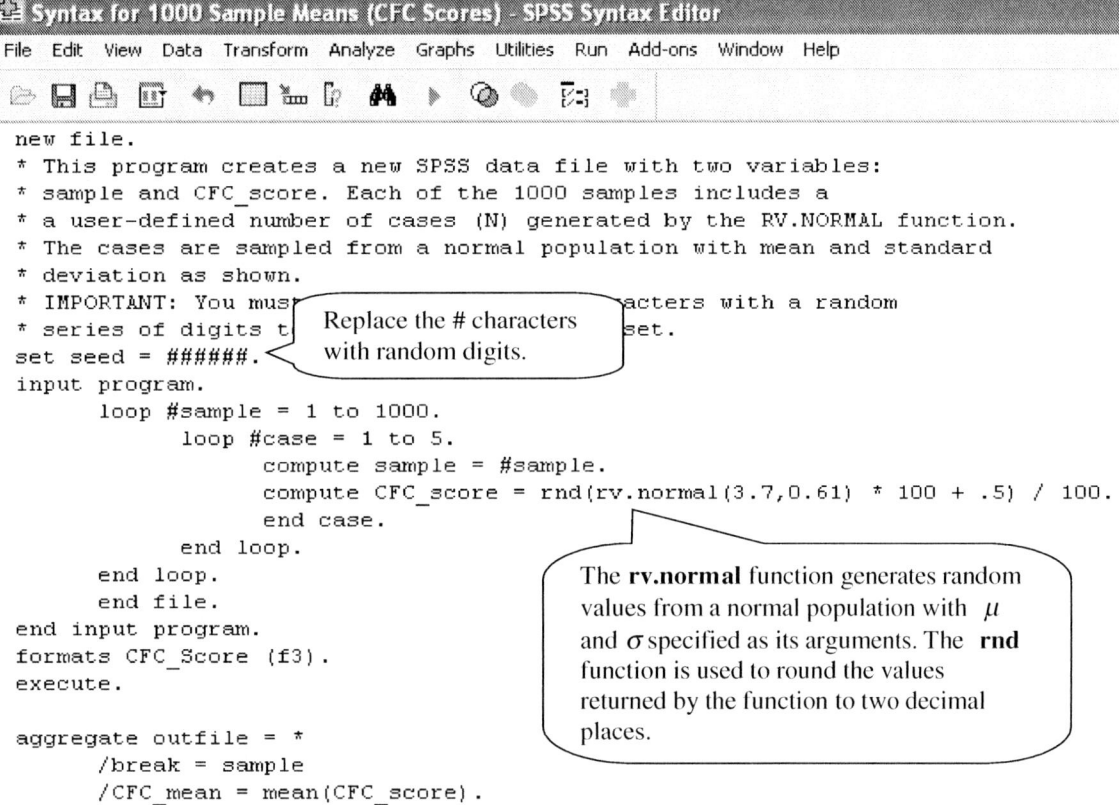

- Click on **Run** in the menu bar, select **All** and press the left mouse button to produce a new SPSS data file of 1000 means computed for samples of 5 CFC scores.

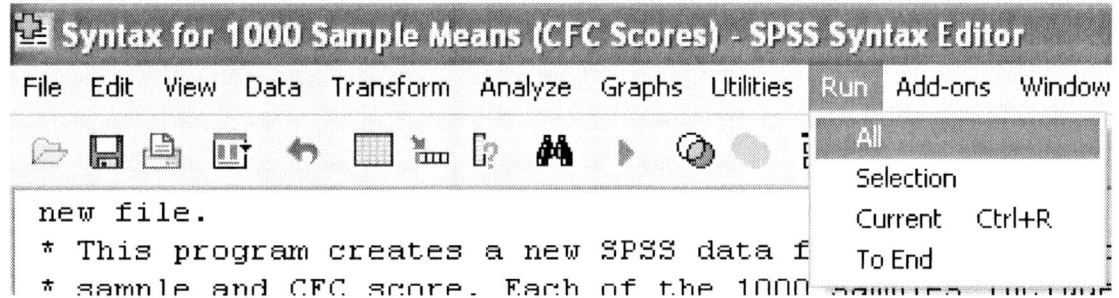

The first 10 rows of the **Data View** window of the **Data Editor** should be similar to following:

	sample	CFC_mean
1	1	3.79
2	2	3.79
3	3	4.17
4	4	3.89
5	5	3.75
6	6	3.90
7	7	3.88
8	8	3.72
9	9	3.73
10	10	3.63

- In this next step we will convert each CFC mean score to a z statistic. From the **Transform** menu, click on **Compute Variable...**

... to produce the **Compute Variable** dialog window. The image below has been cropped to fit on the page.

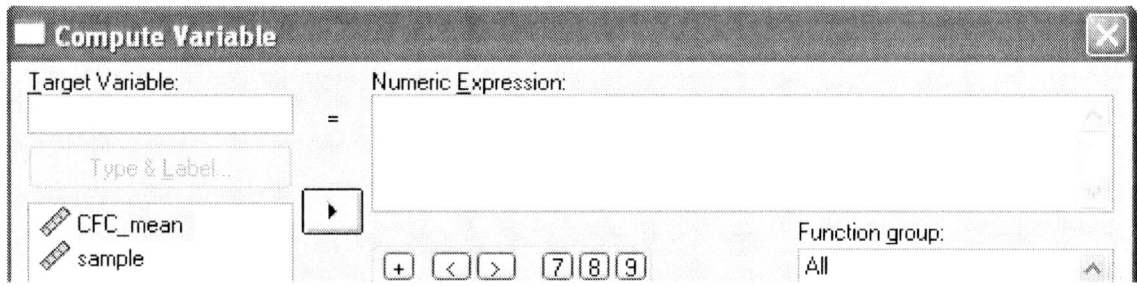

- Position the cursor in the **Target Variable:** field and type **Z_CFC**. Now place the cursor in the **Numeric Expression:** field and type the following formula:

  `(CFC_mean - 3.51) / (0.61 / SQRT(5))`

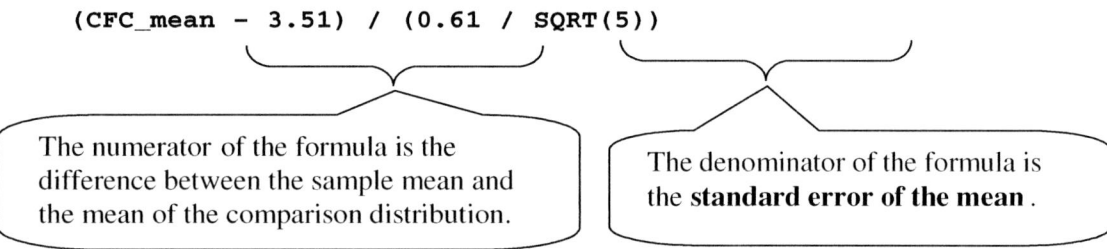

The numerator of the formula is the difference between the sample mean and the mean of the comparison distribution.

The denominator of the formula is **the standard error of the mean**.

The formula converts each CFC mean score to a z statistic. Check to make sure that your screen looks like the following, then click **OK**.

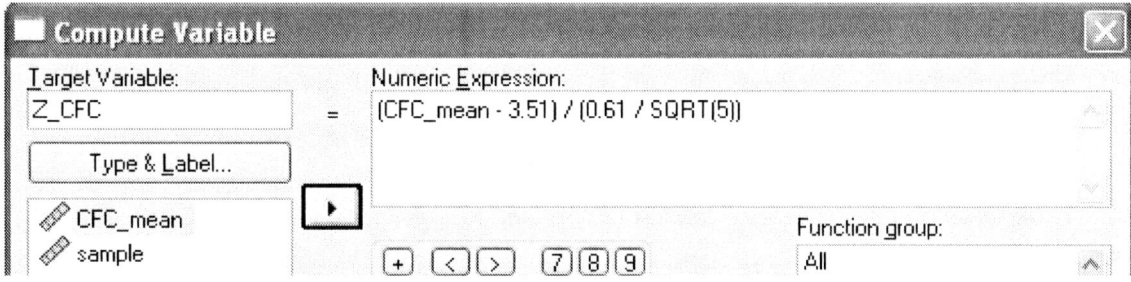

Your Data View window should be similar to the following.

	sample	CFC_mean	Z_CFC
1	1	3.74	.83
2	2	3.79	1.03
3	3	3.95	1.63
4	4	3.46	-.17
5	5	4.22	2.62
6	6	3.83	1.17
7	7	3.77	.95
8	8	3.60	.32
9	9	3.33	-.67
10	10	3.53	.07

- Access the **Compute Variable** dialog window again and type **p_value** in the **Target Variable:** field. Now type the following formula in the **Numeric Expression:** field:

    `2 * (1 - cdfnorm(abs(Z_CFC)))`

The **cdfnorm** function returns the probability of observing a z statistic *less than or equal to* the z statistic entered as its argument. In other words, cdfnorm returns the area under the normal curve to the *left* of the z statistic.

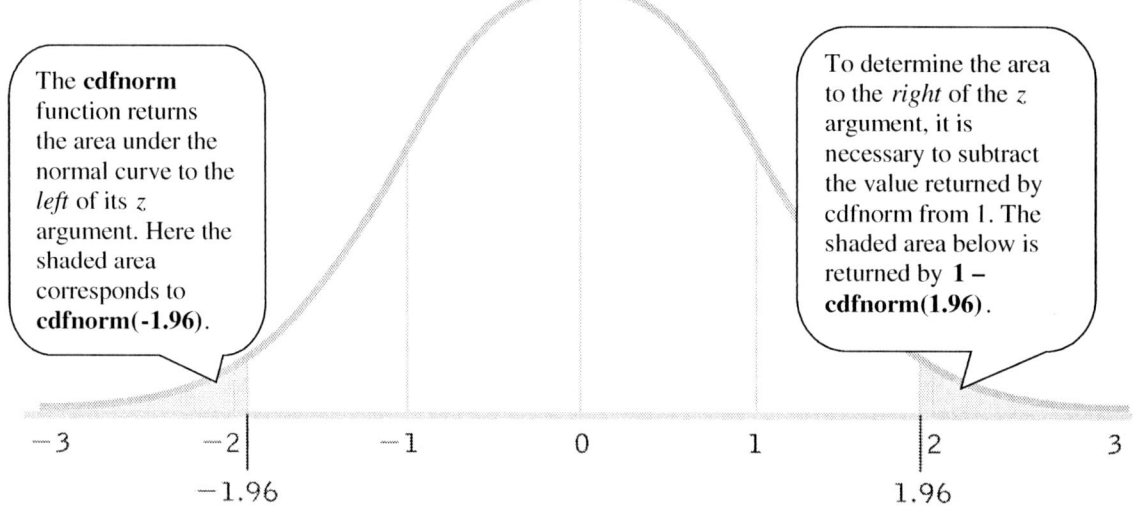

The **cdfnorm** function returns the area under the normal curve to the *left* of its z argument. Here the shaded area corresponds to **cdfnorm(-1.96)**.

To determine the area to the *right* of the z argument, it is necessary to subtract the value returned by cdfnorm from 1. The shaded area below is returned by **1 − cdfnorm(1.96)**.

Because the cdfnorm function returns the area to the left of its z argument, you will get different areas under the curve for positive and negative z statistics:

cdfnorm(-1.96) = .0228

cdfnorm (1.96) = .9772

Therefore, to return the area to the left of a negative z argument *or* the area to the right of that same z argument expressed as a positive value, it is necessary to take the absolute value of z and subtract the value returned by cdfnorm(abs(z)) from 1:

1 - cdfnorm(abs(z))

To return the area to the left of a negative z argument *and* the area to the right of that same z argument expressed as a positive value, it is necessary to subtract the value returned by cdfnorm(abs(z)) from 1 and multiply this difference by 2:

2 * (1 - cdfnorm(abs(z)))

The value returned by 2 * (1 – cdfnorm(abs(z))) is set equal to the variable p_value, so each **p_value** is the probability of observing a z score as extreme (in either tail of the normal distribution) as the one recorded in that row of the **Data Editor**. Put another way, the p_value of each z statistic is the likelihood of observing a mean CFC score as different from the population mean of 3.51 as the one recorded in that row. A *p* value that includes the area in both tails of the normal distribution is called a two-tailed *p* value.

- Click **OK** to generate a column of p_values in the **Data View** window.

  Go to the **Variable View** window and set **Decimals** equal to **2** for the **Z-CFC** variable and equal to **4** for the **p_value** variable. Your screen should be similar to the one below.

	sample	CFC_mean	Z_CFC	p_value
1	1	3.74	.83	.4074
2	2	3.79	1.03	.3013
3	3	3.95	1.63	.1036
4	4	3.46	-.17	.8661
5	5	4.22	2.62	.0089
6	6	3.83	1.17	.2408
7	7	3.77	.95	.3406
8	8	3.60	.32	.7470
9	9	3.33	-.67	.5000
10	10	3.53	.07	.9474

Notice that the *p* value for the mean CFC score of the first sample is .4074. This means that there is about a 41% chance of observing a mean as extreme as 3.74 (≥ 3.74 and ≤ 3.28) if this sample is from a population with $\mu = 3.51$ and $\sigma = .61$—that is, if the null hypothesis is true.

Our next step is to treat each sample mean as the outcome of a different experiment designed to test the null hypothesis that the population mean CFC score is 3.51. This is a nondirectional expression of the null hypothesis, so each test is two-tailed. We will conduct each test at the .05 level of significance

- From the **Transform** menu, select **Compute Variable...** to access the **Compute Variable** dialog window. In the **Target Variable:** field, type **reject_null** as the name of a new variable. In the **Numeric Expression:** field, type **p_value <= .05** as shown in the figure.

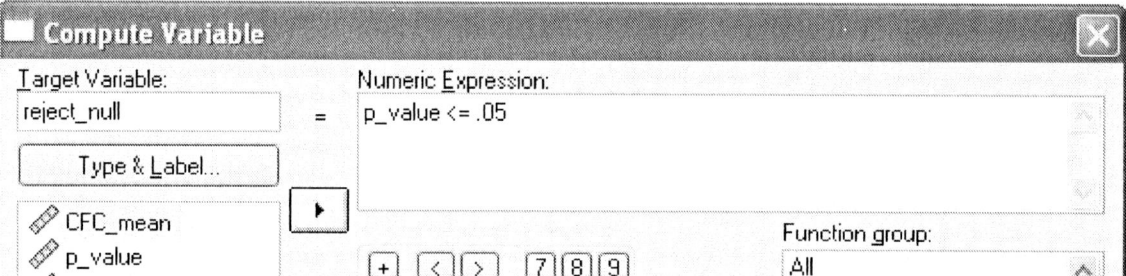

If the value of p_value is less than or equal to .05, then the value **1** will be assigned to **reject_null**; otherwise the value **0** will be assigned. Each **1** thus represents a rejection of the null hypothesis.

- Click the **OK** button to return to the **Data Editor**. The first 10 rows of the **Data View** window should be similar to the following.

	sample	CFC_mean	Z_CFC	p_value	reject_null
1	1	3.74	.83	.4074	0
2	2	3.79	1.03	.3013	0
3	3	3.95	1.63	.1036	0
4	4	3.46	-.17	.8661	0
5	5	4.22	2.62	.0089	1
6	6	3.83	1.17	.2408	0
7	7	3.77	.95	.3406	0
8	8	3.60	.32	.7470	0
9	9	3.33	-.67	.5000	0
10	10	3.53	.07	.9474	0

- Now click on **Analyze** in the menu bar and select **Descriptive Statistics ▶ Frequencies…** from the drop-down menu.

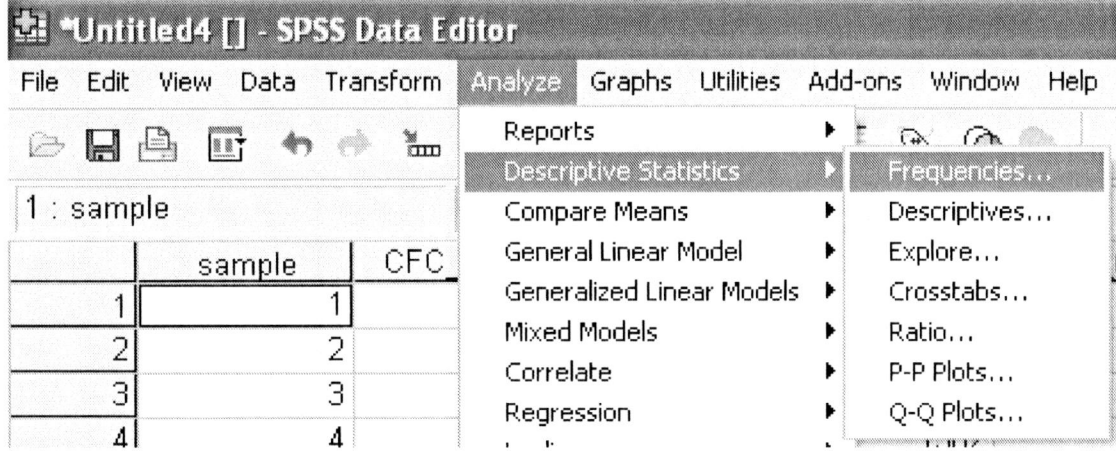

- When the **Frequencies** dialog window appears, select **reject_null** and click the [▸] button to move this variable into the **Variable(s):** field as shown.

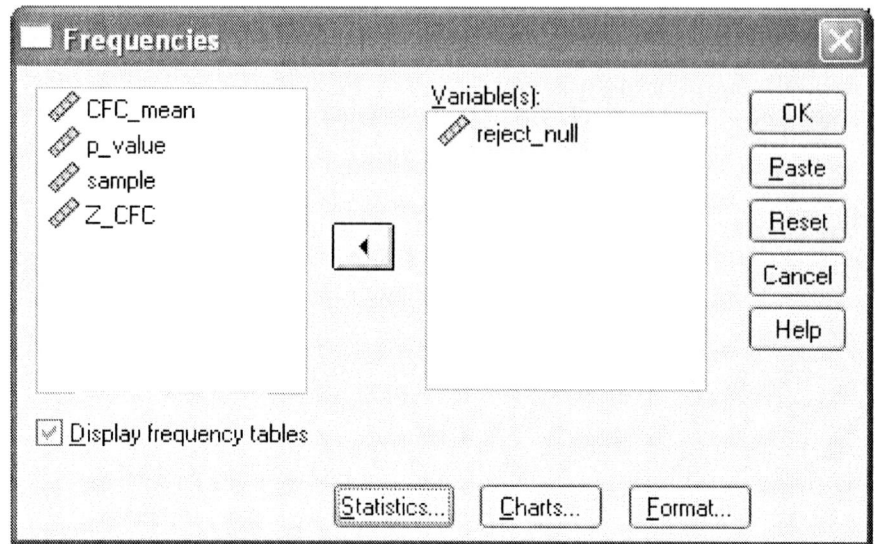

- Click **OK** to produce a frequency output table like the one below.

Of 1000 samples (experiments) based on a sample size of $N = 5$, only 107 (10.7%) resulted in a rejection of the null hypothesis.

reject_null

		Frequency	Percent	Valid Percent	Cumulative Percent
Valid	0	893	89.3	89.3	89.3
	1	107	10.7	10.7	100.0
	Total	1000	100.0	100.0	

- Click on **File** in the menu bar and select **Save As...** from the drop-down menu. When the **Save Output As** dialog window appears, type a name in the **File name:** field and click the **Save** button to save the file to the location named in the **Save in:** field at the top of the window. In the next exercise, we will repeat Exercise 1 for samples of 10, 20, 40, 80, and 160. At the conclusion of each series of steps, we will save the file.

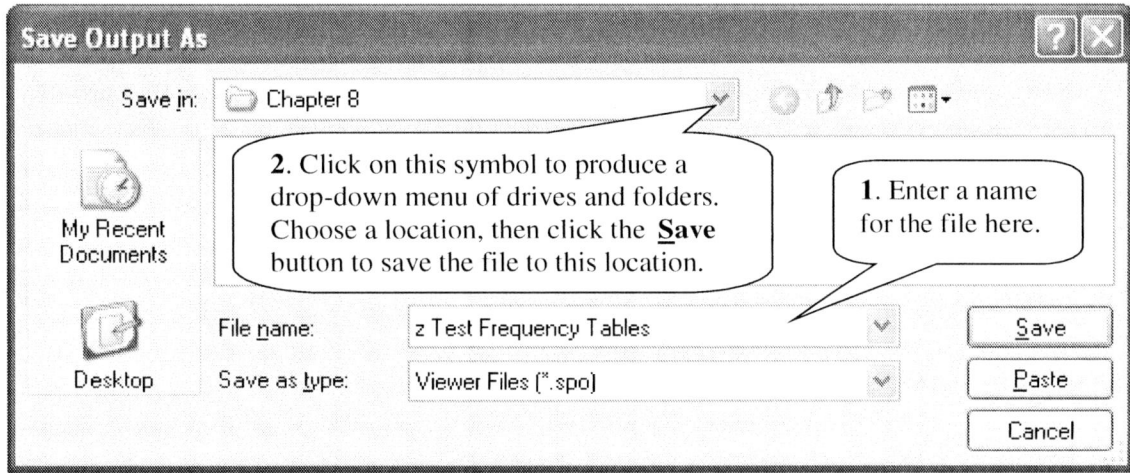

Exercise 2

- Access the **SPSS Syntax Editor** and open the syntax file named **Syntax for 1000 Sample Means (CFC Scores)**.
- Replace the # characters with a sequence of random digits.
- Double the size of the sample by changing the following line in the syntax file.

    ```
    loop #case = 1 to 5
    ```
    Double this value to double the sample size.

- From the menu of the Syntax Editor, click on **Run**, then **All** to run the syntax program.
- From the **Transform** menu, select **Compute Variable...** to access the **Compute Variable** dialog window.
- Type **Z_CFC** (or some name that identifies this variable as a z statistic) in the **Target Variable:** field.
- Type the following expression in the **Numeric Expression:** field:

    ```
    CFC_mean - 3.51) / (0.61 / SQRT(N)
    ```

    where, N = the size of the sample.

- Click **OK** to produce a column of z statistics. Display the z statistics to 2 decimal places.
- Access the **Compute Variable...** dialog window again and type **p_value** in the **Target Variable:** field.
- Type the following expression in the **Numeric Expression:** field:

    `2 * (1 - cdfnorm(abs(Z_CFC)))`

    where, Z_CFC refers to the name of the z statistic.
- Click **OK** to produce a column of p values. Display the p values to 4 decimal places.
- Return to the **Compute Variable...** dialog window and type **reject_null** (or some similar variable name) in the **Target Variable:** field.
- Type **p_value <= .05** in the **Numeric Expression:** field.
- Click **OK** to produce a column of **1**'s and **0**'s. Each **1** represents a rejection of the null hypothesis; that is, each **1** represents a statistically significant outcome (z statistic).
- From the menu bar, select **Analyze, Descriptive Statistics ▶ Frequencies...** to access the **Frequencies** dialog window.
- Move **reject_null** into the **Variable(s):** field and click **OK** to produce a frequency table in the SPSS **Viewer** (output) window.
- **Save** the viewer file to preserve the addition of each frequency table.

Repeat these steps for samples of **20, 40, 80** and **160** cases.

Assignment

Go to the **Data View** window and select **File, New ▶ Data** to produce a new DataSet.

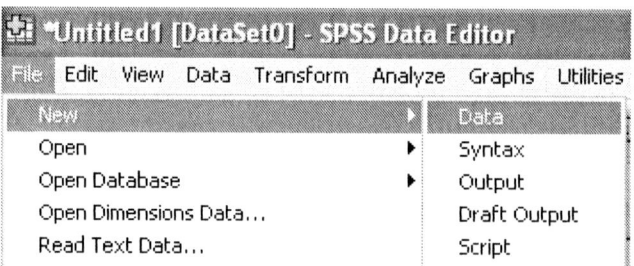

Go to the **Variable View** window and enter **Sample_size** and **Percent_sig** as two new variable names.

Return to the Data View window and enter **5, 10, 20, 40, 80**, and **160** as the values of the **Sample_size** variable.

The values to be entered under **Percent_sig** are the percentages of each set of 1,000 samples that resulted in statistically significant outcomes. These are listed in the frequency tables that you saved in the viewer file.

From the **Graphs** menu, select **Legacy Dialogs ▶ Bar...** to produce the **Bar Charts** dialog window.

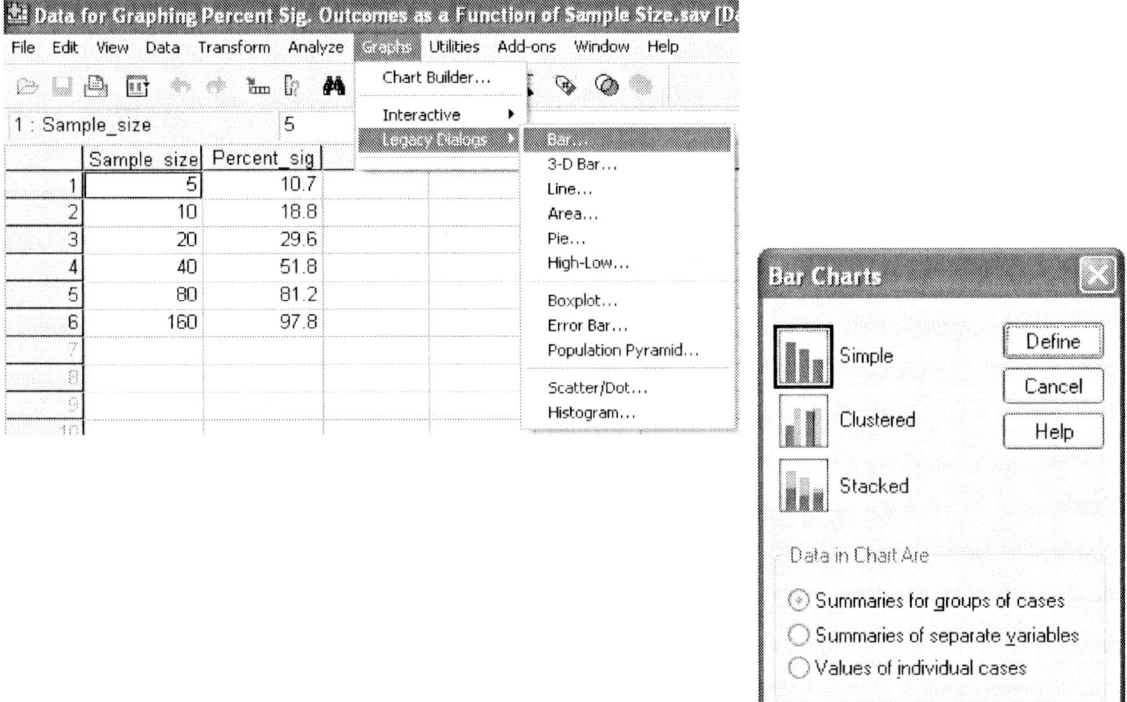

In the **Bar Charts** dialog window, select **Simple**, then click **Define** to produce the **Define Simple Bar: Summaries for Groups of Cases** dialog window.

Select **Sample_size** and move this variable into the **Category Axis:** field.

Click on the radio button next to **Other statistic (e.g., mean)** to activate the **Variable:** field, then move the **Percent_sig** variable into this field.

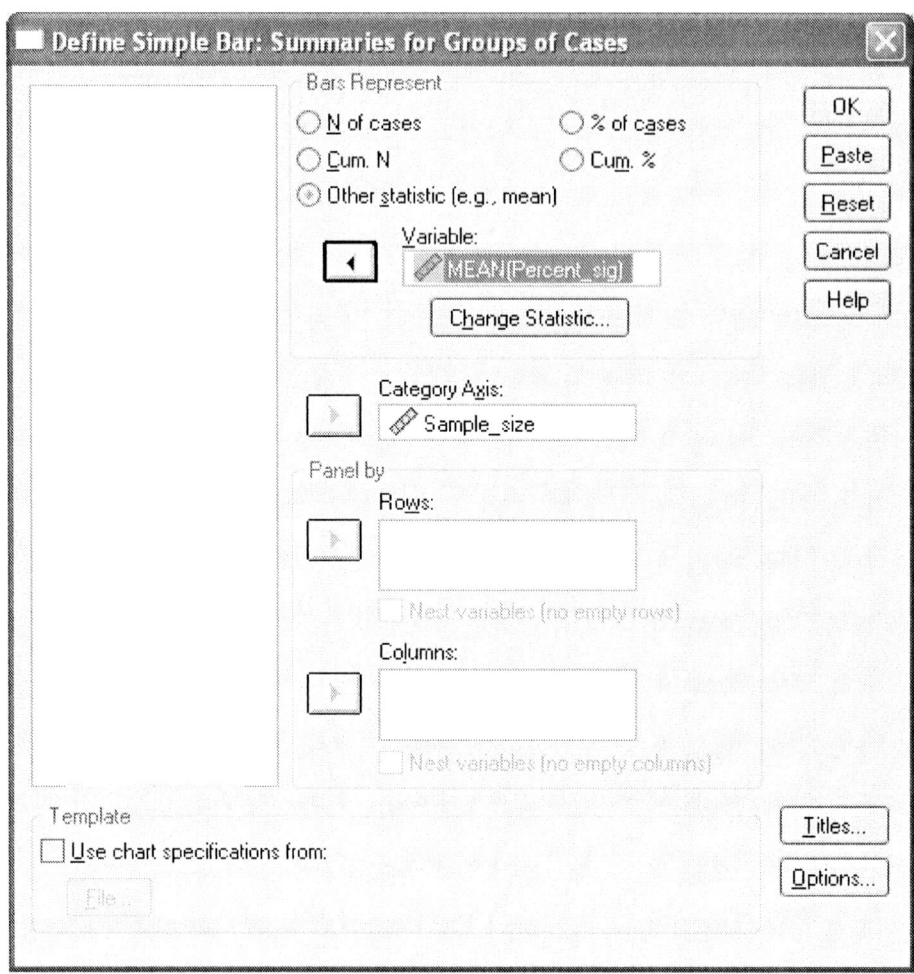

Click **OK** to produce the bar chart.

Questions

1. Describe the relation between sample size, the size of the standard error, the size of the z statistic, and the probability of obtaining a statistically significant outcome (i.e., rejecting the null hypothesis). Support your answer with the frequency tables and bar chart.

2. Given these sampling conditions (i.e., sampling from a normal population with $\mu = 3.7$ and $\sigma = 0.61$), about how large should the sample size be in order to correctly reject the null hypothesis at least 80 percent of the time?

ANSWERS

1. As sample size increases, the standard error decreases, and the size of the z statistic increases. The larger the value of the z statistic, the smaller the p value, increasing the likelihood of obtaining a p value less than or equal to the significance criterion, .05.

reject_null

		Frequency	Percent	Valid Percent	Cumulative Percent
Valid	0	893	89.3	89.3	89.3
	1	107	10.7	10.7	100.0
	Total	1000	100.0	100.0	

reject_null

		Frequency	Percent	Valid Percent	Cumulative Percent
Valid	0	482	48.2	48.2	48.2
	1	518	51.8	51.8	100.0
	Total	1000	100.0	100.0	

reject_null

		Frequency	Percent	Valid Percent	Cumulative Percent
Valid	0	812	81.2	81.2	81.2
	1	188	18.8	18.8	100.0
	Total	1000	100.0	100.0	

reject_null

		Frequency	Percent	Valid Percent	Cumulative Percent
Valid	0	188	18.8	18.8	18.8
	1	812	81.2	81.2	100.0
	Total	1000	100.0	100.0	

reject_null

		Frequency	Percent	Valid Percent	Cumulative Percent
Valid	0	704	70.4	70.4	70.4
	1	296	29.6	29.6	100.0
	Total	1000	100.0	100.0	

reject_null

		Frequency	Percent	Valid Percent	Cumulative Percent
Valid	0	22	2.2	2.2	2.2
	1	978	97.8	97.8	100.0
	Total	1000	100.0	100.0	

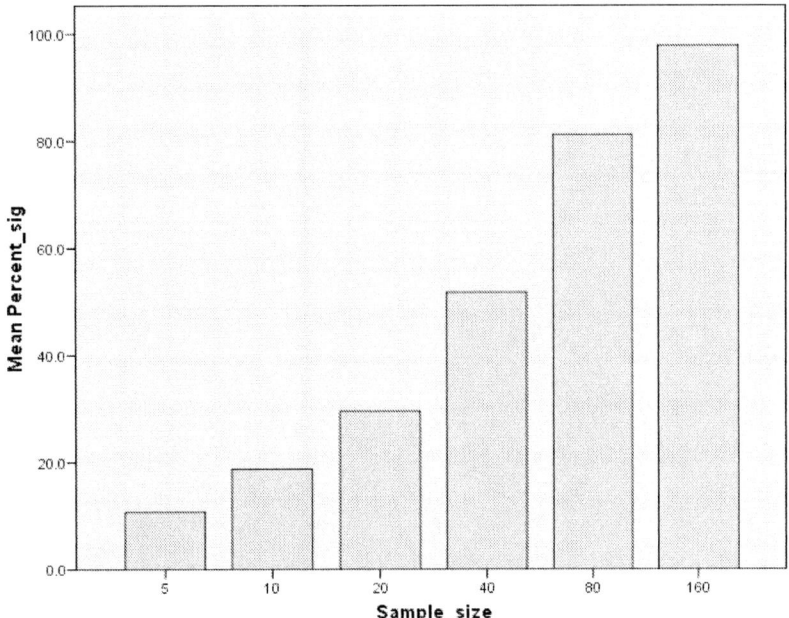

2. According to the histogram, a sample size of at least 80 is required to correctly reject the null hypothesis at least 80 percent of the time. (We know the null hypothesis is false, because we sampled from a population whose mean, 3.7, differs from the mean specified by the null hypothesis, 3.51.)

CHAPTER 9

HYPOTHESIS TESTING WITH *t* TESTS

Comparing Two Groups

INDEPENDENT-SAMPLES *t* TEST

A psychologist believes that a moderate dose of caffeine can improve memory. She designed an experiment in which she randomly assigned half of her available pool of 40 college students to the caffeine condition and half to the placebo condition. Thirty minutes after drinking a cup of fruit juice containing either caffeine (150 mg) or a placebo, participants in both groups studied the same list of 30 words for 30 minutes before being challenged with a test of free recall.

Launch SPSS, select **Type in data** and click **OK**. Go to the **Variable View** window and enter the names of the variables and other settings as shown below.

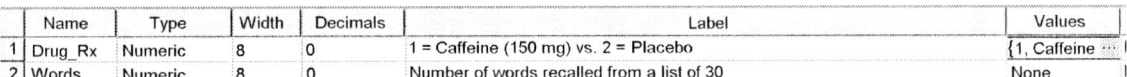

Clicking on the cell under **Values** will cause the gray box to appear, and clicking on the gray box will produce the **Value Labels** dialog window (below). Enter **1** for **Value:** and **Caffeine (150 mg)** as the **Label:** for that value. Click the **Add** button to move the Value: and Label: pair into the field below. Now enter **2** as the second **Value:** and **Placebo** as its **Label:**. The **Value Labels** window should look like this:

Click **Add** then **OK** to return to the Variable View window. Now go back to the **Data View** window and enter the data from the following table.

Drug_Rx	Words	Drug_Rx	Words	Drug_Rx	Words	Drug_Rx	Words
1	18	1	16	2	21	2	17
1	19	1	21	2	19	2	19
1	21	1	22	2	15	2	21
1	26	1	18	2	17	2	15
1	20	1	16	2	18	2	18
1	20	1	24	2	12	2	22
1	22	1	19	2	21	2	16
1	23	1	26	2	18	2	24
1	15	1	25	2	25	2	23
1	21	1	22	2	21	2	23

After checking the data entry for accuracy, save the file. (Use a name that identifies the contents of the file—something like "Caffeine and Memory Data." We'll use this file to complete the set of exercises for Chapter 10.

From the **Analyze** menu, select **Compare Means** ▶ **Independent–Samples T Test...**

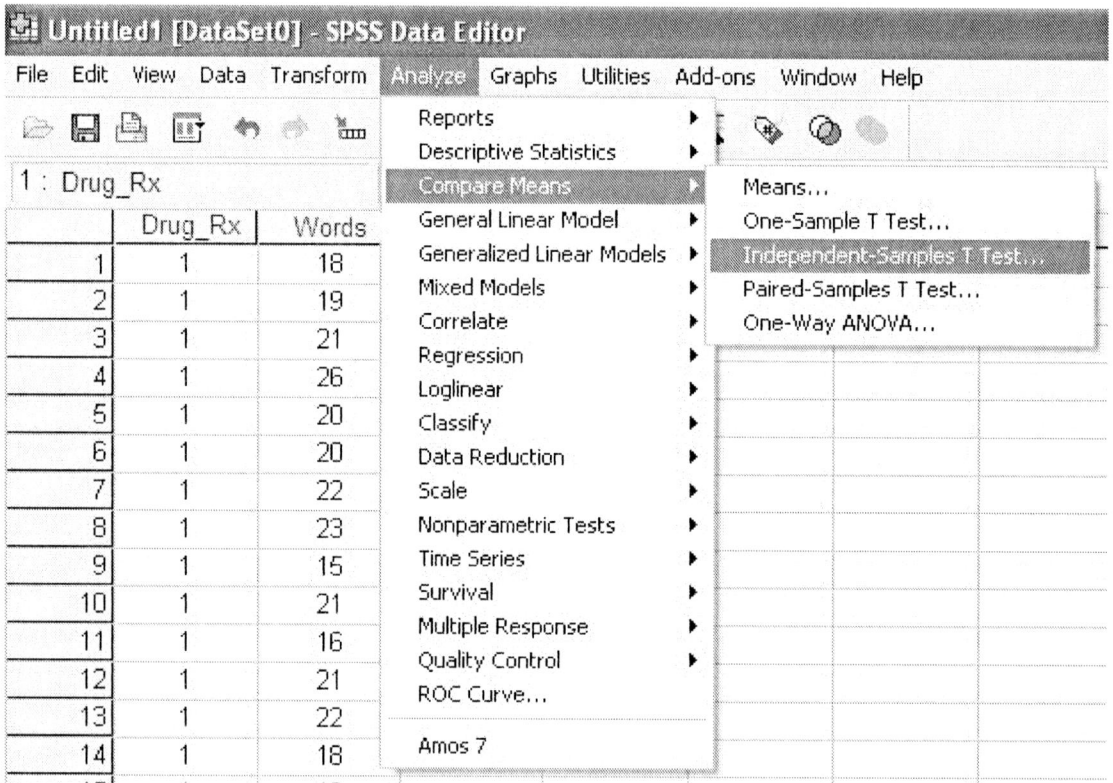

... to produce the **Independent–Samples T Test** dialog window.

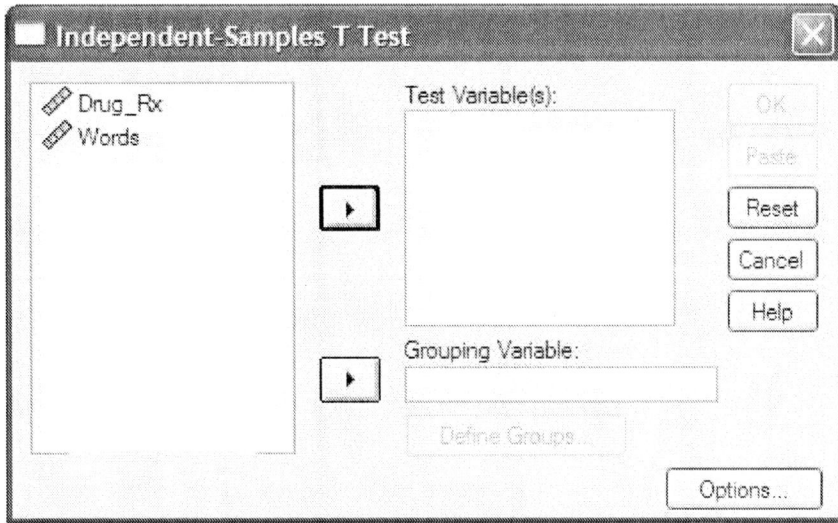

Select **Words** and click the [▶] button to move this variable into the **Test Variable(s):** field. Now move the **Drug_Rx** variable into the **Grouping Variable:** field.

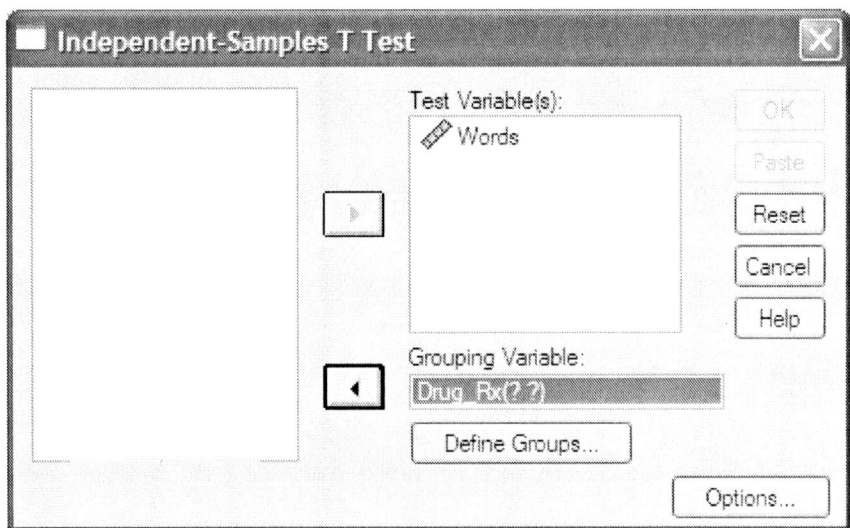

Click on **Define Groups...** to produce the **Define Groups** window. Make sure that the **Use specified values** option is selected. Enter **1** for **Group 1:** and **2** for **Group 2:** as shown.

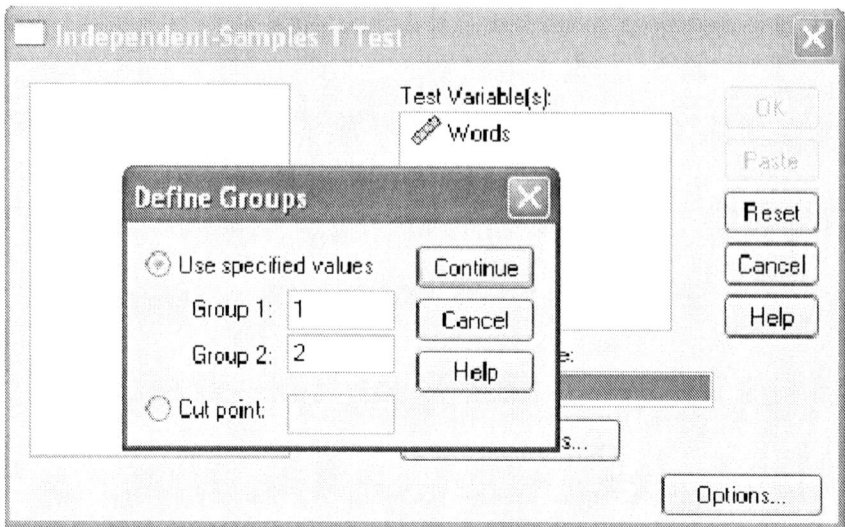

Click **Continue**, then **OK** to produce the **T-Test** output tables. The **Group Statistics** table includes the name of the dependent variable as well as the sample size, mean, standard deviation, and standard error for each group. The values in the table labeled **Independent Samples Test** are used to test the null hypothesis (below).

		Levene's Test for Equality of Variances	
		F	Sig.
Words	Equal variances assumed	.176	.678
	Equal variances not assumed		

If this *p* value is less than or equal to .05, then the equality of variances assumption is rejected, and the values in the second row of the **Independent Samples Test** table are reported. In this example, the equal variances assumption is not rejected, so the values in the first row are

An important assumption of the independent-samples *t* test is that the variances of the two populations are equal. This equality of variances assumption is the null hypothesis tested by **Levene's test**, the results of which are on the left side of the **Independent Samples Test** table. If the **Sig.** value is greater than or equal to .05, then the equal variances assumption is not rejected, and the **t, df,** and **Sig. (2-tailed)** values in the *first* row in the table are used to test the null hypothesis about the effect of caffeine on memory; otherwise, the values in the second row must be used.

Recall that the psychologist hypothesized that a moderate dose of caffeine would improve memory, so the null hypothesis must be expressed as a *directional* hypothesis requiring a *one-tailed test*. The **t–test for Equality of Means** section of the Independent Samples Test output table (below) includes only two-tailed *p* values in the column under **Sig. (2-tailed)**, so you must divide the two-tailed *p* value by 2 to produce the one-tailed *p* value.

		t-test for Equality of Means		
t	df	Sig. (2-tailed)	Mean Difference	Std. Error Difference
1.393	38	.172	1.450	1.041
1.393	37.876	.172	1.450	1.041

Divide this two-tailed *p* value by 2 to get the *p* value for a one-tailed test.

PRESENTING THE RESULTS, APA-STYLE

The *Publication Manual of the American Psychological Association* (5th ed.) prescribes a format for reporting the results of all statistical analyses. The following is an example from the study of the interaction between language and memory by Loftus and Palmer (1974). In this study, participants watched a very brief film of an automobile accident before receiving a questionnaire which included the critical question, "About how fast were the cars going when they _____ into each other?" One group of 50 participants read the word *smashed* in the blank while a second group of 50 participants read the word *hit*. Loftus and Palmer reported the results as follows:

The mean estimate of speed for subjects interrogated with *smashed* was 10.46 mph; with *hit* the estimate was 8.00 mph. These means are significantly different, $t(98) = 2.00$, $p < .05$. (p. 587)

The phrase in which the statistical results are detailed is presented below with comments:

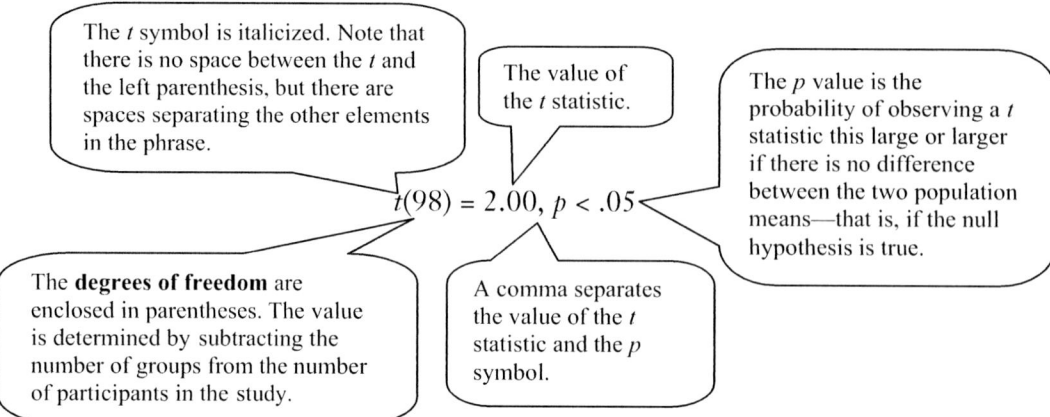

Ruback and Juieng's (1997) study of territorial defense in parking lots offers another example of reporting the results of an independent–samples t test according to APA formatting guidelines. Although these researchers were primarily interested in whether the presence of a waiting driver (an "intruder") affected the time to exit a parking space (departure time), they realized that this relation might be moderated by other variables. After reporting a significant positive correlation between departure time and the number of passengers in the departing vehicle, Ruback and Juieng used independent samples t tests to determine whether number of passengers moderated the relation between departure time and a driver's gender or ethnicity. They reported as follows:

> Male drivers had significantly more passengers in the car with them (M = 1.10) than did female drivers (M = 0.68), $t(198) = 3.14$, $p < .01$, but male drivers and female drivers did not differ in their departure times. Although African American drivers (M = 1.00) had more passengers than did White drivers (M = 0.65), $t(180) = 3.00$, $p < .01$, the two groups did not differ significantly in their departure times. (p. 824)

One may assume that the two studies just cited reported the results of two-tailed tests, because the reported values of the t statistics were greater than the cutoff values for two-tailed tests conducted at the reported significance levels. Had Loftus and Palmer conducted a one-tailed test of the null hypothesis, they may have reported the result as follows: The estimate of the speed of the cars by subjects interrogated with *smashed* (M = 10.46 mph) was significantly greater than the estimate of the subjects in the *hit* condition (M = 8.00 mph), $t(98) = 2.00$, $p < .05$, one-tailed.

Assignment

1. Use APA formatting guidelines to report the results of the independent–samples t test that you conducted to test the null hypothesis that caffeine does not improve recall from verbal memory. Be sure to report the group means and standard deviations as well as the t statistic, degrees of freedom, p value, and the number of tails in the test. State whether the results were statistically significant and supplement your report with the tables from the SPSS output.

PAIRED-SAMPLES t TEST

The same researcher decided to replicate her caffeine study with a repeated measures design. Accordingly, she recruited 20 participants, randomly assigned 10 to the caffeine condition and 10 to the placebo condition, administered the treatments, and recorded the number of words recalled in both groups. The study continued at the same time the next day, but this time each participant switched conditions. A new list of words, matched for length and difficulty with the first list, was studied, and the number of words recalled was recorded.

Go to the **Variable View** window and enter **Caffeine** and **Placebo** as two new variable names. Make sure that **Type** is **Numeric** and **Decimals** is set to **0**. The **Label** entries are optional, but it is generally useful to have more complete descriptions of variables, particularly when a label identifies the codes applied to different values of a nominal variable.

	Name	Type	Width	Decimals	Label	Values
1	Drug_Rx	Numeric	8	0	1 = Caffeine (150 mg) vs. 2 = Placebo	{1, Caffeine...
2	Words	Numeric	8	0	Number of words recalled from a list of 30	None
3	Caffeine	Numeric	8	0	Caffeine condition (half received this treatment on Day 1 and half on Day 2)	None
4	Placebo	Numeric	8	0	Placebo condition (half received this treatment on Day 1 and half on Day 2)	None

Now go to the **Data Editor** and enter, in the order shown, the following data values:

Caffeine: 18, 19, 21, 26, 20, 20, 22, 23, 15, 21, 16, 21, 22, 18, 16, 24, 19, 26, 25, 22

Placebo: 25, 12, 21, 21, 21, 17, 19, 24, 16, 19, 18, 15, 23, 15, 18, 18, 17, 21, 22, 23

After entering the data, the Data Editor should look like this:

	Drug_Rx	Words	Caffeine	Placebo
1	1	18	18	25
2	1	19	19	12
3	1	21	21	21
4	1	26	26	21
5	1	20	20	21
6	1	20	20	17
7	1	22	22	19
8	1	23	23	24
9	1	15	15	16
10	1	21	21	19
11	1	16	16	18
12	1	21	21	15
13	1	22	22	23
14	1	18	18	15
15	1	16	16	18
16	1	24	24	18
17	1	19	19	17
18	1	26	26	21
19	1	25	25	22
20	1	22	22	23

From the **Analyze** menu, select **Compare Means ▶ Paired–Samples T Test...** to produce the **Paired–Samples T Test** dialog window.

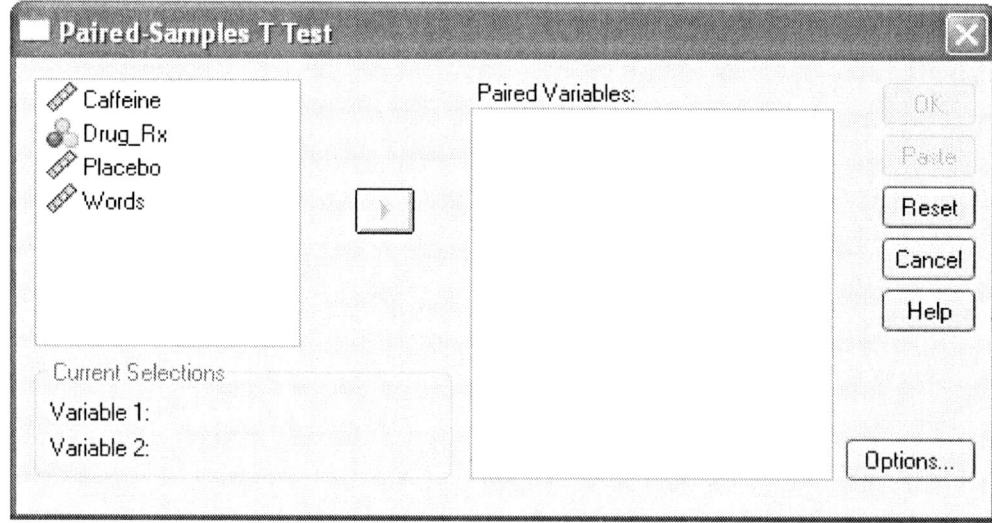

Select **Caffeine** then hold down the Control key on the keyboard as you select **Placebo**. When both variables are selected they will appear under **Current Selections** in the lower left corner of the dialog window:

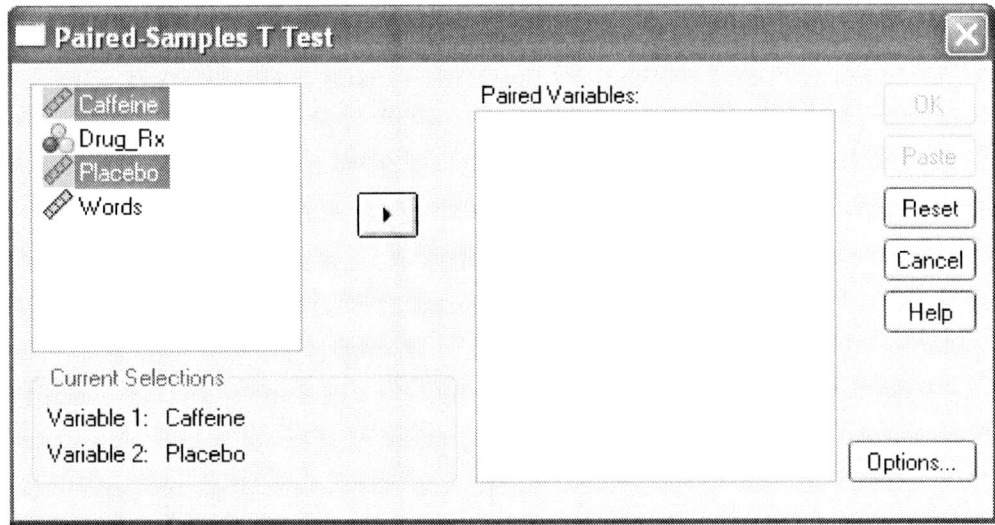

Now click on the ▶ button to move these variables into the **Paired Variable(s):** window. When the dialog window looks like the one below, click **OK** to produce the **T-Test** output tables.

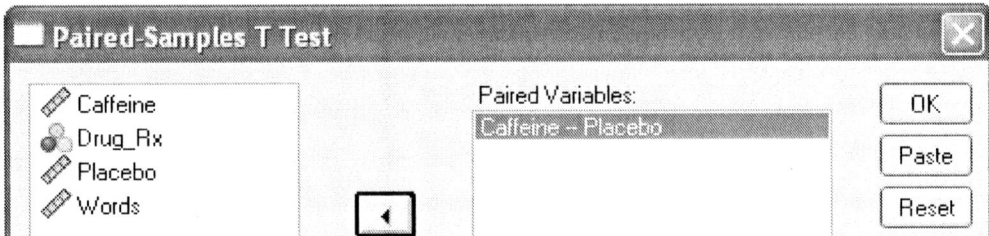

Assignment

2. Describe the results of the paired-samples *t* test according to the formatting guidelines of the APA. Your description should include the means and standard deviations of the dependent variable well as the *t* statistic, degrees of freedom, *p* value, and number of tails in the test. State whether the results were statistically significant and supplement your report with the tables from the SPSS output.

3. The paired-samples *t* test and independent-samples *t* test resulted in different decisions regarding the null hypothesis, despite the fact that the data values (number of words recalled) in the two studies were identical. Explain why the result of the paired-samples *t* test was significant, whereas the result of the independent-samples *t* test was not. (*Hint*: The paired-samples *t* test was used to analyze data from a within-groups design, whereas the independent-samples *t* test was conducted on data from a between-groups design.)

ANSWERS

1. The number of words recalled in the caffeine condition ($M = 20.7$, $SD = 3.2$) was not significantly greater than the number recalled in the placebo condition ($M = 19.25$, $SD = 3.39$), $t(38) = 1.393$, $p = .086$, one-tailed.

Group Statistics

Words	Drug Rx	N	Mean	Std. Deviation	Std. Error Mean
	1	20	20.70	3.197	.715
	2	20	19.25	3.385	.757

Independent Samples Test

		Levene's Test for Equality of Variances		t-test for Equality of Means						
									95% Confidence Interval of the Difference	
		F	Sig.	t	df	Sig. (2-tailed)	Mean Difference	Std. Error Difference	Lower	Upper
Words	Equal variances assumed	.176	.678	1.393	38	.172	1.450	1.041	-.658	3.558
	Equal variances not assumed			1.393	37.876	.172	1.450	1.041	-.658	3.558

2. The number of words recalled in the caffeine condition ($M = 20.7$, $SD = 3.2$) was significantly greater than the number recalled in the placebo condition ($M = 19.25$, $SD = 3.39$), $t(38) = 1.393$, $p = .04$, one-tailed.

Paired-Samples Statisics

		Mean	N	Std. Deviation	Std. Error Mean
Pair 1	Caffeine	20.70	20	3.197	.715
	Placebo	19.25	20	3.385	.757

Paired-Samples Correlations

		N	Correlation	Sig.
Pair 1	Caffeine & Placebo	20	.430	.058

Paired-Samples Test

		Paired Differences							
					95% Confidence Interval of the Difference				
		Mean	Std. Deviation	Std. Error Mean	Lower	Upper	t	df	Sig (2-tailed)
Pair 1	Caffeine - Placebo	1.450	3.517	.786	-.196	3.096	1.844	19	.081

3. The result of the paired-samples, but not the independent-samples, t test was significant because the variability among scores in a within-groups (repeated-measures) design is less than the variability among scores in a between-groups design. The variability among scores in a within-groups design is lower because a major source of variability, individual differences, is eliminated when the same participants serve in both conditions of the study.

CHAPTER 10

HYPOTHESIS TESTING WITH ONE-WAY ANOVA

Comparing Three or More Groups

The **one-way analysis of variance (ANOVA) for between-subjects** (independent-samples) **designs** may be used to analyze interval or ratio (scale) data from a study that includes at least two independent samples of participants. However, because an independent-samples *t* test is traditionally used when there are only two groups of scores, the one-way ANOVA is typically reserved for studies that include at least three groups of participants.

EXERCISE 1
COMPARING THE OUTPUT OF THE INDEPENDENT-SAMPLES *t* TEST AND A ONE-WAY ANOVA

In this first one-way ANOVA exercise, we will compare the results of the independent-samples *t* test from a previous exercise to the results of a one-way ANOVA. This will be followed by a one-way ANOVA to test a null hypothesis after adding a third group of scores to the data set. Launch SPSS, and open the file containing the caffeine and memory data from the Chapter 9 exercises. The file contains hypothetical data for 40 participants who were randomly assigned to a caffeine or a placebo condition.

First, we will repeat the independent-samples *t* test of the null hypothesis that the mean difference between the number of words recalled in Populations 1 (the caffeine population) and 2 (the placebo population) is zero, that is, $\mu_1 - \mu_2 = 0$. From the **Analyze** menu, select **Compare Means** ▶ **Independent-Samples T Test...** to produce the **Independent-Samples T Test** dialog window. Select **Words** and move this variable into the **Test Variable(s):** field. Now move the **Drug_Rx** variable into the **Grouping Variable:** field. Click on **Define Groups...** to produce the **Define Groups** window. Enter **1** for **Group1:** and **2** for **Group 2:**. Click **Continue** to return to the **Independent-Samples T Test** dialog window, then **OK** to produce the **T-Test output** tables.

Now we will conduct a one–way ANOVA to test the null hypothesis that was tested with the independent-samples *t* test.

From the **Analyze** menu, select **Compare Means ▶ One-Way ANOVA...**.

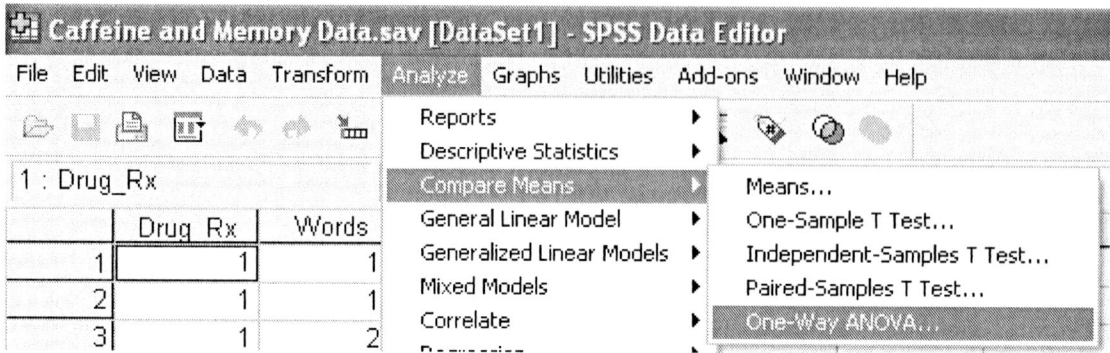

- This will produce the **One-Way ANOVA** dialog window.

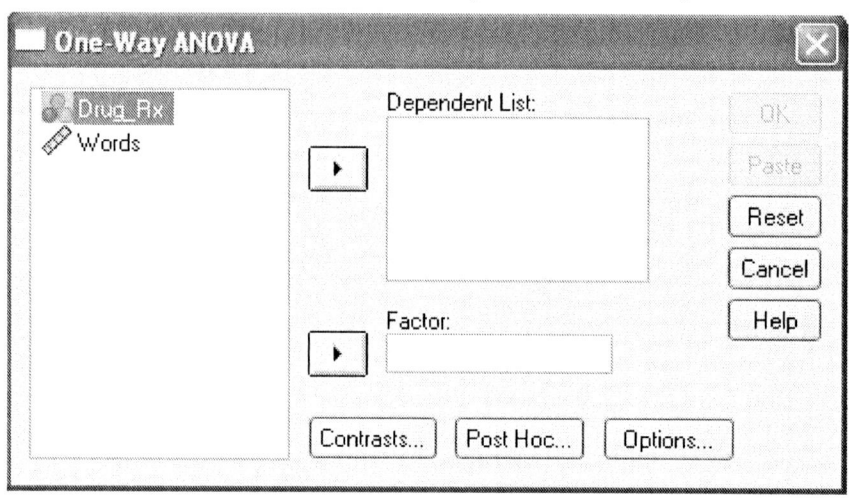

- Select **Words** and move this variable into the **Dependent List:** field. Move the **Drug_Rx** variable into the **Factor:** field. (*Factor* is a synonym for *independent variable*.)

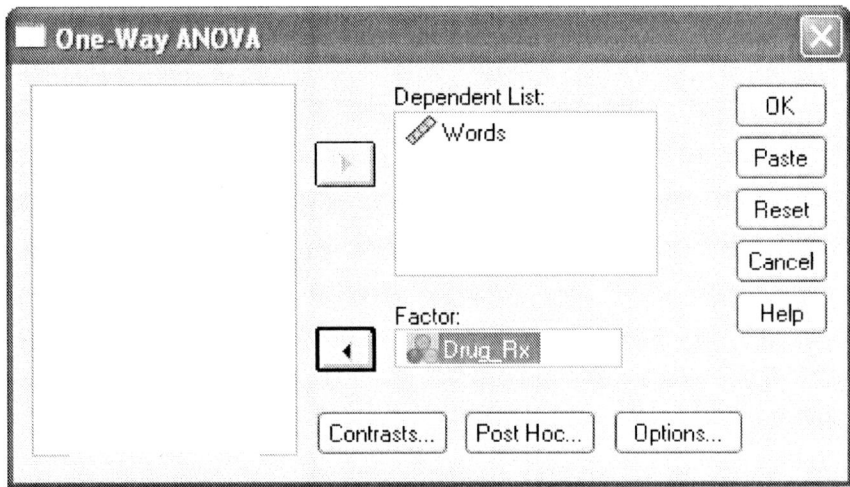

- Now click on the **Options:** tab to produce the **One-Way ANOVA: Options** dialog window. Select the **Descriptive** and **Homogeneity of variance test** (Levene's test) options as shown.

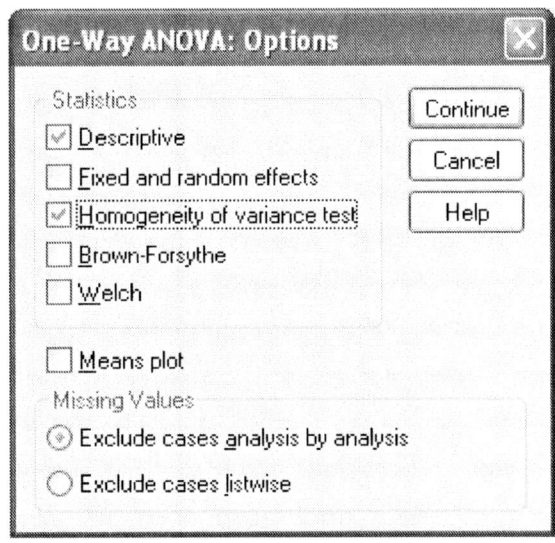

Click **Continue** to return to the **One-Way ANOVA** dialog window, then **OK** to produce the **Descriptives**, **Test of Homogeneity of Variances** and **ANOVA** output tables.

Descriptives

Words

	N	Mean	Std. Deviation	Std. Error
1	20	20.70	3.197	.715
2	20	19.25	3.385	.757
Total	40	19.98	3.332	.527

Test of Homogeneity of Variances

Words

Levene Statistic	df1	df2	Sig.
.176	1	38	.678

ANOVA

Words

	Sum of Squares	df	Mean Square	F	Sig.
Between Groups	21.025	1	21.025	1.939	.172
Within Groups	411.950	38	10.841		
Total	432.975	39			

These one-way ANOVA output tables may be compared to the tables produced by the independent-samples t test procedure that you performed on these data in the Chapter 9 exercise.

Group Statistics

	Drug Rx	N	Mean	Std. Deviation	Std. Error Mean
Words	1	20	20.70	3.197	.715
	2	20	19.25	3.385	.757

		Levene's Test for Equality of Variances		Independent-Samples Test t-test for Equality of Means		
		F	Sig.	t	df	Sig. (2-tailed)
Words	Equal variances assumed	.176	.678	1.393	38	.172
	Equal variances not assumed					

Questions

1. Compare the p values (the values under "Sig.") from the two Levene tests of the equal variances assumption. Did you expect that they would be the same or different? Explain.

2. Compare the values of the t and F statistics from the independent samples t test and the ANOVA, respectively. Explain how they are related. (*Hint*: You can perform an arithmetic operation on the t statistic to produce the F statistic.)

3. Compare the *p* values from the independent-samples *t* test and the ANOVA. Did you expect that they would be the same or different? Explain.

Exercise 2
CONDUCTING A ONE-WAY ANOVA ON DATA FROM THREE GROUPS

In this exercise, we will add a third group of participants. The researcher's decision to add a third group of participants was motivated by her disappointment with the nonsignificant outcome of the independent-samples *t* test. She believes that adding a higher dose of caffeine (300 mg; roughly equivalent to two cups of brewed coffee) will result in support for her hypothesis that caffeine facilitates recall from verbal memory.

Instructions for entering data for Group 3

- Click on the **Data View** tab to access the **Data Editor**.
- Place the cursor in the first blank cell in the column under **Drug_Rx** and type a **3** in this cell.

40	2	23
41	3	
42		

- Copy the **3** that you just typed (right-click and select **Copy**).

- Highlight the next 19 cells, that is, just hold down the left mouse button and drag the cursor through the next 19 cells, stopping when the cell in row **60** is highlighted.
- Right-click and select **Paste**.

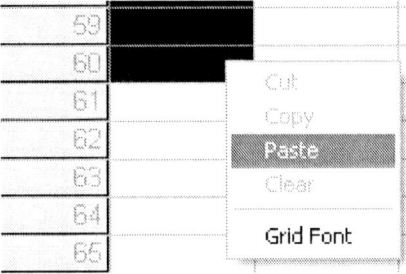

- Starting with row **41** in the column under **Words**, type the data values in the order shown.

  19, 24, 22, 20, 28, 21, 22, 24, 25, 26, 24, 20, 22, 23, 23, 29, 23, 24, 22, 15

Now, we will conduct a one-way ANOVA to test the null hypothesis that the means of the populations of words recalled following the administration of a placebo, a low caffeine dose (150 mg), and a moderate caffeine dose (300 mg) are identical.

- From the **Analyze** menu, select **Compare Means ▶ One-Way ANOVA...** to produce the **One-Way ANOVA** dialog window. Verify that **Words** is in the **Dependent List:** field and **Drug_Rx** variable is in the **Factor:** field.

- Click on the **Options:** tab to produce the **One-Way ANOVA: Options** dialog window. Make sure that the **Descriptive** and **Homogeneity of variance test** options are selected, then click **Continue** to return to the **One-Way ANOVA** dialog window, and **OK** to produce the **Descriptives, Test of Homogeneity of Variances** and **ANOVA** output tables.

Descriptives

Words

	N	Mean	Std. Deviation	Std. Error
1	20	20.70	3.197	
2	20	19.25		
3	20	22.80	3.105	.694
Total	60	20.92	3.500	.452

> A comparison of the group means shows that the high-dose caffeine group remembered more words than the low-dose and placebo groups. The one-way analysis of variance is conducted to determine whether these differences are statistically significant.

Test of Homogeneity of Variances

Words

Levene Statistic	df1	df2	Sig.
.411	2	57	.665

> The equal variances assumption is not rejected, because the *p* value is not less than .05.

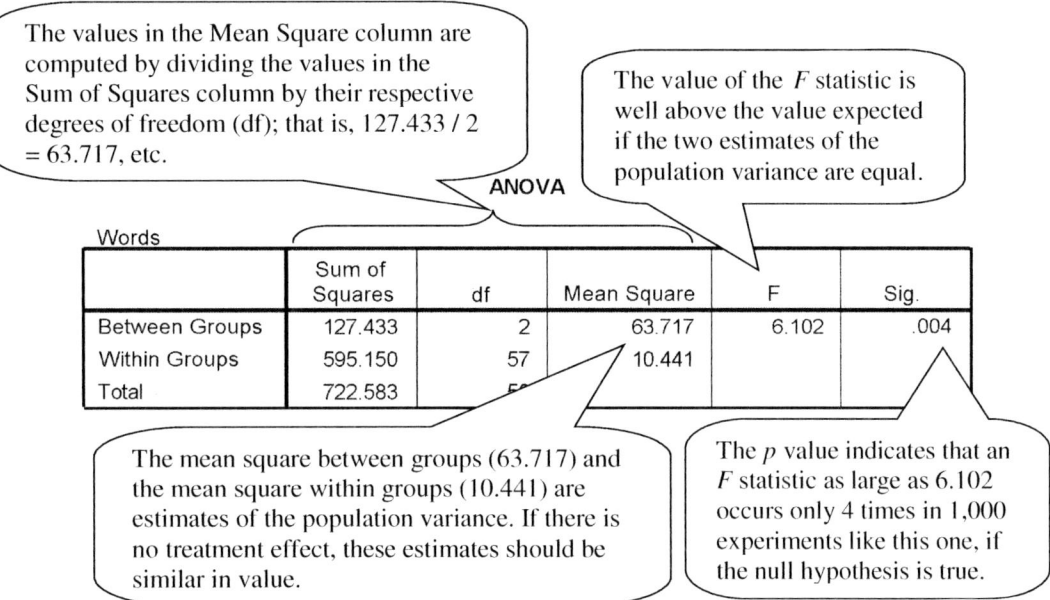

PRESENTING THE RESULTS, APA-STYLE

As noted in the exercises for Chapter 9, the *Publication Manual* of the APA prescribes a format for reporting the results of all statistical analyses. The following is an example from the study of territorial defense in parking lots by Ruback and Juieng (1997, p. 828):

> The first analysis was designed to test whether or not the four levels of intrusion differed significantly. This one-way ANOVA, involving the high intrusion (honking), the low intrusion (no honking), and the two control groups (no intrusion and distraction), indicated a significant difference among the four groups, $F(3, 236) = 13.50, p < .001$.

The phrase in which the statistical results are detailed is presented below with comments:

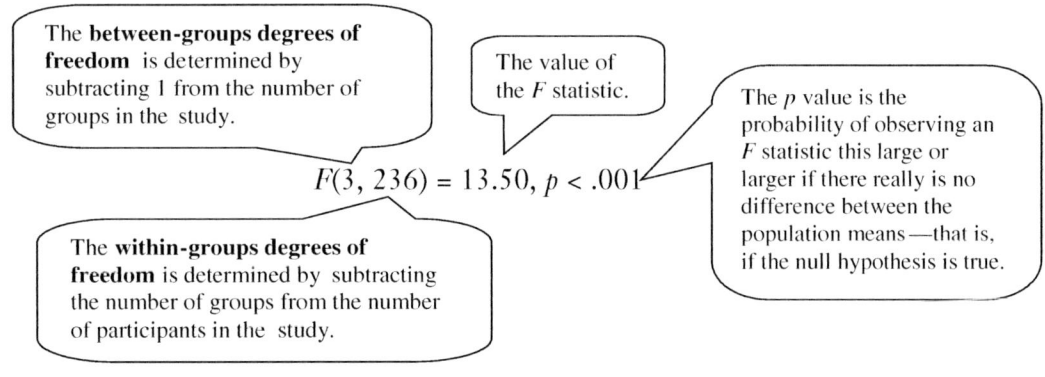

Assignment

Use the APA formatting guidelines (p. 10-7) to describe the results of the analysis of variance. Be sure to include the symbols and statistics as well as the names of the independent and dependent variables in your description. State whether the results were, or were not, statistically significant.

EXERCISE 3
AN EXAMPLE OF A ONE-WAY ANOVA AND POST-HOC COMPARISONS

A significant result for an analysis of variance tells you that the population means are not all the same, but it does not disclose which ones are different. For that, you need to conduct **post-hoc comparisons** (also called *a posteriori comparisons*). These are follow-up analyses designed to identify statistically significant differences between pairs of group means.

First, we will repeat the one-way ANOVA that we conducted in the previous exercise, but this time we'll add some **simple** (i.e., **pairwise**) post hoc comparisons.

- Select **Analyze, Compare Means ▶ One-Way ANOVA...** to produce the **One-Way ANOVA** dialog window. Make sure that **Words** is in the **Dependent List:** field and **Drug_Rx** is in the **Factor:** field.

- Now click on the **Options:** tab to produce the **One-Way ANOVA: Options** dialog window and click on the **Post Hoc...** tab to produce the **One-Way ANOVA: Post Hoc Multiple Comparisons** window.

CHAPTER 10 ■ HYPOTHESIS TESTING WITH ONE-WAY ANOVA

- There are 14 options listed in the section under **Equal Variances Assumed** at the top of the window. Select the box to the left of **Tukey** and click **Continue** to return to the **One-Way ANOVA** dialog window. Click **OK** to produce the **Multiple Comparisons** output tables.

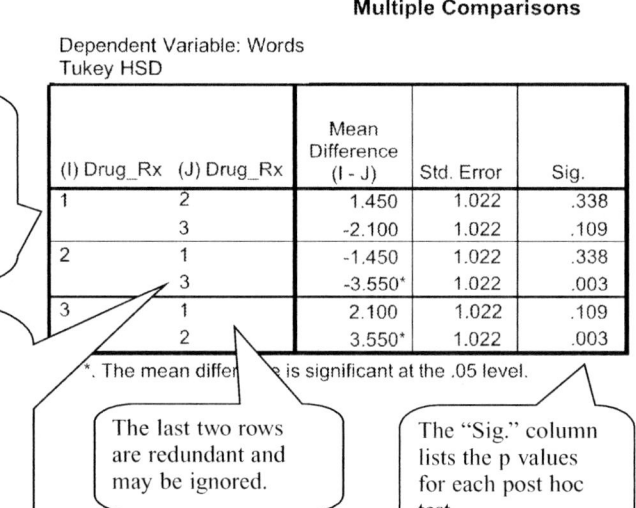

The first two rows of the table show that the mean of the low-dose caffeine group (Group 1) is not significantly different from either the mean of the placebo group ($p = .338$) or the mean of the moderate-dose caffeine group ($p = .109$).

The third row is a repeat of the test in the first row (the positions of the means are just reversed) and is thus redundant. The fourth row shows that the mean of the placebo group (Group 2) is significantly different from the mean of the high-dose caffeine group ($p = .003$). Note that significant mean differences are indicated by an asterisk.

The last two rows are redundant and may be ignored.

The "Sig." column lists the p values for each post hoc test.

The **Tukey HSD** (honestly significantly different) test is frequently selected as a post-hoc test because it is considered neither too conservative nor too liberal. The results of a one-way analysis of variance and post-hoc comparisons for this hypothetical study may be reported as follows.

> A one-way analysis of variance revealed a significant effect of drug treatment on the number of words remembered in a test of free recall, $F(2, 57) = 6.102$, $p = .004$. Post-hoc comparisons (Tukey HSD) showed that participants in the high-dose caffeine group remembered significantly more words ($M = 22.8$, $SD = 3.1$) than participants in the placebo group ($M = 19.25$, $SD = 3.39$), $p = .003$. There were no other significant group differences.

A second example is from a study by Ruback, Pape, and Doriot (1989) of users of public telephones in a shopping mall in Atlanta. The researchers manipulated the number of individuals waiting to use the phone by having either zero, one, or two male confederates approach the area within 30 seconds of the time each subject lifted the receiver to make a call. Because the researchers could not locate a single public telephone with enough traffic to conduct an experiment, a public station with two adjacent telephones was used, and one of the confederates in the two-confederate condition used the other phone while the second confederate stood a little to the side and behind, but within 3 feet of, the caller. The authors used an analysis of variance to examine the effect of the subject's gender and the number of confederate "intruders" on the amount of time each subject remained at the telephone. They used the Newman-Keuls post-hoc test to identify differences between group means. Ruback et al. reported their findings as follows:

> The only significant effect was for number of confederates, $F(2, 50) = 3.23$, $p < .05$. A post-hoc Newman-Keuls test of the means ($p < .05$) revealed that subjects intruded on by two confederates were at the phone longer ($M = 237.4$ secs) than were subjects intruded on by one confederate ($M = 107.0$ secs) and subjects not intruded on by a confederate ($M = 81.5$ secs). The latter two conditions did not differ significantly from each other. (p. 239)

EXERCISE 4
ONE-WAY ANOVA AND POST-HOC COMPARISONS WITH FOUR GROUPS

In this exercise, you will add a fourth group of participants to the design. The researcher's decision to add a fourth group of participants representing a *zero control group* (no treatment of any kind, not even a placebo) was motivated by a colleague's disbelief in the *placebo effect*. A **placebo effect** is a manifestation of the power of suggestion. For example, roughly half of the participants in a randomized clinical trial of a new medication designed to relieve pain may be given a placebo, a capsule that looks, feels, and tastes like the capsule that includes the new medication but which does not include the medication. A double-blind procedure is usually employed such that neither the participants nor the individuals administering the capsules know whether the participant is receiving the medication or a placebo. A sizable percentage of the participants given the placebo may report pain relief—an outcome that is, by definition, a placebo effect. Kirsch and Sapirstein (1999) estimated that 50% of the response to antidepressant medication is due to the placebo effect, with 25% attributable to the pharmacological properties of the medication, and 25% to other factors such as the physician-patient relationship.

- Add the following data values (number of words recalled) for Group 4:

  14, 20, 19, 17, 23, 13, 18, 18, 21, 16, 15, 19, 16, 11, 17, 22, 14, 21, 24, 10.

- Conduct a one-way ANOVA on the data from this four-group design and follow the omnibus ANOVA with a set of Tukey *HSD* post-hoc comparisons.

CHAPTER 10 ■ HYPOTHESIS TESTING WITH ONE-WAY ANOVA

Questions

4. Use the APA formatting guidelines to describe the results of the analysis of variance. Be sure to include the appropriate statistical symbols and statistics as well as the names of the independent and dependent variables in your description of the results of the overall analysis of variance, and support your description with copies of the appropriate SPSS output tables. Report the results of the Tukey post-hoc tests. For all significant mean differences, enclose group means and standard deviations in parentheses and provide the p value from the Tukey test. For each report that involves a p value, state whether the results were, or were not, statistically significant.

5. Describe any evidence of a possible placebo effect. (*Hint*: Think of the logic of hypothesis testing and the fact that the zero control group was added to the design to disclose a possible placebo effect.)

ANSWERS

1. The p values from the two Levene tests of the equal variances assumption are identical as should be the case when the same test is used more than once to analyze the same set of data.

2. Squaring the t statistic produces the F statistic—that is, $t^2 = F$, and $t = \sqrt{F}$.

3. The p values from the t test and the ANOVA are identical. This follows from the relation between the t and F statistics identified in the answer to Question 2. Put another way, when there are two groups of scores the independent samples t test and the one-way ANOVA are algebraically equivalent, so the p values should be the same.

4. A one-way ANOVA revealed a significant caffeine treatment effect, $F(3, 76) = 9.03$, $p < .0005$. Follow-up group comparisons using Tukey's HSD test revealed that memory performance following the higher (300 mg) dose of caffeine ($M = 22.8$, $SD = 3.11$) was significantly different from both the placebo ($M = 19.25$, $SD = 3.39$, $p = .008$) and zero control ($M = 17.4$, $SD = 3.89$, $p < .0005$) conditions. The number of words recalled following the lower (150 mg) dose of caffeine ($M = 20.7$, $SD = 3.2$) was significantly greater than the number recalled following the zero control condition ($p = .015$) but not following the placebo treatment ($p = .535$). Finally, there were no significant differences between either the placebo and zero control conditions ($p = .320$) or the two caffeine conditions ($p = .215$).

Descriptives

Words

	N	Mean	Std. Deviation
1	20	20.70	3.197
2	20	19.25	3.385
3	20	22.80	3.105
4	20	17.40	3.858
Total	80	20.04	3.883

Test of Homogeneity of Variances

Words

Levene Statistic	df1	df2	Sig.
.693	3	76	.559

ANOVA

Words

	Sum of Squares	df	Mean Square	F	Sig.
Between Groups	312.938	3	104.313	9.030	.000
Within Groups	877.950	76	11.552		
Total	1190.888	79			

Multiple Comparisons

Dependent Variable: Words
Tukey HSD

(I) Drug_Rx	(J) Drug_Rx	Mean Difference (I - J)	Std. Error	Sig.
1	2	1.450	1.075	.535
	3	-2.100	1.075	.215
	4	3.300*	1.075	.015
2	1	-1.450	1.075	.535
	3	-3.550*	1.075	.008
	4	1.850	1.075	.320
3	1	2.100	1.075	.215
	2	3.550*	1.075	.008
	4	5.400*	1.075	.000
4	1	-3.300*	1.075	.015
	2	-1.850	1.075	.320
	3	-5.400*	1.075	.000

*. The mean difference is significant at the .05 level.

5. The null hypothesis tested to determine whether there is evidence of a placebo effect is as follows:

> The mean number of words recalled following treatment with a placebo is the same as the mean number of words recalled in the absence of any systematic treatment.

In symbols, $\mu_{placebo} = \mu_{zero\ control}$

This hypothesis was not rejected ($p = .320$), so there is no evidence of a placebo effect in this study. The research hypothesis states that the mean number of words recalled following treatment with a placebo is not the same as the mean number of words recalled in the absence of any systematic treatment. A rejection of the null hypothesis would provide support for this hypothesis.

You may be thinking that the absence of a significance difference between the placebo and low-dose caffeine group ($p = .535$) provides evidence of a placebo effect. However, the logic of hypothesis testing does not regard a failure to reject the null hypothesis as evidence supporting it.

CHAPTER 11

TWO-WAY ANOVA

Understanding Interactions

Do drivers "defend their territory" by taking longer to leave a parking space when another driver is waiting to take it? This question was addressed in a replication of parts of two studies reported by Ruback and Juieng (1997). In this set of exercises you will analyze the data from this replication by conducting two factorial ANOVAs. A **factorial ANOVA** is used when the experimental design includes at least two independent variables, each with two or more levels.

The data file for this exercise is entitled "Parking Data for Exercise 11" on the data CD. Double-clicking on this file will launch SPSS and load the file into the **Data Editor** window. The first 10 cases are shown below:

	Intruder_cond	gender	numpass	dir_exit	dep_time
1	1	1	1	2	29
2	1	2	0	1	31
3	1	2	1	1	12
4	1	2	1	1	31
5	1	1	0	1	24
6	1	2	1	2	14
7	1	2	3	1	21
8	1	2	0	1	15
9	1	1	0	2	60
10	1	2	0	1	80

From the **Analyze** menu, select **General Linear Model ▶ Univariate...**

	Intruder_cond	gender	numpass	dir_exit	dep_time
1	1	1	1	2	29
2	1	2	0	1	31
3	1	2	1	1	12
4	1	2	1	1	31
5	1	1	0	1	24
6	1	2	1	2	14
7	1	2	3	1	21
8	1	2	0	1	15
9	1	1	0	2	60
10	1	2	0	1	80

to produce the **Univariate** dialog window (below). Select **dep_time** and click on the ▶ button to move this variable into the **Dependent Variable:** box on the right. Now select **Intruder_cond** and move this independent variable into the **Fixed Factor(s):** field; do the same with the **gender** variable. After moving the variables, the Univariate window should look like this:

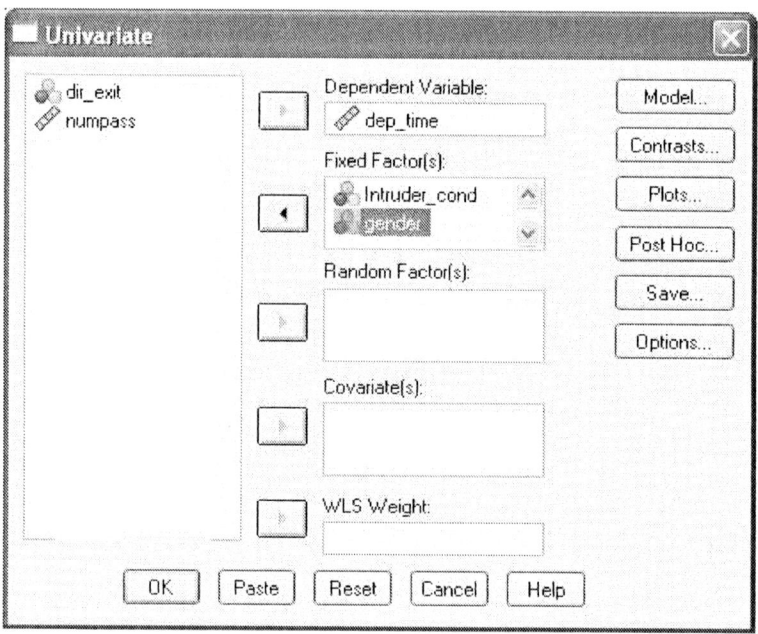

Now click on the **Options...** tab (bottom tab on the right side of the window) to produce the **Univariate: Options** dialog window; click in the box to the left of **Descriptive statistics** (under **Display** on the left side of the window), and click **Continue** to return to the Univariate dialog window.

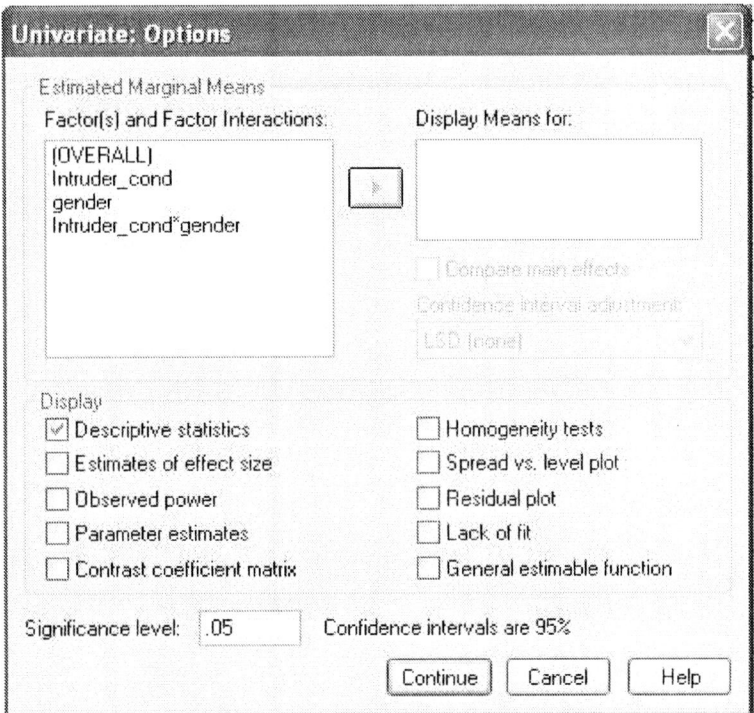

Now click **OK** to close the Univariate window and produce the output.

The first of three output tables is labeled **Between-Subjects Factors** and lists each of the factors in the analysis as well as the numbers of participants representing each level of each factor. For example, the first two rows tell us that 96 drivers were in the intruder condition (code = 1), and 95 drivers were in the no-intruder condition (code = 2). The next two rows tell us that there were 91 female drivers (code = 1) and 100 male drivers (code = 2)

The table labeled **Descriptive Statistics** lists the means, standard deviations, and number of drivers in each condition (cell or combination of intruder condition and gender of driver) of the study. For example, the two rows list the statistics for female and male drivers in the intruder condition. The statistics in the rows labeled "Total" are for the factor listed in the first column, ignoring the levels of the factor listed in the second column. The last row in the table lists the statistics for the combination of all levels of all factors. A more traditional format for presenting the means for a 2 × 2 factorial design is shown on the next page. A generic form of the table is presented first followed by a blank table.

Factor A

	Level 1	Level 2	
Factor B Level 1	A_1B_1	A_2B_1	B_1
Level 2	A_1B_2	A_2B_2	B_2
	A_1	A_2	

Intruder Condition

	Intruder	No Intruder	
Gender of Driver Female			
Male			

You may wish to fill in the blanks in the second table with the appropriate means from the SPSS output. The table may be particularly helpful as you answer the following questions.

1. Which condition resulted in the lowest mean departure time? The highest?

2. Compare the intruder vs. no-intruder conditions. Which condition resulted in the slower departure time?

3. Now compare the means for the female and male drivers. Which group had the slower departure time?

The third table in the output, labeled **Tests of Between-Subjects Effects**, includes the results of a 2 (Intruder Condition: intruder vs. no intruder) × 2 (Gender: male vs. female drivers) between-groups factorial ANOVA. The column labeled **Source** lists the different sources of variance. You may ignore the first two rows, labeled "Corrected Model" and "Intercept." The next three rows list the names of the factors as well as the intruder condition × gender of the driver interaction. The column labeled **Type III Sum of Squares** lists the between-groups sums of squares (SS_B) for the two factors and their interaction as sources of variance or "treatments." The bottom row in this column, labeled **Error,** lists the within-groups sum of squares (SS_W). The **df, Mean Square, F,** and **Sig.** columns include the degrees of freedom, population variance estimates, F statistics, and p values, respectively, for each of the sources of variance.

4. For each of the following questions, provide the appropriate evidence to support your answer. Be sure to present the results in the editorial style of the American Psychological Association.

    a. Was there a main effect of intruder condition?

    b. Was there a main effect of gender?

    c. Was there an interaction effect? If so, was it *qualitative* or *quantitative*?

    d. Interpret the result of the test for an interaction effect.

In the Results section of Study 1, Ruback and Juieng (1997) wrote: "Because number of people in the departing car was related to time it took to depart, $r(198) = .24$, $p < .001$, we used this variable as a grouping factor in subsequent analyses. A 2 × 2 ANOVA of the departure times was conducted using intrusion and number of people in the departing car as grouping variables, with number in the car being dichotomized into (a) only one person in the car or (b) more than one person in the car" (pp. 824–825).

A correlation between number of passengers and departure time was also observed in this study, $r(190) = .148$, $p = .041$. In this next exercise, you will follow the example of Ruback and Juieng by dichotomizing the number of passengers variable before conducting a 2 (Intruder Condition: intruder vs. no intruder) × 2 (number of passengers: 0 vs. 1 or more) ANOVA for just the male drivers. This ANOVA will not include female drivers because their departure times were similar in the intruder and no-intruder conditions.

The first part of this exercise requires that you select just the male drivers for analysis. First, click on **Data … Select Cases …** to produce the **Select Cases dialog window.** In the Select Cases dialog window, click on the radio button next to **If condition is satisfied,** then click on the large **If** button to produce the **Select Cases: If** dialog window. In the Select Cases: If dialog window, select gender from the list of variables and click on the ▶ button to move this variable into the box on the right. Type **= 2** so that the expression in the box now reads **gender = 2.** Click **Continue** to return to the Select Cases dialog window, then **OK** to return to the **Data Editor** window. Your screen should look like this, with slashes through the cases that correspond to female drivers:

	intruder_cond	gender	numpass	dir_exit	dep_time	filter_$
1	1	1	1	2	29	0
2	1	2	0	1	31	1
3	1	2	1	1	12	1
4	1	2	1	1	31	1
5	1	1	0	1	24	0
6	1	2	1	2	14	1
7	1	2	3	1	21	1
8	1	2	0	1	15	1
9	1	1	0	2	60	0
10	1	2	0	1	80	1
11	1	2	1	1	90	1
12	1	1	1	1	38	0
13	1	2	1	2	107	1
14	1	2	2	2	33	1
15	1	1	0	1	45	0

The next task is to recode the numpass variable into a different variable (call it numpass2) with two values: 1 = 0 passengers, 2 = 1 or more passengers. From the **Transform** menu options select **Recode into Different Variables...** to produce the Recode into Different Variables dialog window. When this window appears, select **numpass** from the list of variables and click the ▶ button to move this variable into the field on the right. Place the cursor in the **Name:** box under **Output Variable** and type the name of the recoded variable (**numpass2**). In the **Label:** box, type **1 = 0 passengers, 2 = 1 or more passengers**. Now click on the **Old and New Values** box near the center of the window to produce the **Recode into Different Variables: Old and New Values** dialog window. The cursor should be blinking in the **Value:** box under **Old Value** in the upper left corner of the window. The first old value to be recoded is 0, so type **0** in this box, then position the cursor in the **Value:** box under **New Value** and type **1** as the new value. Now click the **Add** button to enter the recode request to the **Old -->New** list. To recode the rest of the values of numpass, click the **Range, value through HIGHEST:** button (the next-to-last radio button on the left side of the window) and type **1** in the box. Type **2** in the Value: box under **New Value** and click the **Add** button to cause all values of numpass that are 1 and higher to be recoded as **2**. Click **Continue** to return to the Recode into Different Variables dialog window. When the Recode into Different Variables dialog window appears, click the **Change** button to execute the recode requests, and click **OK** to return to the Data Editor window. Your Data Editor window should now include numpass2 as a new variable with two values: 1 to indicate drivers with no passengers and 2 to denote drivers with at least one passenger:

	Intruder_cond	gender	numpass	dir_exit	dep_time	filter_$	numpass2
1	1	1	1	2	29	0	2
2	1	2	0	1	31	1	1
3	1	2	1	1	12	1	2
4	1	2	1	1	31	1	2
5	1	1	0	1	24	0	1
6	1	2	1	2	14	1	2
7	1	2	3	1	21	1	2
8	1	2	0	1	15	1	1
9	1	1	0	2	60	0	1
10	1	2	0	1	80	1	1
11	1	2	1	1	90	1	2
12	1	1	1	1	38	0	2
13	1	2	1	2	107	1	2
14	1	2	2	2	33	1	2
15	1	1	0	1	45	0	1

5. Conduct a 2 (Intruder Condition: intruder vs. no intruder) × 2 (number of passengers: 0 vs. 1 or more) ANOVA and interpret the output by answering the following questions. Be sure to support your answers by citing the appropriate statistics from the SPSS output.

   a. Was there a main effect of intruder condition?

   b. Was there a main effect of number of passengers?

   c. Was there an interaction? If so, was it qualitative or quantitative?

   d. Interpret the result of the test for an interaction effect.

In the brief introduction to their naturalistic observation study (Study 1), Ruback and Juieng (1997) observed that "Because a parking space has minimal value to a departing driver, intrusion should facilitate a speedier departure. However, because concerns with identity and control are so tied to driving, it was predicted that intrusion would induce territorial defense." (p. 823). In their discussion of the results of this study, they wrote:

> In this observational study, departing drivers took longer to leave their parking spaces when they were intruded upon by another driver than when they were not. Although longer departure times following intrusion may indicate territorial behavior, causality cannot be inferred with this

observational study because other factors may be operating. For instance, the presence of the intruding cars may have distracted the departing drivers, causing them to need more time to leave the parking space. A related possibility is that departing drivers took longer to leave when intruded upon because they wanted to be careful to avoid a collision with the intruding car. (p. 825)

In their follow-up field experiment (Study 2), Ruback and Juieng (1997) attempted to separate intrusion from distraction by having a confederate drive slowly past drivers who were about to leave. They reported that "... drivers who were intruded upon ($M = 36.78$ s) did not stay significantly longer than did those who were distracted ($M = 31.09$ s), $F(1, 236) = 2.09$, ns" (p. 828). In their discussion of this finding, Ruback and Juieng noted that "the distraction condition may not have been a pure manipulation of distraction, in that even though the distracting car was not waiting for the departing driver, the presence of the distracting car could have primed departing drivers about the value of the space they were about to leave" (p. 829).

Ruback and Juieng did not record the direction of exit of the departing drivers they observed. If drivers were distracted by the presence of another vehicle, or if "they wanted to be careful to avoid a collision with the intruding car," then one may reasonably assume that they would have been more distracted, or would have exercised more caution, when backing toward than away from that vehicle. See the figure below.

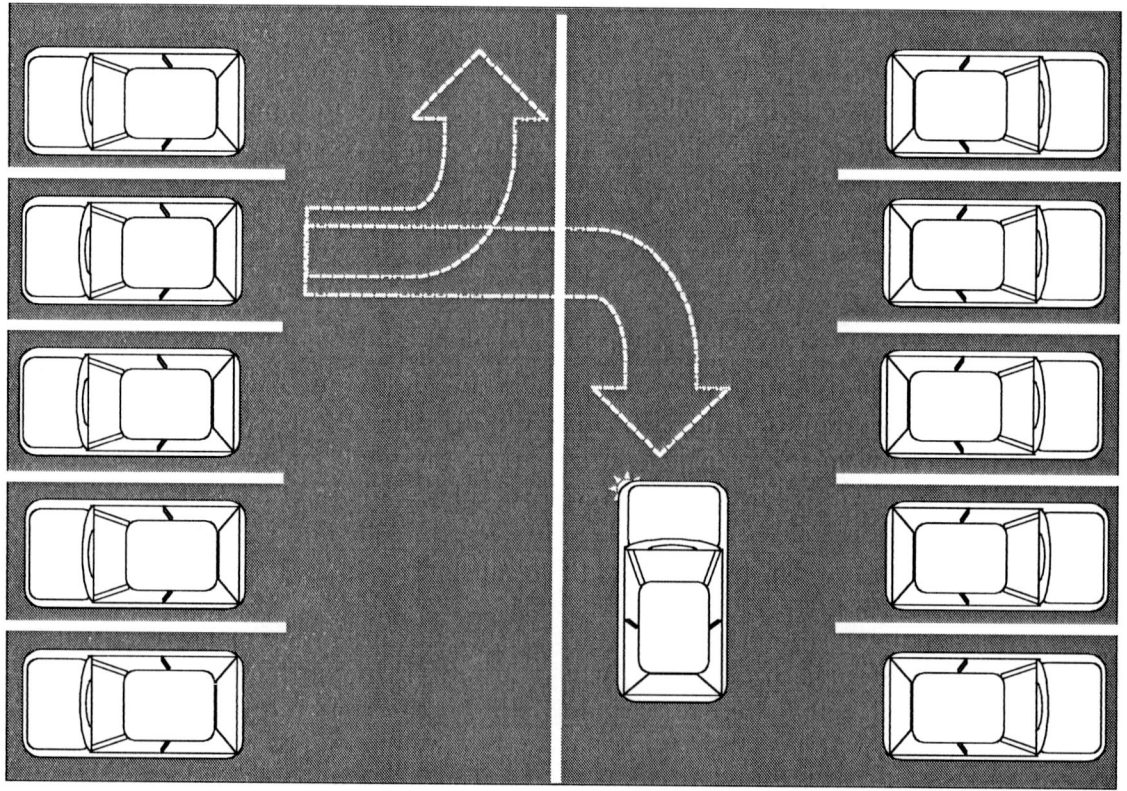

6. Use an independent-samples *t* test to analyze the effect of the variable dir_exit (direction of exit: 1 = toward, 2 = away) on departure time. Report the results in the style of the American Psychological Association by following a brief statement of the result of the *t* test with a comma and the following syntax: $t(df) = x.xx, p = .xxx$, 2-tailed.

7. Do the results of these exercises support the hypothesis that drivers exhibit territorial defense of parking spaces by taking longer to exit in the presence of an intruder? Explain your answer.

ANSWERS

1. The lowest mean was recorded for male drivers in the no-intruder condition ($M = 21.45$ s, $SD = 11.808$ s, $n = 47$), whereas the highest mean was for female drivers in the no-intruder condition ($M = 35.23$ s, $SD = 22.644$ s, $n = 48$).

2. The slowest departure times were observed in the intruder ($M = 31.45$ s, $SD = 21.704$ s, $n = 96$) condition. Drivers in the no-intruder condition ($M = 28.41$ s, $SD = 19.302$ s, $n = 95$) exited their spaces about 3 seconds sooner.

3. Female drivers had slower departure times ($M = 33.88$ s, $SD = 21.296$ s, $n = 91$). Male drivers ($M = 26.35$ s, $SD = 19.253$ s, $n = 100$) exited parking spaces around 7.5 seconds faster than female drivers.

4. a. There was no main effect of intruder condition, $F(1, 187) = 1.207$, $p = .273$.

   b. There was a main effect of gender, $F(1, 187) = 7.053$, $p = .009$. The departure times of male drivers ($M = 26.35$ s) were significantly faster than those of female drivers ($M = 33.88$ s).

   c. There was a significant intruder condition x gender interaction, $F(1, 187) = 4.328$, $p = .039$. This is a *qualitative* interaction, because the effect of intruder condition was opposite for male and female drivers.

   d. The significant interaction effect indicates that the effect of the intruder condition depended upon the gender of the departing driver. When an intruder was present, female drivers left about 3 seconds sooner than in the no-intruder condition. In contrast, male drivers remained in "their" parking spaces about 9 seconds *longer* when an intruder was present vs. when there was no intruder.

5. a. There was a main effect of intruder condition, $F(1, 96) = 6.923$, $p = .01$. Male drivers exited "their" parking spaces significantly more slowly in the presence of an intruder.

   b. There was also a main effect of number of passengers, $F(1, 96) = 10.194$, $p = .002$. Male drivers accompanied by one or more passengers took significantly longer to leave the parking spaces ($M = 32.08$ s, $SD = 22.117$ s, $n = 50$) than those who were not accompanied by passengers ($M = 20.62$ s, $SD = 13.883$ s, $n = 50$).

   c. There was no interaction between intruder condition and number of passengers, $F(1, 96) = .464$, $p = .497$.

   d. The absence of an interaction effect means that male drivers were not differentially influenced by the presence of passengers in the intruder and no–intruder conditions.

6. The departure times when backing toward ($M = 30.52$ s, $SD = 18.021$ s, $n = 54$) vs. away ($M = 32.64$ s, $SD = 25.866$ s, $n = 42$) from an intruder were not significantly different, $t(94) = -0.474$, $p = .637$, 2-tailed.

7. Male, but not female, drivers took longer to leave parking spaces when an intruder was present and when they were accompanied by one or more passengers, but there is no evidence that the effect of intrusion was affected by the presence of passengers. These

results offer tentative support for the territoriality hypothesis, although it is difficult to separate the effect of an intruder as a "threat" to one's "property" from the effect of an intruder as a distraction when one is leaving a parking space. However, one may argue as follows: If the presence of a waiting driver causes drivers to exit more slowly because they are distracted or because they are concerned about having an accident, then it is reasonable to suppose that those concerns would be magnified for drivers exiting toward rather than away from an intruder. However, this study provided no evidence that drivers may have been more distracted or may have exercised extra caution when backing toward a waiting driver. This result does not support the argument that longer departure times in the presence of an intruder may be explained by an appeal to distraction or the exercise of additional caution while backing out.

CHAPTER 12

BEYOND HYPOTHESIS TESTING

Confidence Intervals, Effect Size, and Power

The purpose of this set of exercises is to demonstrate a statistical inference procedure called **interval estimation**. As an alternative to hypothesis testing, a researcher may compute a **confidence interval** that is centered around the sample mean (M), and use this interval to simultaneously test a number of null hypothesized values of a population mean (μ).

EXERCISE 1

Launch SPSS and navigate to the data CD. Locate the syntax file named **Syntax for 1000 Sample means (100,15)** and open it. Now select **Run**, then **All** (as shown below) to execute the syntax program and create the data file.

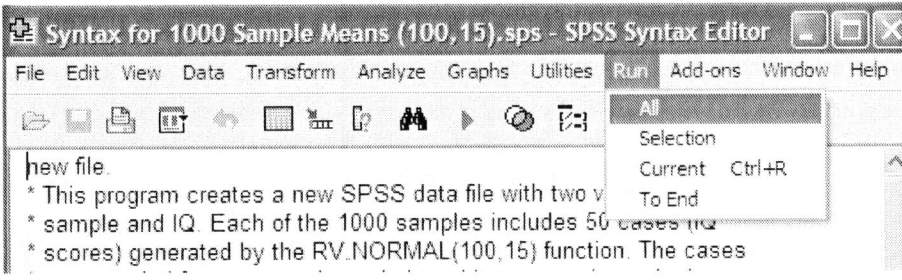

The syntax program generated an SPSS data file that includes two variables, **sample** and **IQ_mean**. The values of the sample variable are simply the sample numbers (1 to 1000), and the values of the IQ_mean variable are means of samples of 50 values randomly selected from a normal population with μ 100 and σ 15. The **Data Editor** should be similar to this:

	sample	IQ_mean	var	var	var
1	1	100.60			
2	2	101.16			
3	3	101.14			
4	4	99.66			
5	5	97.30			

We will construct a **95% confidence interval** around each of the sample means in the IQmeans data file. Each confidence interval (CI) is defined by its lower and upper limits. The formulas for the lower and upper limits are as follows:

$$CI_{UL} = M + z_{\frac{\alpha}{2}}(\sigma_M) = M + 1.96\left(\frac{\sigma}{\sqrt{N}}\right) = M + 1.96\left(\frac{15}{\sqrt{50}}\right)$$

$$CI_{LL} = M - z_{\frac{\alpha}{2}}(\sigma_M) = M - 1.96\left(\frac{\sigma}{\sqrt{N}}\right) = M - 1.96\left(\frac{15}{\sqrt{50}}\right)$$

where,

CI_{UL} is the upper limit of the confidence interval

CI_{LL} is the lower limit of the confidence interval

M is the sample mean

$\pm z_{\frac{\alpha}{2}}$ are the critical z scores that define the two-tailed rejection region of the null hypothesis tested at a significance level of $\alpha = .05$; when $\alpha = .05$, $\pm z = \pm 1.96$

σ_M is the standard error of the mean

From the **Transform** menu, select **Compute Variable...** to produce the **Compute Variable** dialog window and create a new variable named **CI95_LL**. Type **CI95_LL** in the **Target Variable:** field, then move **IQ_mean** into the **Numeric Expression:** field and complete the expression so that it reads as follows:

IQ_mean − 1.96 * 15 / SQRT(50)

Click **OK**. The formula computes the **lower** limit of a 95% confidence interval for each of the sample means in the data file.

Use **Transform, Compute Variable…** to create a new variable named **CI95_UL**. In the **Target Variable:** box type **CI95_UL** (the name CI95_LL should still be in the field, so just change the "U" to an "L"). Edit the expression in the **Numeric Expression:** field (this should require nothing more than changing the minus sign to a plus sign) to read:

$$IQ\_mean + 1.96 * 15 / SQRT(50)$$

Click **OK**. The formula computes the **upper** limit of a 95% confidence interval for each of the sample means.

Each of the 95% confidence intervals that you just computed is an interval estimate of the true value of the population mean. Each interval estimate is centered around a sample mean (M), which is your best estimate of the true value of the population mean (μ). The intervals are **95%** confidence intervals because the level of confidence is computed as the **additive inverse** of the significance level: **CI% = 100% − alpha% = 100% − 5% = 95%**. We are permitted to say that we are 95% confident that any given interval contains the true value of the population mean. In the next step, we will count the number of confidence intervals that include the true value of the population mean.

Use **Transform, Compute Variable…** to produce the **Compute Variable** dialog window and create a new variable named **decision**. Type **decision** in the **Target Variable:** field. In the **Numeric Expression:** field, type:

$$CI95\_UL >= 100 \text{ \& } CI95\_LL <= 100$$

and click **OK**. For each pair of confidence limits the expression will return **1** if the population mean is within the interval, **0** if it is not. Go to the **Variable View** window and set **Decimals** to zero for the decision variable.

If you typed the formulas correctly, the first 10 rows of the **Data Editor** window should be similar to this:

	Sample	IQ_mean	CI95_LL	CI95_UL	decision
1	1	100	96	104	1
2	2	104	100	108	1
3	3	101	97	105	1
4	4	100	96	104	1
5	5	101	97	105	1
6	6	95	91	99	0
7	7	98	94	102	1
8	8	98	94	102	1
9	9	103	99	107	1
10	10	100	96	104	1

From the **Analyze** menu, select **Descriptive Statistics ▶ Frequencies...** to produce a count of the number of 95% confidence intervals that include the true value of the population mean. When the **Frequencies** window appears, move **decision** into the **Variable(s):** field and click **OK**.

> We know the true value of the population mean in this and all other computer simulation exercises, because we set up the population to have a mean of 100 and a standard deviation of 15. Because we know the population parameters we can detect whether each of the confidence intervals that we constructed really includes the true value of the population mean ($\mu = 100$).

Questions

1. Assuming that the null hypothesis is true, what is the *expected* percentage of 95% confidence intervals that include the value 100?

2. What is the *actual* percentage of confidence intervals that include the value 100? Support your answer with the SPSS output.

3. Suppose that a school psychologist in a certain school district believes that the 8th-grade students in her district are unusual but she isn't sure how their relative difference might be expressed on a standard IQ test. She hypothesizes that the mean IQ score in this population of 8th-grade students is not 100.

    State the **null hypothesis** that the school psychologist is interested in testing.

4. Now suppose that the samples of IQ scores in the IQMeans data file are samples of 8th-grade students from this psychologist's district. Thus each confidence interval represents a test of the null hypothesis (the one that you wrote as your answer to Question 3, if you are correct). Based on the confidence intervals that you constructed, what percentage of the time will this school psychologist conclude that she is correct—that is, what percentage of the time will she conclude that the mean IQ in the population of 8th-graders in her district really is different from 100? Put another way: Of this large number of tests of the null hypothesis, what percentage of them will allow the school psychologist to reject the null hypothesis and conclude that the mean IQ score among 8th grade students in her school district is not 100?

5. You may wish to reread the text box on top of this page before you answer this question: What percentage of the school psychologist's rejections of the null hypothesis are correct rejections? Explain your answer.

CHAPTER 12 ■ BEYOND HYPOTHESIS TESTING

EXERCISE 2

Repeat Exercise 1, but this time use the syntax file named **Syntax for 1000 Sample means (110,15)**. Execute each step of this exercise exactly as you did in Exercise 1.

Questions

6. What is the *actual* percentage of confidence intervals that include the value 100? Support your answer with the SPSS output.

7. Each confidence interval is a test of the null hypothesis that you identified in Question 3. Of this large number of confidence intervals, what percentage of them will allow the school psychologist to reject the null hypothesis and conclude that the mean IQ score among 8th-grade students in her school district is not 100?

8. Recall that this is a computer simulation as you answer this question: What percentage of the school psychologist's rejections of the null hypothesis are correct rejections? Explain your answer.

9. Assuming that your answer to Question 6 above is a number greater than zero, what does this percentage represent?

    A. correct decisions   B. Type I errors   C. Type II errors

10. Explain your answer to Question 9.

ANSWERS

EXERCISE 1

1. Expect 950, or 95%, of the confidence intervals to include the null-hypothesized value of the population mean (100).

2. Answers will vary because of the random number seed. According to the output table below, **94.1 percent** of the confidence intervals included the population mean, 100. This is reasonably close to the expected rate of 95 percent.

decision

		Frequency	Percent	Valid Percent	Cumulative Percent
Valid	0	59	5.9	5.9	5.9
	1	941	94.1	94.1	100.0
	Total	1000	100.0	100.0	

3. The null hypothesis that the school psychologist is interested in testing is as follows: **The mean IQ score in the population of 8th-grade students in her district is 100.** Note that the null hypothesis is always the opposite of the research hypothesis.

4. According to the output table above, the school psychologist will conclude that she is correct—that is, she will conclude that the average IQ in the population of 8th-graders in her district really is different from 100—about **5.9 percent** of the time. In other words, the school psychologist will reject the null hypothesis about 5.9 percent of the time.

5. Each time the school psychologist rejects the null hypothesis she is making a Type I error, so **none** of her rejections are correct. We know that all of her rejections are Type I errors because we set up the population mean to be 100—the value specified by the null hypothesis.

EXERCISE 2

6. According to the output table below, **0.1 percent** of the confidence intervals include the population mean, 100. This is not surprising given that the population mean for this exercise is 110.

decision

		Frequency	Percent	Valid Percent	Cumulative Percent
Valid	0	999	99.9	99.9	99.9
	1	1	.1	.1	100.0
	Total	1000	100.0	100.0	

CHAPTER 12 ■ BEYOND HYPOTHESIS TESTING

7. According to the previous output table, the school psychologist will conclude that she is correct—that is, she will conclude that the average IQ in the population of 8th-graders in her district really is different from 100—about **99.9 percent** of the time. In other words, the school psychologist will reject the null hypothesis about 99.9 percent of the time.

8. Each time the school psychologist rejects the null hypothesis she is making a correct decision, so **all** her rejections are correct. We know that all her rejections are correct decisions because we set up the population mean in this exercise to be 110 instead of 100 as it was in Exercise 1. We set up the null hypothesis to be false, so each decision to reject it is a correct decision.

9. Each of the confidence intervals that contain the null-hypothesized value of the population mean (100) is a Type II error (choice C).

10. The confidence intervals that resulted in a failure to reject the null hypothesis are Type II errors because the null hypothesis was set up to be false in this exercise. A Type II error occurs when the researcher fails to reject a false null hypothesis.

CHAPTER 13

CHI SQUARE

Expectations Versus Observations

THE CHI-SQUARE TEST FOR GOODNESS OF FIT

Chi-square tests are conducted when the variables of interest are measured on a **nominal** scale. Examples of such variables, also termed **categorical variables**, include *gender, political party affiliation, ethnicity, religious preference, diagnostic category, favorite color*, and so forth. There are two chi-square tests. In this set of exercises we will use the **chi-square test for goodness of fit** to test the null hypothesis that the frequency distributions of the values of *a single* nominal variable in two populations are the same. The research hypothesis states that the distributions of frequencies in the two populations are not the same.

EXERCISE 1

A large national of adult respondents, aged 25 to 65, were asked whether they preferred coffee, tea, soft drinks, or some other caffeinated beverage. The results are displayed in the table on the left. A survey of the preferences of 1,000 college students yielded the observed frequencies (f_o) displayed in the table on the right. Use the **.01** level of significance to test the null hypothesis that the two frequency distributions are from identical populations.

Adult Sample

Beverage Preference	Percent
Coffee	40
Tea	25
Soft drinks	30
Other	5
Total	100

Sample of College Students

Beverage Preference	f_o
Coffee	320
Tea	190
Soft drinks	485
Other	5
Total	1000

- Launch SPSS and select **Type in data** from the opening "What would you like to do" menu options. Click the **Variable View** tab to access the

Variable View window. In the **Name** column, type **Bev_pref** as the name of the category variable and **Observed_Freq1** as the name of the observed frequencies variable. Both variables should be **Numeric** with **Decimals** set to **0**.

- Click in the first cell under **Values** to produce a gray box on the right side of the cell. Click on the gray box to access the **Value Labels** dialog window. Enter "1" in the **Value:** field, then **Tab** into the **Label:** field, type "Coffee," and either click the **Add** button or press the **Enter** key to complete the entry.

Click the **Add** button to move the **Value:** and the **Label:** into the list field at the bottom of the window.

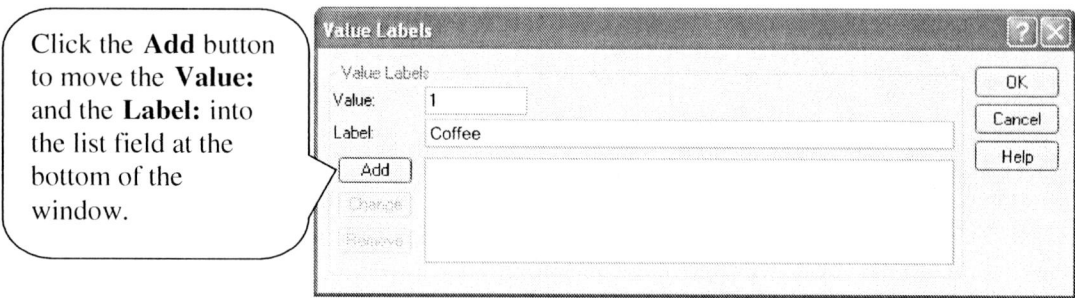

- Use "2," "3," and "4" as the values for "Tea," "Soft drinks," and "Other," respectively. There are two options to correct entry errors. Clicking on an incorrect entry will cause the **Value:** and **Label:** to be displayed in the Value Labels fields. The first option is to click on the **Remove** button to erase the entry; the second is to edit the entry by typing a new Value: or Label: and clicking the **Change** button. When the **Value Labels** dialog window looks like the one below, click **OK** to return to the **Variable View** window.

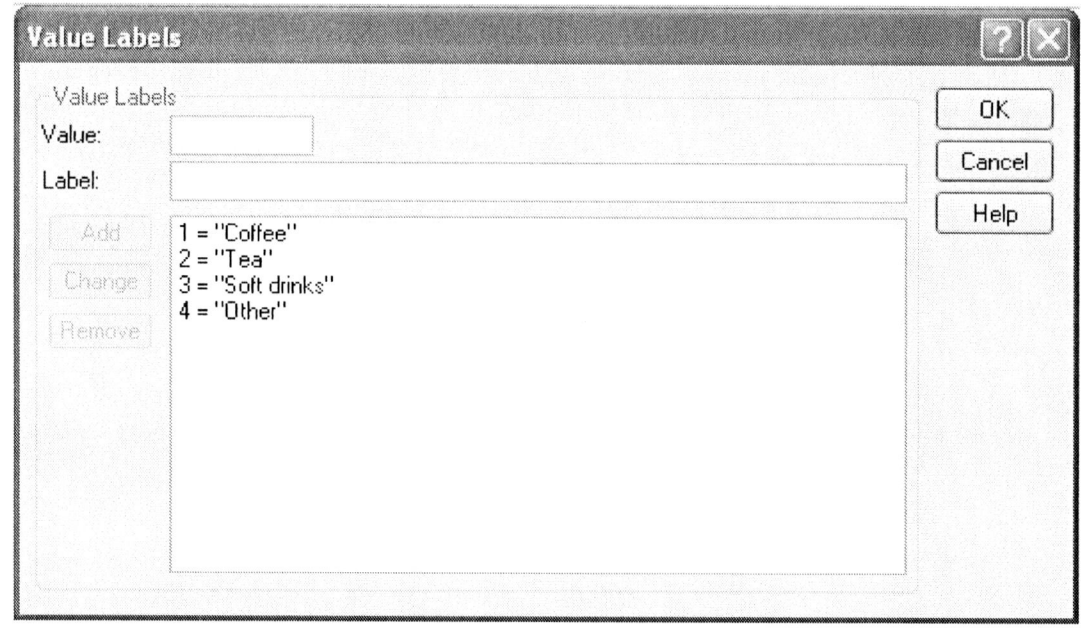

The Variable View window should look like this.

	Name	Type	Width	Decimals	Label	Values	Missing	Columns	Align	Measure
1	Bev_pref	Numeric	8	0		{1, Coffee}...	None	11	Right	Nominal
2	Observed_Freq1	Numeric	8	0		None	None	11	Right	Scale

- Select the **Data View** tab to access the **Data Editor** window. Enter the label values (**1, 2, 3,** and **4**) under **Bev_pref.** and enter the observed frequencies for the sample of college students (under f_o in the table on p. 13-1) in the **Observed_Freq1** column.

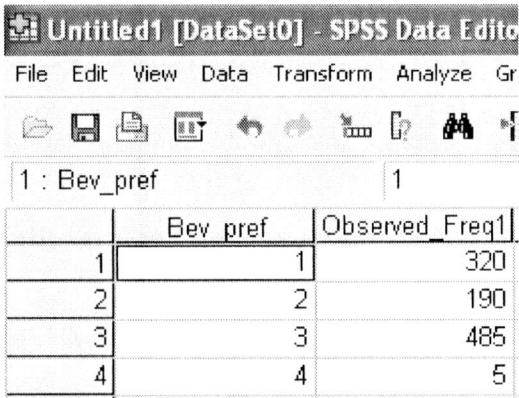

- From the **Data** menu, select **Weight Cases...** to access the **Weight Cases** dialog window.

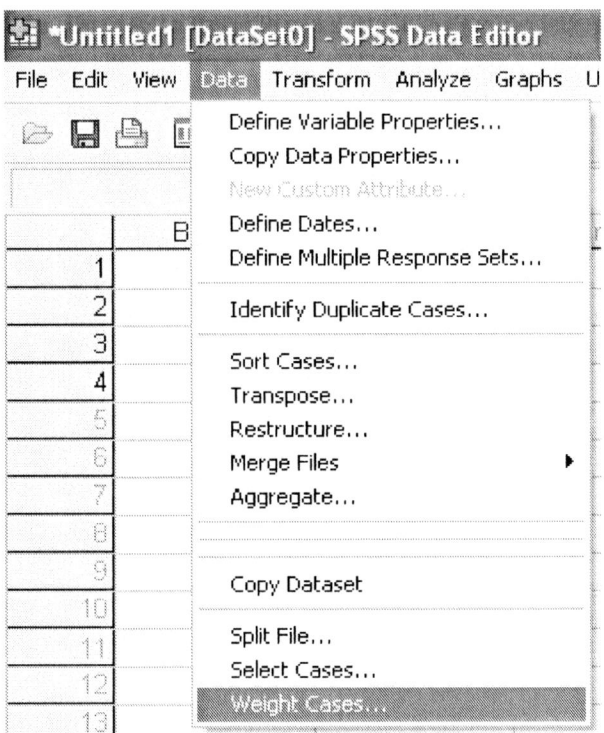

- Select the **Weight cases by** radio button and click the ▶ button to move **Observed_Freq1** into the **Frequency Variable:** field. Click **OK** to return to the **Data Editor** window.

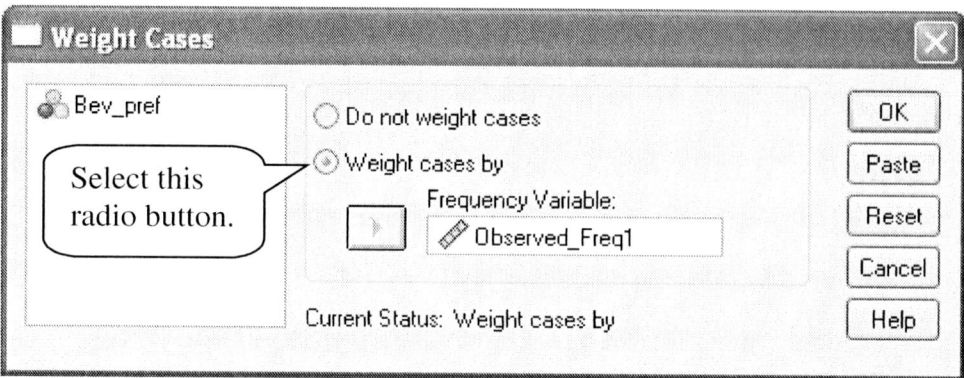

- From the **Analyze** menu, select **Nonparametric Tests** ▶ **Chi-Square...** to access the **Chi-Square Test** dialog window. Select **Bev_pref** and click the ▶ button to move this variable into the **Test Variable List:** field. Under **Expected Values** select the **Values:** radio button. Enter **40** in the field to the right of the **Value:** radio button and click the **Add** button to complete the entry. (SPSS will convert the percentages into relative frequencies.)

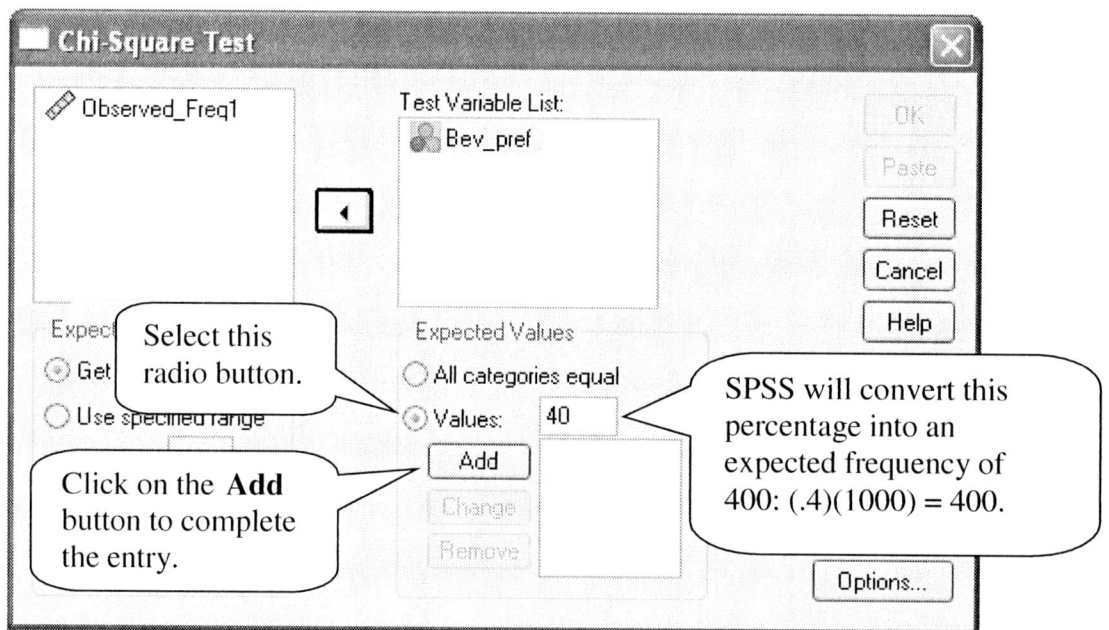

When all of the expected values have been entered, the **Expected Values** section of the dialog window should look like this:

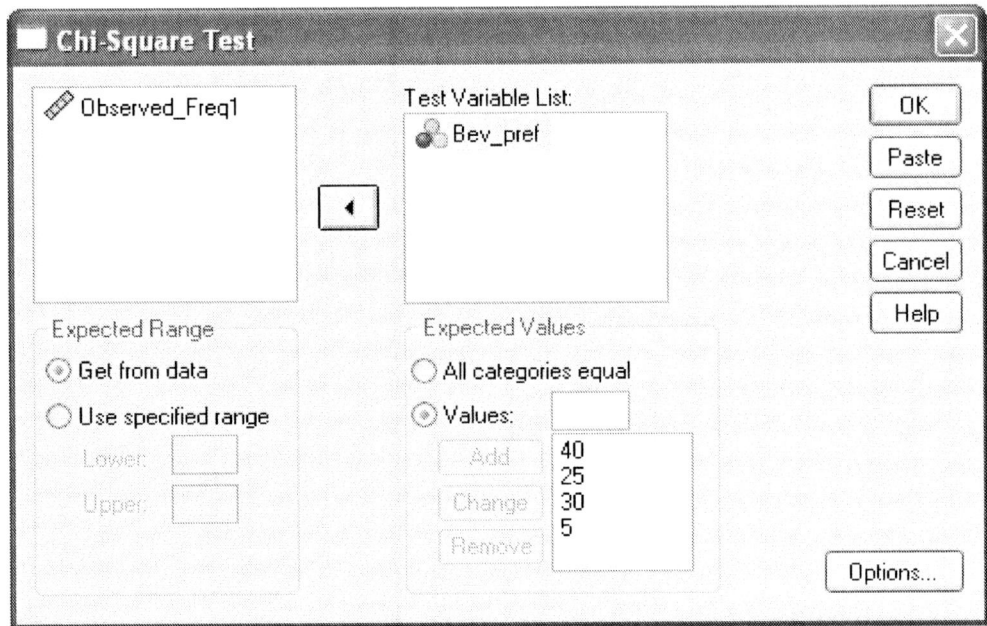

- Click **OK** to produce the two chi-square output tables.

Bev_pref

	Observed N	Expected N	Residual
1	320	400.0	-80.0
2	190	250.0	-60.0
3	485	300.0	185.0
4	5	50.0	-45.0
Total	1000		

The value of Total is the sample size N.

Each residual is the difference between the observed and expected frequency.

Test Statistics

	Bev_pref
Chi-Square [a]	184.983
df	3
Asymp. Sig.	.000

a. 0 cells (.0%) have expected frequencies less than 5. The minimum expected...

The magnitude of the chi-square statistic is proportional to the differences between the observed and expected frequencies listed in the Residual column in the table above.

The p value is the probability of observing a chi-square statistic at least as large as the one observed (184.983) if the null hypothesis is true. If the p value is less than the significance criterion, then the null hypothesis is assumed to be false and rejected accordingly. SPSS reports p values less than .0005 as ".000."

PRESENTING THE RESULTS OF A CHI-SQUARE ANALYSIS, APA-STYLE

The APA editorial style requires that a report of the results of a chi-square analysis include the symbols for the chi-square statistic, sample size, and the p value as well as the values of the chi-square statistic, the degrees of freedom, the sample size, and p. The following example is from pp. 138–139 of the *APA Publication Manual* (5th ed.):

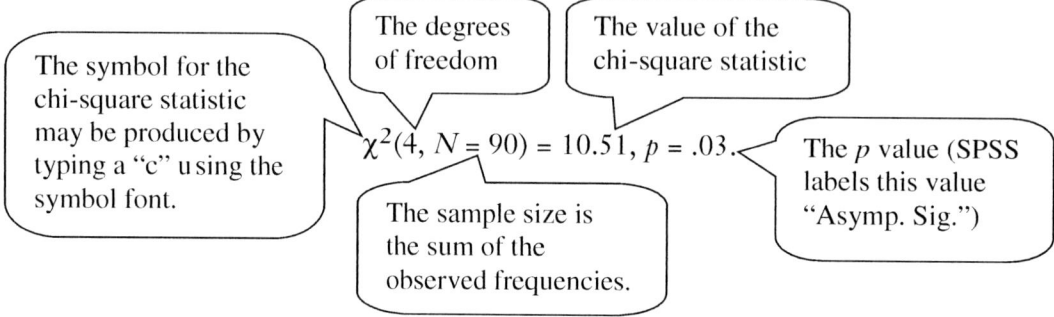

Assignment 1

1. Use the editorial style of the APA to describe the result of the chi-square analysis. Be sure to include all the elements in the example above and state whether the result does or does not support the research hypothesis.

EXERCISE 2

In a brand-blind preference test, 135 participants were asked to select a preferred laundry detergent after using four of the market-leading brands for a 1-week trial period. The results, expressed as the number of participants favoring each of the four brands, are displayed below. Use the .05 level of significance to test the null hypothesis that the four brands are equally preferred in the population.

Brand	f_o
A	46
B	31
C	27
D	31

- Go to the **Variable View** window and enter **Brand_pref** as the name of the category variable and **Observed_Freq2** as the name of the observed frequencies variable. Both variables should be **Numeric** with **Decimals** set to **0**.

- Access the **Value Labels** dialog window and enter the labels displayed in the table on p. 13-6 (i.e., 1 = Brand A, 2 = Brand B, etc.). After entering the values and labels, click **OK** to return to the **Variable View** window.

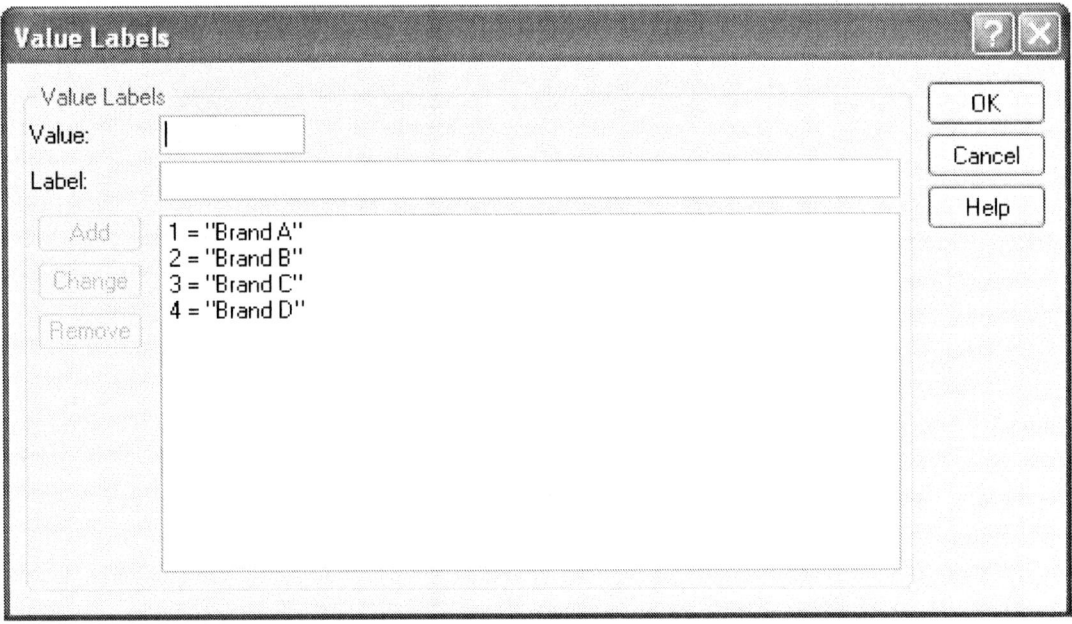

- Go to the **Data Editor** window and enter the label values (**1, 2, 3,** and **4**) under **Brand_pref**, then enter the observed frequencies for the sample of participants (under f_o in the table on p. 13-6) in the **Observed_Freq2** column.

- From the **Data** menu, select **Weight Cases...** to access the **Weight Cases** dialog window. Select the **Weight cases by** radio button and move **Observed_Freq2** into the **Frequency Variable:** field. Click **OK** to return to the **Data Editor** window.

- From the **Analyze** menu, select **Nonparametric Tests ▶ Chi-Square...** to access the **Chi-Square Test** dialog window. Select **Brand_pref** and click the ▶ button to move this variable into the **Test Variable List:** field. Under **Expected Values** select the **All categories equal:** radio button.

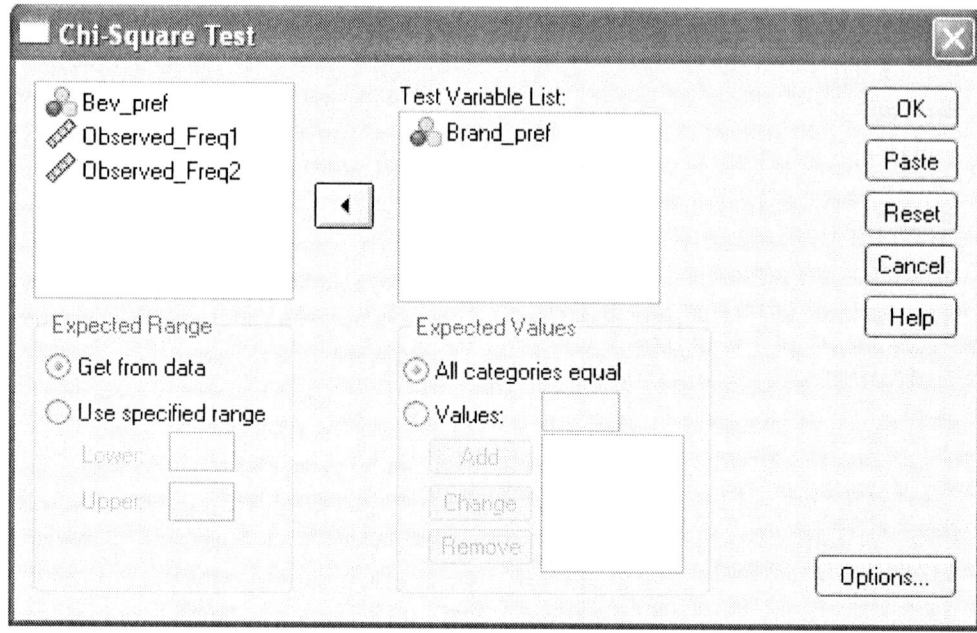

- Click **OK** to produce the SPSS output tables.

Assignment

2. Use the editorial style of the APA to describe the results of the chi-square analysis. Be sure to include all the elements in the example on p. 13-6 and state whether the result does or does not support the research hypothesis.

EXERCISE 3

The faculty handbook at a small liberal arts college advises faculty to teach their courses at a level of difficulty that produces the following symmetrical grade distribution: A's (10%), B's (20%), C's (40%), D's (20%), and F's (10%). The midterm grade distribution for Dr. Smith's most difficult course (enrollment of 50 students) is as follows: A's (20%), B's (40%), C's (32%), D's (6%), F's (2%). Use the .05 level of significance to test the null hypothesis that Dr. Smith's grade distribution does not differ from the distribution described in the faculty handbook.

Follow the steps in Exercise 1 to produce the SPSS output tables. These are summarized as follows:

- Go to the **Variable View** window and enter the **Grade** as the name of the category variable and **Observed_Freq3** as the name of the observed frequencies variable. Both variables should be **Numeric** with **Decimals** set to **0**.
- Access the **Value Labels** dialog window and enter the labels displayed in the table (i.e., 1 = A, 2 = B, etc.). After entering the values and labels, click **OK** to return to the **Variable View** window.
- Go to the **Data Editor** window and enter the label values (**1, 2, 3, 4,** and **5**) under **Grade**. Convert the percentages for the 50 students to frequencies (i.e., multiply each proportion by 50) and enter these in the **Observed_Freq3** column.
- From the **Data** menu, select **Weight Cases...** to access the **Weight Cases** dialog window. Select the **Weight cases by** radio button and move **Observed_Freq3** into the **Frequency Variable:** field. Click **OK** to return to the **Data Editor** window.
- From the **Analyze** menu, select **Nonparametric Tests ▶ Chi-Square...** to access the **Chi-Square Test** dialog window. Select **Grade** and click the ▶ button to move this variable into the **Test Variable List:** field. Under **Expected Values** select the **Values:** radio button. Enter the recommended grade distribution percentages (**10, 20, 40, 20,** and **10**) in the field to the right of the **Value:** radio button and click the **Add** button to complete each entry. (SPSS will convert the percentages into relative frequencies.)
- Click **OK** to produce the SPSS output tables.

Assignment3

3. Use the editorial style of the APA to describe the results of the chi-square analysis. Be sure to include all of the elements in the example on p. 13-6 and state whether the result does or does not support the research hypothesis.

CHI-SQUARE TEST FOR INDEPENDENCE

In this set of exercises we will conduct a **chi-square test for independence** to test a null hypothesis which states that two nominal variables are independent (unrelated) in the population.

The data for this exercise are based on results reported by Loftus and Palmer (1974). Participants in their study watched a brief film of a multi-car accident before completing a questionnaire about the film. The manipulated variable was the phrasing of a question that asked each participant to estimate the speed of the cars when they "hit" vs. "smashed into" each other. Fifty participants were assigned to each experimental condition, and 50 were assigned to a control condition that did not include this question. One week later participants from all three groups were invited back to the laboratory to complete a second questionnaire that included the question, "Did you see any broken glass?"

Launch SPSS, and select the **Type in data** option. Navigate to the data CD and load the file **Memory Reconstruction Data**. The values of the variable **Verb_condition** are as follows: 1 = *smashed*, 2 = *hit*, and 3 = *control*. The values of the **Response** variable are responses to the question, "Did you see any broken glass?" (1 = yes, 2 = no).

- From the **Analyze** menu, select **Descriptive Statistics** ▶ **Crosstabs...**

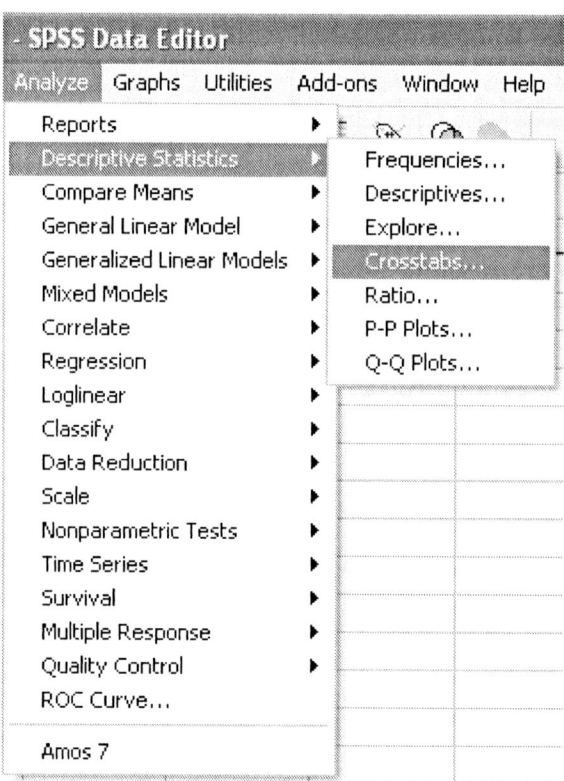

- When the **Crosstabs** dialog window appears, select **Response** and move this variable into the **Row(s):** field, then select **Verb-condition** and move this variable in the **Column(s):** field.

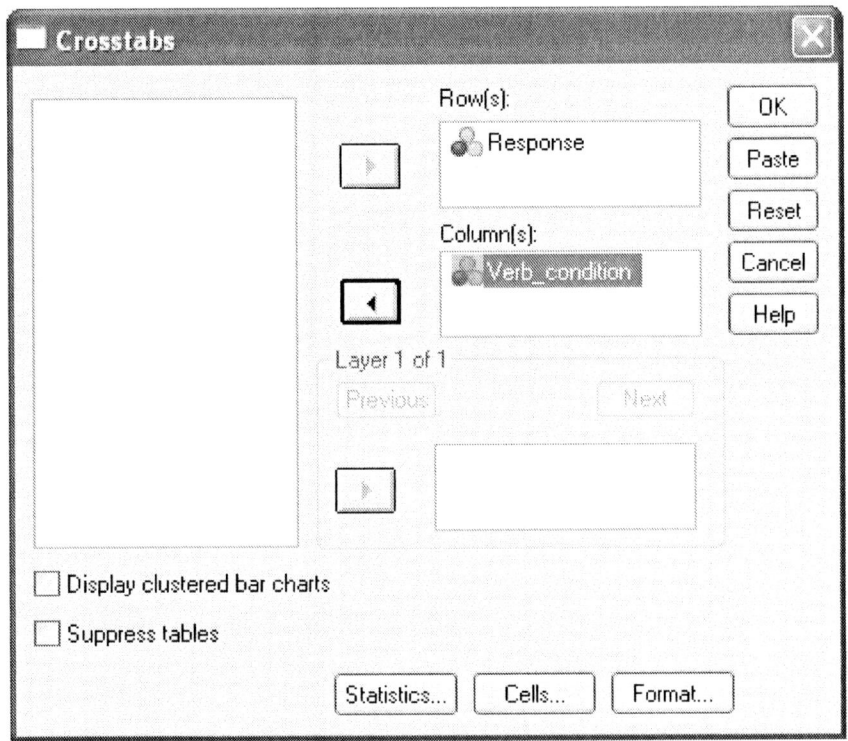

- Click on the **Statistics...** button to produce the **Crosstabs: Statistics** dialog window. Select **Chi-square** and **Phi and Cramér's V**, then click **Continue** to return to the **Crosstabs** dialog window.

- Now click on the **Cells...** button to produce the **Crosstabs: Cell Display** window. Select the **Observed** and **Expected** options under **Counts**, as well as the **Row** and **Column** options under **Percentages**. The window displayed below is a truncated version of the full window.

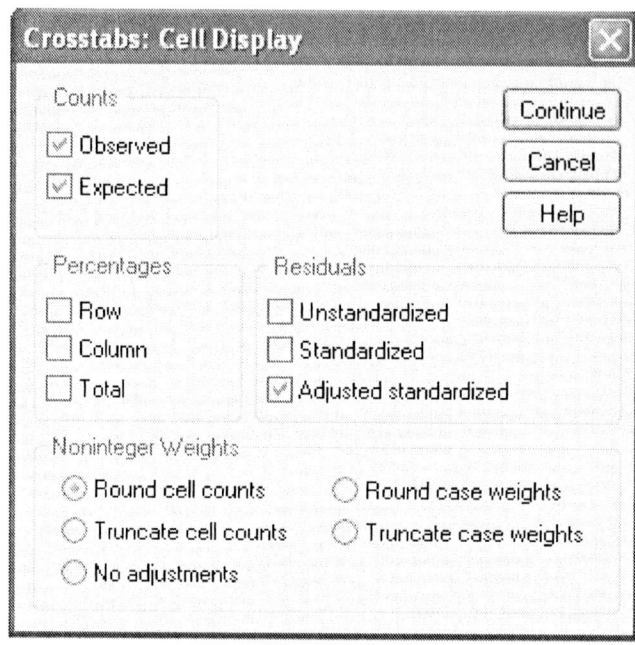

- Click **Continue** to return to the **Crosstabs** dialog window, then **OK** to produce the output.

The **Case Processing Summary** table includes information about sample size (N) and missing data. A second table, labeled **Response * Verb_condition Crosstabulation**, is better known as a **2 × 3 contingency table**. This table lists the **observed** (labeled **Count**) and **expected** (**Expected Count**) **frequencies**, as well as the **adjusted standardized residuals** for each cell of the table.

PRESENTING THE RESULTS OF THE HYPOTHESIS TEST, APA STYLE

The following table, labeled **Chi-Square Tests**, lists three statistics and their associated *p* values. The test that is most commonly used is the **Pearson Chi-Square**, named for its inventor, Karl Pearson.

Chi-Square Tests

	Value	df	Asymp. Sig. (2-sided)
Pearson Chi-Square	7.780[a]	2	.020
Likelihood Ratio	7.430	2	.024
Linear-by-Linear Association	6.369	1	.012
N of Valid Cases	150		

a. 0 cells (.0%) have expected count less than 5. The minimum expected count is 9.67.

The value of the chi-square statistic is **7.780**. The *p* value (**.020**) is the probability of observing a chi-square statistic this extreme under the assumption that the null hypothesis is true. Degrees of freedom for the chi-square test for independence are determined by computing the product of (the number of rows − 1) and (the number of columns − 1). For this example, ***df* = (3 − 1)(2 − 1) = 2(1) = 2**.

Loftus and Palmer (1974) described the result as follows:

> An independence chi-square test on these responses was significant beyond the .025 level, $\chi^2(2) = 7.76$. The important result ... is that the probability of saying "yes," $P(Y)$, to the question about broken glass is .32 when the verb *smashed* is used, and .14 with *hit*. Thus *smashed* leads both to more "yes" responses and to higher speed estimates. (p. 587)

Assignment

4. Review the example of reporting the results of a chi-square analysis on p. 13-6, and edit the paragraph from the report by Loftus and Palmer (1974) to conform to current APA guidelines.

5. Look at the footnote in the above output table labeled **Chi–Square Tests**. Following Lewis and Burke (1949), the majority of statisticians have advised that the results of a chi-square test for independence are valid to the extent that each of the expected frequencies in a chi-square contingency table is at least 5. However, in a more recent review of the literature, Delucchi (1983) concluded that very low expected frequencies for each cell could be tolerated (that is, would not inflate the Type I error

rate) as long as the total number of participants was at least 5 times the number of cells in the contingency table.

Based on this more recent guideline, are the results of this chi-square analysis valid? Defend your answer.

6. Review the discussion (pp. 603–604 in the text) pertaining to **adjusted standardized residuals**. Identify the cells in the contingency table whose observed frequencies are different from their expected frequencies.

7. What is the **effect size** for this study? Use the table below (from p. 599 in the text) to label the effect size.

TABLE 13-10. CONVENTIONS FOR DETERMINING EFFECT SIZE BASED ON CRAMER'S V

Jacob Cohen (1992) developed guidelines to determine whether particular effect sizes should be considered small, medium, or large. The effect-size guidelines vary depending on the size of the contingency table. There are different guidelines based on whether the smaller of the two degrees of freedom (row or column) is 1, 2, or 3.

EFFECT SIZE	WHEN $df_{ROW/COLUMN} = 1$	WHEN $df_{ROW/COLUMN} = 2$	WHEN $df_{ROW/COLUMN} = 3$
Small	0.10	0.07	0.06
Medium	0.30	0.21	0.17
Large	0.50	0.35	0.29

ANSWERS

CHI-SQUARE TEST FOR GOODNESS OF FIT

1. The research hypothesis is supported. In the population of college students like those observed in this sample, the distribution of preferences for caffeinated beverages is different from the distribution of preferences in the adult population, $\chi^2(3, N = 1000) = 184.983, p < .0005$.

2. There is no evidence from this study to support the hypothesis that one brand of laundry detergent is preferred over another, $\chi^2(3, N = 135) = 6.244, p = .100$.

Test Statistics

	Brand_pref
Chi-Square [a]	6.244
df	3
Asymp. Sig.	.100

a. 0 cells (.0%) have expected frequencies less than 5. The minimum expected cell frequency is 33.8.

3. The research hypothesis is supported: The distribution of grades in Dr. Smith's class is almost certainly different from the distribution of grades recommended in the faculty handbook, $\chi^2(4, N = 50) = 23.9, p < .0005$.

Test Statistics

	Grade
Chi-Square [a]	23.900
df	4
Asymp. Sig.	.000

a. 0 cells (.0%) have expected frequencies less than 5. The minimum expected cell frequency is 5.0.

CHI-SQUARE TEST FOR INDEPENDENCE

4. Compared to participants who were not asked to estimate the speed of the cars in the accident and those who read a question that included the verb *hit*, participants who read the word *smashed* were more than twice as likely to recall seeing broken glass in the scene, $\chi^2(2, N = 150) = 7.78, p = .020$.

5. There were 150 participants in the study, and this number is greater than 5 times the number of cells (5 × 6 = 30). According to this criterion, the results of this chi-square analysis are valid.

6. The absolute values of the adjusted standardized residuals in the cells that correspond to the *smashed* condition (Verb_condition = 1) exceed 2.5. According to criteria discussed in the text, the observed frequencies for these cells are different from the expected frequencies.

Response * Verb_condition Crosstabulation

			Verb_condition			Total
			1	2	3	
Response	1	Count	16	7	6	29
		Expected Count	9.7	9.7	9.7	29.0
		Adjusted Residual	2.8	-1.2	-1.6	
	2	Count	34	43	44	121
		Expected Count	40.3	40.3	40.3	121.0
		Adjusted Residual	-2.8	1.2	1.6	
Total		Count	50	50	50	150
		Expected Count	50.0	50.0	50.0	150.0

7. The effect size is .228. According to Cohen's criteria, this is between a small and a medium effect size.

CHAPTER 14

BEYOND CHI SQUARE

Nonparametric Tests with Ordinal Data

As discussed in the text, nonparametric analyses are used primarily under two conditions: (1) when the data are measured on an ordinal scale, and (2) when "the underlying population distribution is greatly skewed, a situation that often develops when we have a small sample size" (p. 622 in the text). You were introduced to the most commonly used nonparametric tests in the previous chapter: the chi-square tests for goodness of fit and independence. In this set of exercises, we will use SPSS to compute three alternatives to the parametric statistics described in Chapters 5 and 9. First, we will compute Spearman's rho, the nonparametric alternative to the Pearson correlation described in Chapter 5. Then we will use SPSS to compute the Wilcoxon signed ranks statistic as a nonparametric alternative to the paired-samples t test introduced in Chapter 9. Finally, we will compute the Mann-Whitney U statistic as a nonparametric alternative to the independent-samples t tests that were also introduced in Chapter 9.

EXERCISE 1
COMPUTING THE SPEARMAN RANK-ORDER CORRELATION COEFFICIENT

- Launch SPSS. If you have not disabled the opening window, select **Type in data**, click the **OK** button, and click on the **Variable View** tab to access the **Variable View** window.

- Type **Country** as the name of the first variable. Click in the cell under **Type**, then click on the gray box to access the **Variable Type** dialog window. In the Variable Type window, click on the radio button next to **String**. The default setting for the **Width** of the variable name is **8** characters. There are 13 characters in "United States," so change the number of **C**h**aracters:** in the string variable to **15** as shown.

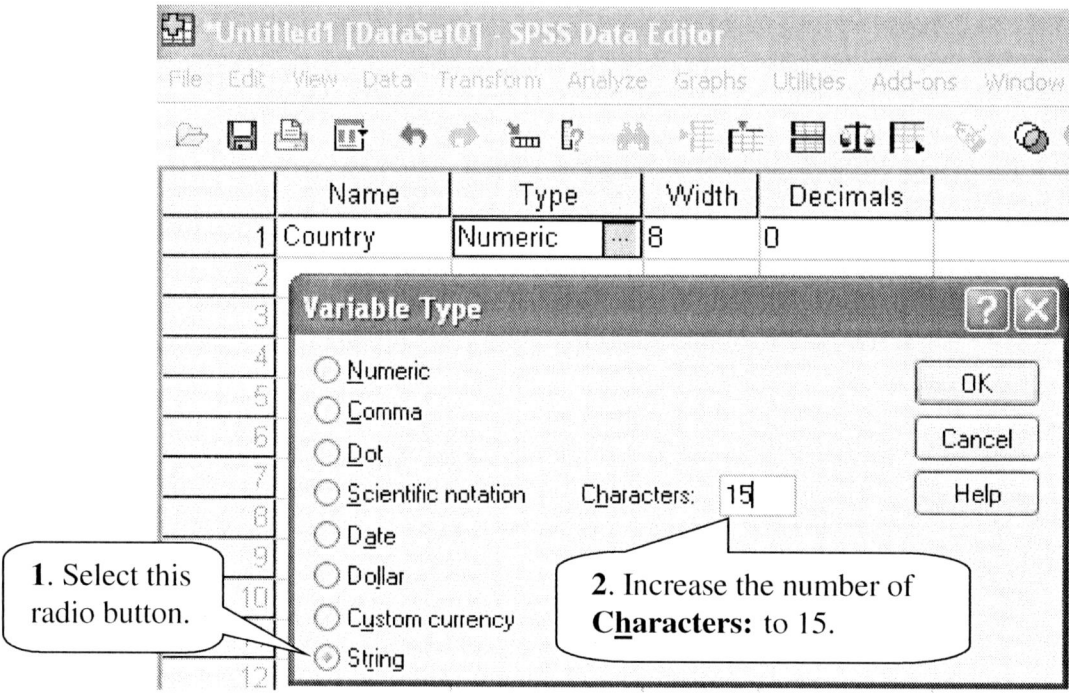

- Click the **OK** button to return to the **Variable View** window.
- Enter **Pride_Score** and **Compet_Rank** as shown.

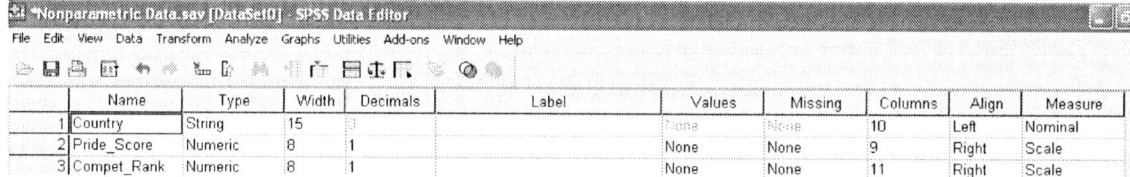

- Enter the following data into the **Data Editor**.

COUNTRY	PRIDE SCORE	COMPETITIVENESS RANK
United States	4.0	1
South Africa	2.7	10
Austria	2.4	2
Canada	2.4	3
Chile	2.3	5
Japan	1.8	7
Hungary	1.6	8
France	1.5	6
Norway	1.3	4
Slovenia	1.1	9

- When you are finished, the **Data View** window should look like the one below.

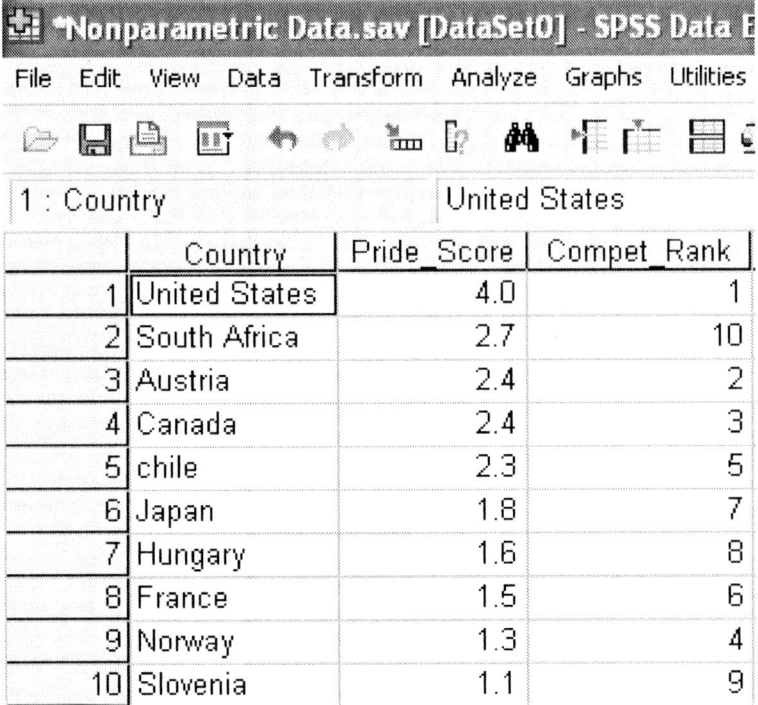

- From the **Analyze** menu select **Correlate ▶ Bivariate...** to produce the **Bivariate Correlations** dialog window. Click on the box next to **Spearman**, then move the variables, **Pride_Score** and **Compet_Rank**, into the **Variables:** field. (It is not necessary to convert the values of Pride_Score to ranks. SPSS will do this for us.)

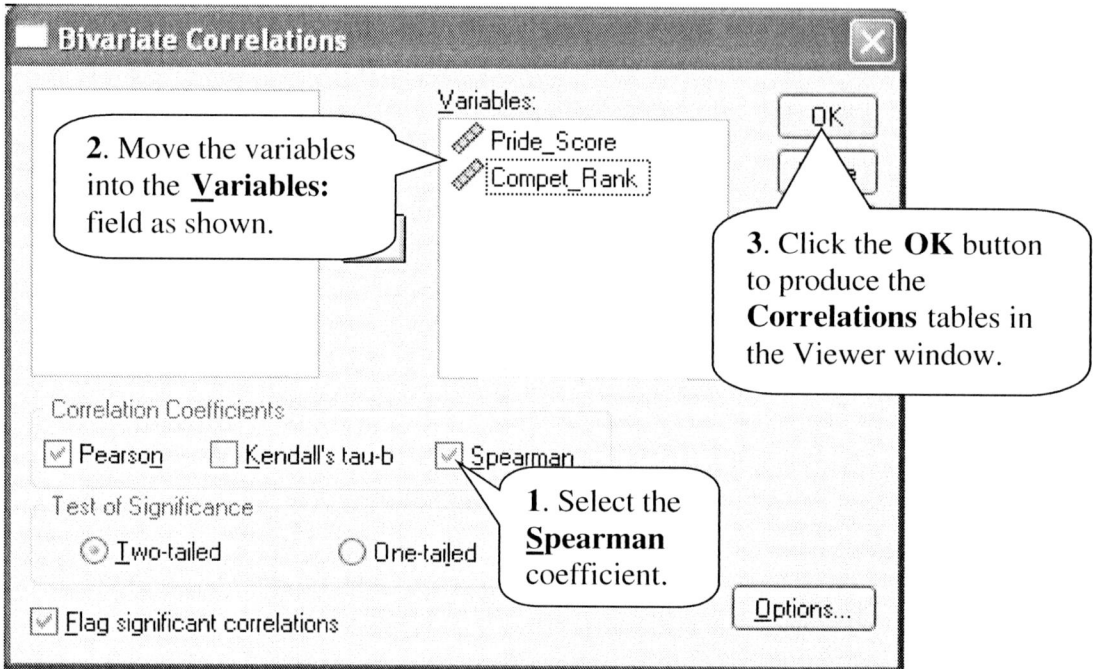

- Click **OK** to produce the Correlations tables for the Pearson and Spearman formulas in the **SPSS Viewer** window.

Questions

1. What is the value of the Spearman correlation coefficient for these variables? Support your answer with the appropriate output table.
2. Compare the Spearman and Pearson coefficients. Why are these correlation coefficients different?

EXERCISE 2
THE WILCOXON SIGNED-RANKS TEST

- From the **File** menu, select **Data ▶ New** to open a new data window in the Data Editor.

- Go to the **Variable View** window and enter the variables as follows:

	Name	Type	Width	Decimals	Label	Values	Missing	Columns	Align	Measure
1	Country	String	15	0		None	None	10	Left	Nominal
2	Period_1	Numeric	8	2	1995-1996	None	None	8	Right	Scale
3	Period_2	Numeric	8	2	2003-2004	None	None	8	Right	Scale

- Go to the **Data View** window and enter the data from the table:

COUNTRY	1995–1996	2003–2004
United States	3.11	4.00
Australia	2.10	2.90
Ireland	3.36	2.90
New Zealand	2.62	2.60
Canada	2.56	2.40
Great Britain	2.09	2.20

- After completing the data entry, the **Data Editor** should look similar to this:

	Country	Period_1	Period_2
1	United States	3.11	4.00
2	Australia	2.10	2.90
3	Ireland	3.36	2.90
4	New Zealand	2.62	2.60
5	Canada	2.56	2.40
6	Great Britain	2.09	2.20

It is not necessary to convert these interval measures to ranks. SPSS will compute the difference between each pair of variable values, rank the differences from smallest to largest, and assign a rank of 1 to the smallest difference, 2 to the next-smallest difference, etc.

From the **Analyze** menu, select **Nonparametric Tests ▶ 2 Related Samples...**

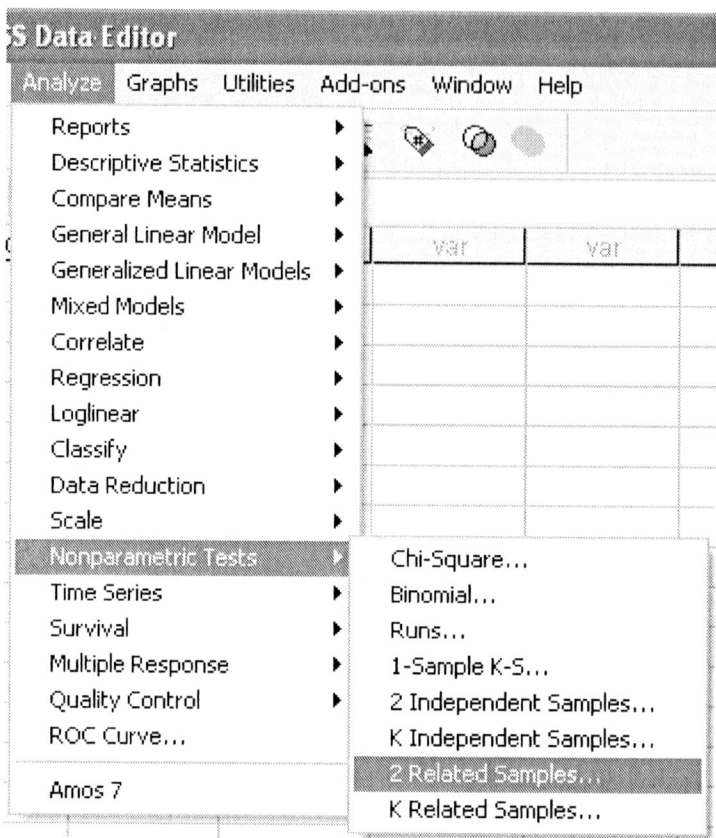

- In the **Two-Related-Samples Tests** dialog window, select **Period_1**, then hold down the Shift key or the Control (Ctrl) key while you select **Period_2**. Both variables should now appear under **Current Selections** in the lower left corner of the window.

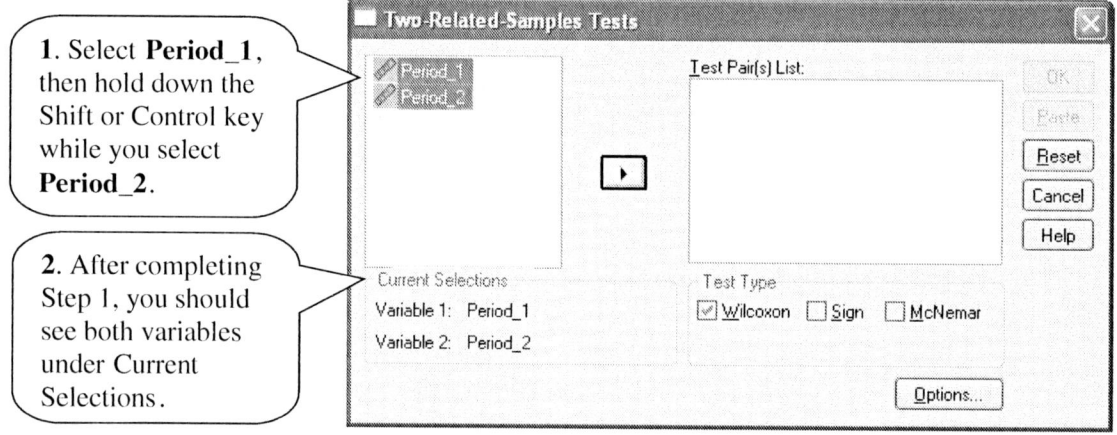

1. Select **Period_1**, then hold down the Shift or Control key while you select **Period_2**.

2. After completing Step 1, you should see both variables under Current Selections.

- Click the ▶ button to move the pair of variables into the **Test Pair(s) List:** field. Locate the Test Type section of the window and make sure that the box next to **Wilcoxon** is checked.

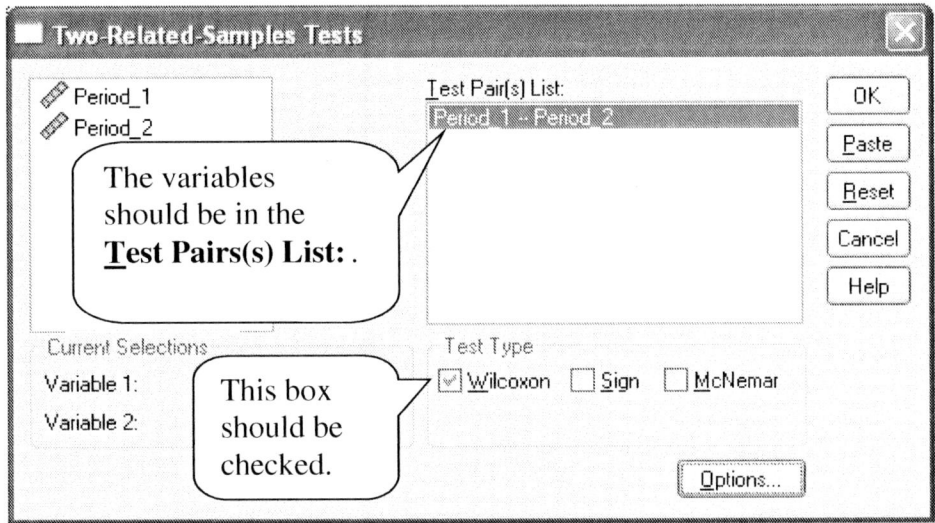

- Click the **OK** button to generate the two output tables.

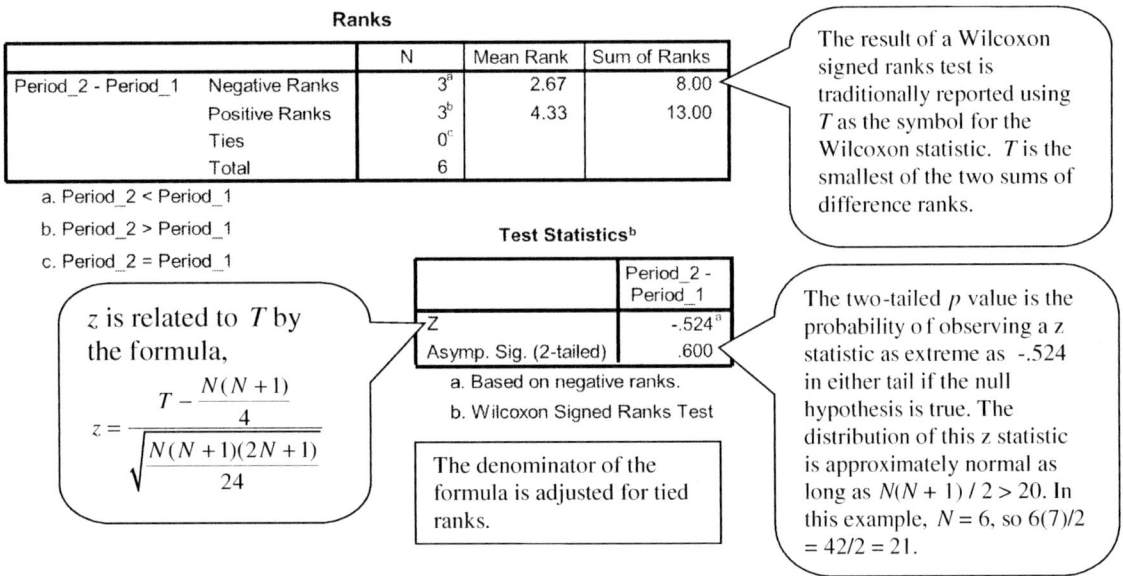

Question

3. Are the accomplishment-related national pride rankings different in the two periods? Explain your answer.

Exercise 3
THE MANN-WHITNEY U TEST

- From the **File** menu, select **Data ▶ New** to open a new data window in the **Data Editor**.
- Go to the **Variable View** window and enter the variables as follows:

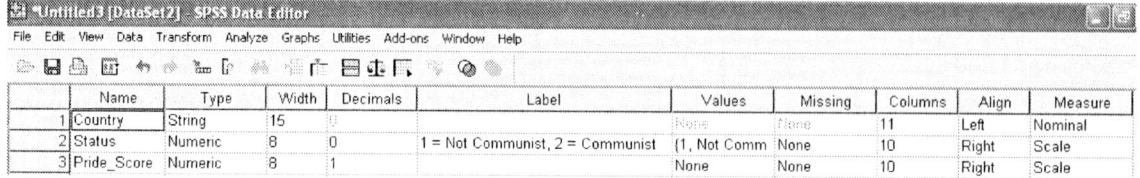

- The **Value Labels** dialog window is accessed by clicking in the second cell under **Values** and clicking on the gray box that appears. Values are assigned to labels as follows:

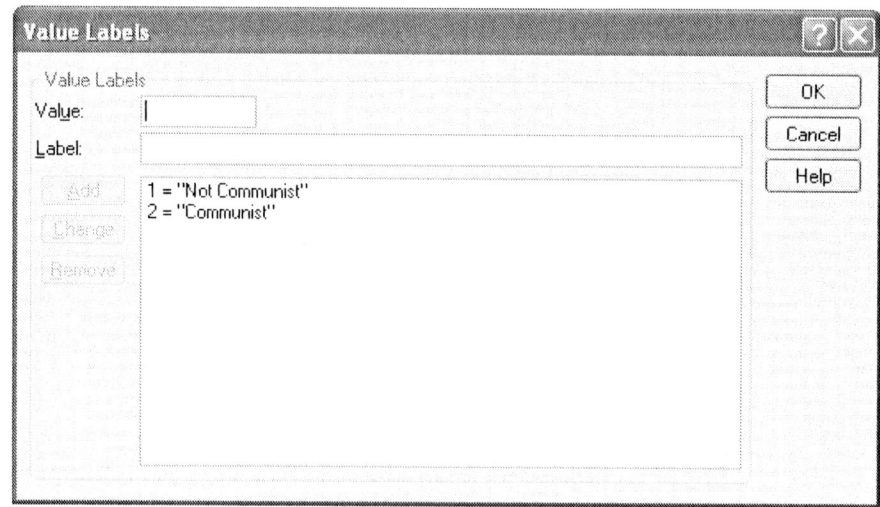

- Go to the **Data View** window and enter the data from the table:

COUNTRY	STATUS CODE	PRIDE SCORE
Not Communist		
Ireland	1	2.90
Austria	1	2.40
Spain	1	1.60
Portugal	1	1.60
Sweden	1	1.20
Communist		
Hungary	2	1.60
Czech Republic	2	1.30
Slovenia	2	1.10
Slovakia	2	1.10
Poland	2	0.90

- After completing the data entry, the Data Editor should look similar to this:

	Country	Status	Pride_Score
1	Ireland	1	2.9
2	Austria	1	2.4
3	Spain	1	1.6
4	Portugal	1	1.6
5	Sweden	1	1.2
6	Hungary	2	1.6
7	Czech Republic	2	1.3
8	Slovenia	2	1.1
9	Slovakia	2	1.1
10	Poland	2	.9

It is not necessary to convert the values of Pride_Score to ranks. SPSS will combine the values of Pride_Score for the two groups, rank the scores from smallest to largest, and compute the average rank for the two groups.

- From the **Analyze** menu, select **Nonparametric Tests** ▶ **2 Independent Samples...**

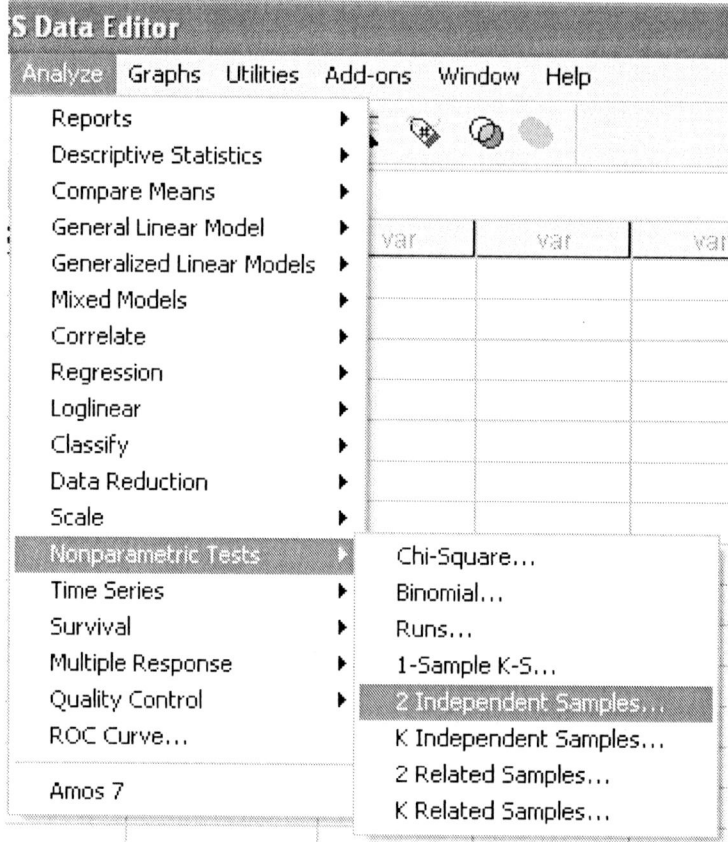

- In the **Two-Independent-Samples Tests** dialog window, select **Pride_Score** and move this variable into the **Test Variable List:** field. Select **Status** and move this variable into the **Grouping Variable:** field.

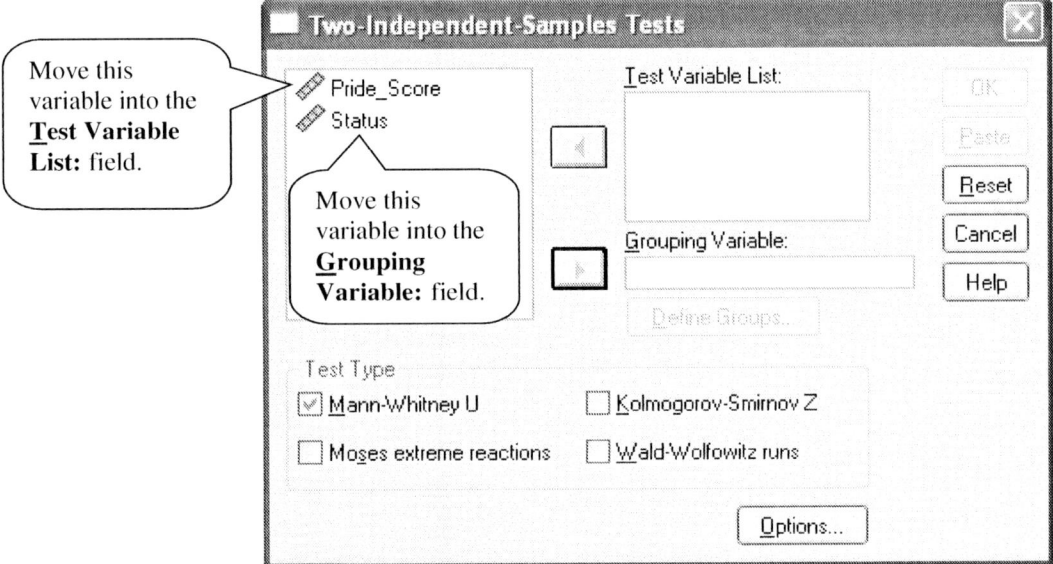

- Click on **Define Groups…** to access the **Two-Independent-Samples Tests: Define Groups** dialog window.

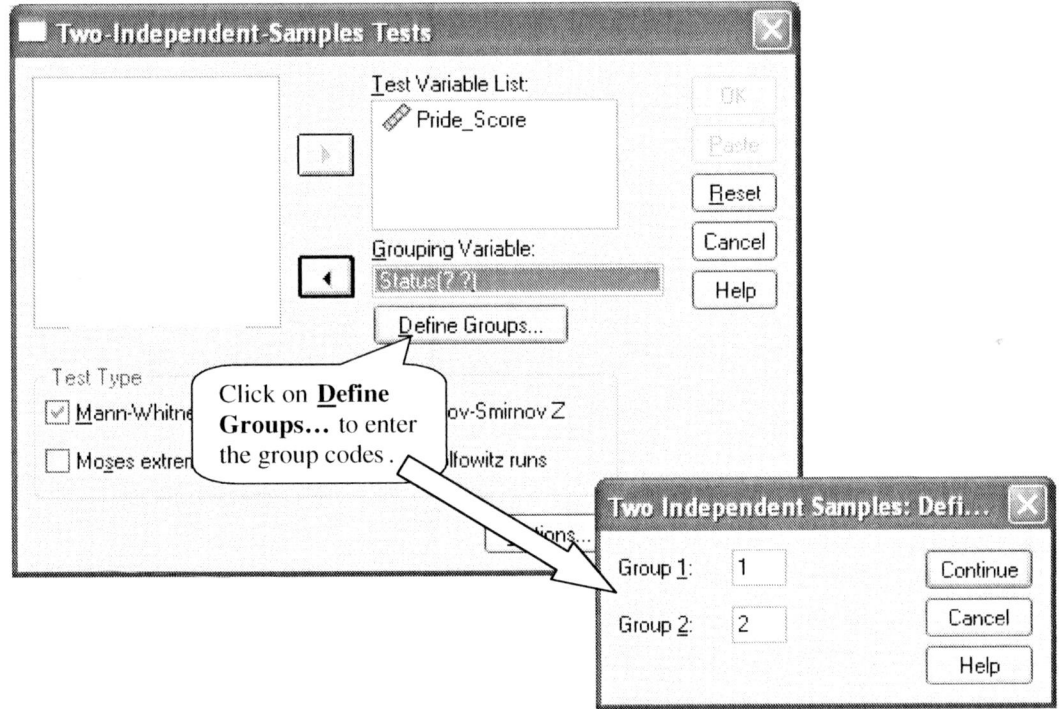

- Click the **OK** button to generate the two output tables.

Ranks

	Status	N	Mean Rank	Sum of Ranks
Pride_Score	1	5	7.40	37.00
	2	5	3.60	18.00
	Total	10		

Test Statistics[b]

	Pride_Score
Mann-Whitney U	3.000
Wilcoxon W	18.000
Z	-2.015
Asymp. Sig. (2-tailed)	.044
Exact Sig. [2*(1-tailed Sig.)]	.056[a]

a. Not corrected for ties.
b. Grouping Variable Status

z is related to U by the formula,

$$z = \frac{U - \frac{N_1 N_2}{2}}{\sqrt{\frac{N_1 N_2 (N_1 + N_2 + 1)}{12}}}$$

The normal approximation to U is reasonable if the larger N is at least 20 and the sample sizes are not too different.

When N is small (as in this example) the exact significance level should be reported.

Question

4. Are the accomplishment-related national pride rankings different in the populations of recently communist and recently noncommunist countries? Explain your answer.

ANSWERS

1. As shown in the table, the Spearman correlation coefficient is .401.

Correlations

			Compet_Rank	Pride_Score
Spearman's rho	Compet_Rank	Correlation Coefficient	1.000	.401
		Sig. (2-tailed)	.	.250
		N	10	10
	Pride_Score	Correlation Coefficient	.401	1.000
		Sig. (2-tailed)	.250	.
		N	10	10

2. The Pearson and Spearman correlations are not the same because SPSS does not convert the values of Pride_Score to ranks before computing the Pearson correlation coefficient. However, the Pearson and Spearman formulas are interchangeable when the values of both variables are entered as ranks.

Correlations

		Compet_Rank	Pride_Score
Compet_Rank	Pearson Correlation	1.000	-.519
	Sig. (2-tailed)	.	.124
	N	10	10
Pride_Score	Pearson Correlation	-.519	1.000
	Sig. (2-tailed)	.124	.
	N	10	10

3. According to the Wilcoxon signed ranks test, the hypothesis that the accomplishment-related national pride rankings in the two periods are different is not supported. The p value is .6, considerably above the significance criterion of .05.

4. According to the Mann Whitney U test for independent ranks, the hypothesis that the accomplishment-related national pride rankings in recently communist and noncommunist countries are different is not supported, although this outcome would be described as "marginally significant" by most researchers. The p value is .056, just above the significance criterion of .05.